STEALTH

STEALTH

THE SECRET CONTEST TO INVENT INVISIBLE AIRCRAFT

PETER WESTWICK

OXFORD
UNIVERSITY PRESS

OXFORD
UNIVERSITY PRESS

Oxford University Press is a department of the University of Oxford.
It furthers the University's objective of excellence in research, scholarship,
and education by publishing worldwide. Oxford is a registered trade mark of
Oxford University Press in the UK and in certain other countries.

Published in the United States of America by Oxford University Press
198 Madison Avenue, New York, NY 10016, United States of America.

Library of Congress Cataloging-in-Publication Data
Names: Westwick, Peter J., author.
Title: Stealth : the secret contest to invent invisible aircraft
/ Peter Westwick.
Other titles: Secret contest to invent invisible aircraft
Description: New York, NY : Oxford University Press, [2020] |
Identifiers: LCCN 2019015749 | ISBN 9780190677442 (hardcover)
Subjects: LCSH: Stealth aircraft—United States—History. | Stealth
aircraft—Design and construction. | B-2 bomber—History. | F-117 (Jet
attack plane)—History. | Aeronautics, Military—Research—United
States—History—20th century. | Aeronautics, Military—Research—United
States—History—21st century.
Classification: LCC UG1242.S73 W47 2020 | DDC 623.74/6—dc23
LC record available at https://lccn.loc.gov/2019015749

1 3 5 7 9 8 6 4 2
Printed by LSC Communications
United States of America

CONTENTS

LIST OF ILLUSTRATIONS

INTRODUCTION

On a moonless night in January 1991 a dozen aircraft appeared in the skies over Baghdad. Or rather, didn't appear. The airplanes arrived in the dark, their black outlines cloaking them from sight. More importantly, their odd, angular shapes, which made them look like flying origami, rendered them virtually invisible to Iraq's formidable air-defense radars.

The aircraft were F-117As, better known as the Stealth Fighter, and they were part of the opening salvo of Operation Desert Storm, the international effort, led by US forces, to reverse Iraq's invasion of Kuwait. American television viewers were transfixed by video footage of F-117s dropping laser-guided bombs down the airshafts of Baghdad buildings. No Stealth aircraft were lost in the Gulf War.[1]

The technology behind the F-117 and the similarly stealthy B-2 bomber marked a military breakthrough. The F-117 is more than 60 feet long and 40 feet across, but to radar it looks as small as a ball bearing. The far larger B-2 has the radar footprint of a Frisbee.

Just as remarkable, Stealth's inventors, at two different aerospace firms, wound up with contrasting airplanes. Just look at the two planes and the differences are apparent: on the one hand, the sharply angular F-117; on the other, the smoothly rounded B-2.

Why is one Stealth plane angular and the other curved? The answer to that simple question reveals several tensions at the core of this story: between the two companies, Lockheed and Northrop; between the disciplines of radar physics and aeronautical engineering; and between design philosophies, especially involving the role of computers versus human intuition in aircraft design. These tensions played out in an

I.1
An F-117 in flight.
Source: U.S. Air Force.

I.2
A B-2 in flight.
Source: courtesy of Northrop Grumman Corporation.

exceptional cast of characters, from bookish engineers to jovial prank-sters to hard-driving managers.

This book is about where those aircraft came from and why they look the way they do. It tells the story of engineers at Lockheed and Northrop and their epic contest to build these two planes, a competition conducted under the highest levels of secrecy in the Cold War. In a fantastically fertile five-year period in the mid- to late 1970s, engineers at the two firms arrived at different solutions to achieve the same breakthrough: aircraft essentially invisible to radar.

There is a tendency in military history to view a new technology as a deus ex machina: a new weapon (the longbow at the Battle of Agincourt, the machine gun in the First World War, and, perhaps the greatest deus ex machina of them all, the atomic bomb in the Second World War) suddenly appears on the scene and revolutionizes warfare. But where did the technology come from? Why did it appear at that particular time? Why did one side get it and not another? In short: how did it come to be? These questions are often ignored because military history tends to tell stories either from the top down, the presidents-and-generals view of grand strategy, or from the bottom up, the trench-level view of the combat soldier.

There is another view, between that of the general's genius and the soldier's courage, what the historian Paul Kennedy has called "history from the middle": the story of the engineers and midlevel military officers who champion new military technologies. In Kennedy's case, it was the engineers who turned the tide in World War II with the P-51 Mustang, antisubmarine warfare, amphibious assault, and antitank weapons.[2] Similarly, Stealth originated with engineers at Lockheed and Northrop and won the backing of technical program managers in the military long before either generals or frontline soldiers knew about it.

That is not to say that these engineers always agreed. However fierce the competition was between the two firms, the technical battles within the firms were as fierce, or even fiercer. Stealth, in other words, was a contest on three levels: between the US and the Soviet Union; between Lockheed and Northrop; and *within* Lockheed and Northrop.

An early British airplane builder, Howard Theophilus Wright (no relation to the American brothers), declared in 1912, "The successful aeroplane, like many other pieces of mechanism, is a huge mass of compromise."[3] He did not, however, suggest how engineers might reach compromise. On a typical day in the advanced design department of Northrop in Hawthorne, in the mid-1970s, engineers in their offices would lift their heads from their work like startled animals as the shouted arguments of John Cashen and Irv Waaland, Northrop's principal Stealth designers, shattered the tranquility. Cashen and Waaland would have been comforted, and probably not surprised, to learn that twenty miles away in Burbank, similar arguments echoed down the hallways of Lockheed. The popular image of the aerospace engineer is rational, dispassionate, and reserved. These engineers were certainly rational but not at all dispassionate. And their passion enabled the invention of Stealth.

That passion was needed because Stealth faced determined resistance on many levels. On the technical level, a number of engineers, including some of the most legendary names in the aircraft business, thought it couldn't be done. At the corporate level, some managers thought the dubious prospects were not worth a major investment of company finances. At the strategic and political level, some argued there were better ways to solve the problem of Soviet air defenses, by flying low and fast, for instance, or using electronic jammers.

Engineers at Lockheed and Northrop overcame this resistance to Stealth, and this book examines the two programs side by side, revealing key differences in their approaches along with similarities. The differences started with their routes to Stealth: one through aircraft, the other more through spacecraft, the latter an important, unrecognized source for Stealth.

They differed also in their reliance on computers. Computers entered first of all in the design process, where Lockheed leaned heavily on computer codes to analyze radar diffraction, while Northrop depended more on physical intuition. A critical but often less appreciated role for computers stemmed from flight controls, often known as fly-by-wire. Lockheed's first design was unstable in all three directions;

one of Northrop's Stealth aircraft spun like a weather vane in the yaw axis. Stealth aircraft depended on computers not just for their design but also to stay in the air. In other words, the key parts of Stealth were not just the outside of the plane, the parts you could see, but also the guts inside the plane, the electronics you couldn't see. The Stealth program thus represented a momentous change in the aerospace industry, as electrical engineers displaced the old-school aeronautical engineers. And the two firms differed in their embrace of computerized flight control.

Finally, the two firms diverged in another disciplinary dispute. Ever since the Wright brothers, aircraft design had been dominated by aerodynamics. Most aircraft designers, including Lockheed's famous Kelly Johnson, came out of aeronautical engineering. For Stealth, these aeronautical traditionalists were challenged by physicists and engineers who specialized not in airflow but in electromagnetic waves. These tensions caused many of the arguments that roiled design offices, but they also proved creative, and their resolution by each firm determined the shape of the airplanes and the outcome of the contests.

The two firms, however, also had characteristics in common. One was the shop floor. It was one thing to produce a slick-looking airplane on a blueprint, another thing altogether to turn that into flying hardware. Stealth aircraft were not unique in this regard, but they provide an especially telling example of hardware that pushed beyond existing limits of materials and tooling. Both firms had to integrate design and manufacturing, and both nevertheless struggled to realize their designs. The story of Stealth involved machine tools as well as computers and drafting tables, and blue collars as well as white collars.

Lockheed and Northrop had one other obvious commonality: geography. Of all the major US aircraft companies, the ones that created Stealth aircraft were in Southern California, based twenty miles apart across the LA basin. This was not a coincidence. Southern California had long attracted visionaries and dreamers, nourishing a culture of boundary-pushing. That creative culture made Southern California more known for the entertainment industry than for aerospace: for Imagineering, not engineering. But aerospace not only underpinned the regional economy, it also tapped the creative, entrepreneurial culture—including, as we shall see, some surprising connections between Stealth and Disneyland.

These themes all came together in two central episodes: the competitions between Lockheed and Northrop for what became the F-117 and the B-2 bomber. But there was an intermediate step between the two planes that has been largely lost to history. Called Tacit Blue, it provided the crucial stepping-stone from the flat and faceted F-117 to the curvy B-2 flying wing. It also sparked a connection between the otherwise isolated design teams, one that yielded a surprising source for the flying wing concept.

Stealth was a product not only of a particular place but also of a particular time. Stealth aircraft may have made their public debut in the Gulf War, but the fateful decisions and crucial innovations occurred in the 1970s, for reasons both strategic, such as the American experience in the Vietnam War, and technological, including the availability of digital electronic computers—and also, perhaps, cultural.

After the seemingly limitless expansion of American economic and military strength after World War II, the 1970s were an uneasy decade of inflation and unemployment, and of declining faith in the government after Vietnam and Watergate. California governor Jerry Brown called it an "era of limits," and in a famous speech in 1979 President Jimmy Carter spoke of a national "crisis of confidence . . . a crisis that strikes at the very heart and soul and spirit of our national will."[4]

The 1970s were also, however, a time of great political, economic, and cultural ferment, a transition in many ways from postwar America to our postindustrial, globalized world. The tectonic shifts included a burst of technological creativity, some of it with the express aim of overcoming the era's perceived limits, leading to the personal computer, genetic engineering—and Stealth.[5]

That technological upheaval in turn reflected a broader lesson. Stealth was not just a product of the 1970s but rather drew on decades of R&D, which itself reflected a national willingness to make long-term investments in uncertain ventures. And those investments came from both the public and the private sectors. Stealth represented a vast integration of the state and private industry, what is commonly called the military-industrial complex. In order to demonstrate the superiority of an unfettered free market over a command economy in the Cold War, the US embraced a strong public-private partnership.

The Cold War military-industrial complex often carries negative connotations, of a corrupting intrusion of the state into private enterprise and, in the other direction, of private interests into public policy. And indeed Stealth, as some observers argued, could seem like a waste of money and brainpower, enabled by official secrecy and encouraged by pork-barrel politics, all just to produce yet another weapon and a new lap of the arms race. But from a later vantage point, from a time when high-tech boosters insist that the government has no role in innovation, Stealth may provide another example of a successful public-private partnership, and it may thus hold enduring lessons.

The decisive role of Stealth aircraft in the Gulf War demonstrated the fruits of that partnership and popularized talk of a "Revolution in Military Affairs"—a revolution first glimpsed by Soviet strategists.[6] Soon after the Gulf War, the Soviet Union—the adversary whose presence motivated the invention of Stealth—ceased to exist. There is a saying that "the Cold War was won in El Segundo," meaning that scientists and engineers, the denizens of El Segundo and other LA aerospace suburbs, won the Cold War by confronting the Soviets with an arms race they couldn't win. Others have argued instead that scientists and engineers *prolonged* the Cold War by driving the arms race, leading the US to the brink of bankruptcy and the world to the edge of Armageddon.

This book will consider both arguments, but it will also present a third view: that Stealth offered an *alternative* to nuclear weapons, a way out of the looking-glass labyrinth of nuclear strategy. Stealth helped launch a reconsideration of strategic fundamentals, albeit one that, in the end, ran up against the inertia of nuclear strategy.

Writing about Stealth presents certain challenges. It was one of the nation's most tightly held secrets, although it was also the subject of persistent leaks. Many documents and technical details remain classified, and some Stealth workers still refuse to discuss the topic at all. For that reason, some engineers (and some historians) believe it premature, and perhaps fruitless, to attempt a history of Stealth.

Like other aspects of the Cold War, the subject of Stealth is too important to wait for that distant day, decades hence, when all the sources are accessible. And aside from some technical details, one can glean much of the story from available sources, including oral histories along with documents. Where these sources present conflicting accounts I have tried to arrive at the most likely version.

I did not set out to write a history of Stealth. For several years I have directed the Aerospace History Project, a collaboration between USC and the Huntington Library to document the history of Southern California's aerospace industry. In the course of assembling our aerospace archive, I realized that Stealth represented a remarkable story, featuring a cast of interesting characters and raising important issues about modern military technology. I also realized that existing books have not told this story, in part because classification has restricted access to sources.

Our project has collected a number of unclassified sources on Stealth, in documents and especially in oral histories with a number of key figures at Lockheed and Northrop. While some information about Stealth remains classified—for instance, the precise radar cross sections of the F-117 and B-2—the general concepts are now forty years old, and it is possible to discuss Stealth in some technical detail. I have also drawn on sources at other archives that provide new insights on the broader technological and strategic context of the late Cold War.

The history of Stealth requires dealing with some technical concepts, but I have tried to avoid overwhelming the reader with frequency bands, side lobes, and surface currents, let alone differential equations. For the technical terms that are unavoidable, the glossary at the back of the book provides general definitions. Similarly, I have tried not to drown readers in the alphabet soup of SPOs, FSDs, PDRs, IOCs, and so on that characterizes military program management. Finally, the notes provide exemplary rather than exhaustive citations.

STEALTH

CHAPTER ONE

ROOTS OF THE REVOLUTION

Stealth is as old as hunting. The need to sneak up on prey—or to hide from predators—inspired early humans to blend into the landscape, to imitate the animal world, from the leopard's spots to the zebra's stripes. The French word *camouflage*, to disguise or conceal, captured some of the idea. Shakespeare understood it: Malcolm's soldiers in *Macbeth* disguised themselves as trees (Birnam Wood) on their march to Dunsinane. The emergence of modern militaries first brought brightly colored uniforms (thus the British "redcoats"), to instill pride and distinguish friend from foe, but as the lethal range of weapons increased in the nineteenth century, armies began shifting to khaki or olive drab to blend in rather than stand out.[1]

Camouflage became prevalent in World War I, including and perhaps especially for aircraft. First the French and Germans and then the British and Americans began painting the undersides of airplanes white or pale blue to match the sky, and the topsides with darker greens to match the earth when viewed from above, sometimes throwing in polygons or pointillist patterns to confuse the eye.[2]

The wartime effort drew more on artists than on scientists, but late in the war the US National Research Council organized a committee on aircraft camouflage, led by a civilian physicist named Matthew Luckiesh, on loan from General Electric. The committee undertook a research program out of Langley Field in Virginia, starting with the assumption that, since the human eye distinguishes objects through differences in brightness and color, an invisible airplane would need the same brightness and color as its background. Moreover, since natural backgrounds often vary in light, shade, and color, patterns would usually be better than uniform tones—but the patterns should still have the same average color and brightness as the background. The committee thus took systematic data on the brightness and hues of land, sky, and water, and on the best sizes and shapes of camouflage patterns. Luckiesh summarized some of the results in articles entitled "The Visibility of Airplanes," published after the war.[3]

The end of the war largely ended these initial forays into invisible aircraft before they settled on an optimum approach. Interest in air defenses faded, and with it the need to hide aircraft. Air-power theorists in the 1920s and 1930s instead began talking about the airplane as a decisive, omnipotent weapon. In particular, they viewed strategic bombing—that is, the deliberate targeting of civilian populations and industrial centers—as the key to warfare.[4] As Germany rebuilt its air forces under Hitler, the British realized that airborne bombers posed a dire threat, erasing their traditional defensive advantage as an island nation. In the familiar formulation, voiced by former prime minister Stanley Baldwin in 1932, "The bomber will always get through." The primary approach to detect incoming aircraft, involving giant concrete acoustic mirrors, could at best pick up bombers at 15 miles, which gave only half the time needed to scramble fighters to intercept them. Baldwin added, regarding the possibility of air defense, "It cannot be done, and there is no expert in Europe who will say it can." In air exercises in 1934 half the bombers in a simulated raid on London reached their targets.[5]

But there were in fact some experts who said otherwise. In late 1934 the British formed a Committee for the Scientific Survey of Air Defence, sometimes known as the Tizard Committee after its chairman, the scientist Henry Tizard. Its initial focus was a fantastic proposal from Nikola Tesla. Earlier that year the visionary inventor of electrical and radio devices, now seventy-eight years old and increasingly eccentric, had announced the invention of a particle beam that would destroy airplanes in flight. The so-called death ray—Tesla himself shunned the term—received wide publicity, especially after newspapers reported that the Germans were conducting experiments on it (and that Guglielmo Marconi, another famed inventor, was also working on it). The British committee quickly disproved the death ray idea, including the possibility that high-power radio waves might be used to fry pilots. In the process, however, they stumbled across earlier reports that airplanes flying near radio receivers tended to interfere with the signals. The scientists thought this technique might be applied to detect aircraft, so they cooked up a quick test using a BBC transmitter and an airborne bomber. It worked: the radio waves broadcast by the transmitter hit the airplane, echoed off it, and were picked up by the radio antenna. Within a year the system could detect planes at a distance of 75 miles.[6]

The result, dubbed radar, for *RAdio Detection And Ranging*, was the wonder weapon of World War II. Not only could radar reveal the presence of an airplane; the time between a pulse transmission and reception provided the range, and the direction of the signal yielded the target's altitude and bearing. And radar worked at night, and through clouds. It worked even better than the suggestion offered by one enterprising Londoner for finding German bombers at night during the Blitz: "Take cat in airplane: aim guns where cat is looking"—a proposal apparently not pursued, alas, by the British.[7]

The scale of radar research in the US during World War II was bigger than the Manhattan Project. A joint US-British effort pushed radar transmitters to shorter wavelengths, from meters to down to a few centimeters, known as the microwave region, for higher target resolution and for antennas small enough to fit on airplanes. The Germans had nothing comparable, and the Japanese lagged even further. Germany had started a radar program at the same time as Britain, but its leaders failed to appreciate its importance (radar was seen as a defensive weapon, and Hitler wanted offensive weapons), and its program did not enjoy the funding or scientific manpower of the Allied counterpart.[8]

Radar proved crucial to the Allied war effort, for submarine and ship detection, airplane and ship navigation, and proximity fuzes for antiaircraft and artillery shells. It helped the Royal Air Force win the Battle of Britain, enabled the strategic bombing of Germany and Japan, and aided the carrier war in the Pacific and the antisubmarine campaign in both theaters. Thus the common sentiment among both scientists and historians: while the atomic bomb may have ended World War II, radar won it.[9]

Radar tilted the balance in the air back toward the defender, but no sooner had radar waves been introduced in combat than each side began trying to counteract them, in an early form of electronic warfare. The British and Germans developed countermeasures to jam or spoof enemy radars, leading to the long-running "Battle of the Beams" in the skies over the English Channel. Both sides also tried radar-absorbing materials on aircraft. The German project was known by the code name *Schornsteinfeger*, or chimney sweep, because the absorbers often incorporated carbon black. Since submarine periscopes and snorkels stuck out from the ocean surface and appeared on radar displays, the Germans coated them with radar-damping rubber or plastic sheets. At the MIT Radiation Laboratory in the US, a team led by Otto Halpern, an émigré Jewish physicist from Austria, developed materials known as HARP, for Halpern Anti-Radar Paint. These were actually more like rubber sheets, with one version for ships and another for aircraft, although the latter—a rubber mat sprinkled with aluminum flakes— was so thin, about .025 inches, that it was indeed like a coat of paint. Another Rad Lab invention, called the Salisbury Screen after its inventor, Winfield W. Salisbury, used a thin reflective sheet, although it only worked for radar waves of a selected wavelength.[10]

The Germans also began to develop a remarkable airplane, the Horten 229, a sleek flying wing that seemed to incorporate charcoal as a radar-absorbent coating. The Ho-229's resemblance to the later B-2 has sparked speculation that the Germans designed the first stealth airplane, but recent analyses have cast doubt on the use of charcoal, and the Horten designers apparently chose the flying wing not for radar evasion but to enhance aerodynamic performance—the same appeal, we shall see, that the flying wing held for Jack Northrop.[11]

As the postwar peace rapidly gave way to the Cold War, the pendulum seemed to swing back in favor of the offense. New jet aircraft made air defense both more difficult and at the same time, because of nuclear bombs, more imperative. The Soviets had a justified fear of surprise attack, having lost some four thousand planes in the first week of the German invasion in 1941. The Soviets put so much emphasis on air defense that they made it a separate military service, known as

PVO-Strany. From 1945 to the early 1960s the Soviets spent more on air defenses than they did on nuclear forces. Even after the advent of strategic missiles they continued to commit enormous resources to air defense, about 15 percent of the total military budget in the late 1960s and early 1970s—about as much as they spent on their navy.[12]

These "unknown troops," as one of their commanders called them, developed a series of radar-guided surface-to-air missiles known in the US by the NATO designation "SA-," starting with the SA-1 in the mid-1950s. The SA-2 made its mark on history by shooting down the high-flying U-2 spy plane of Francis Gary Powers in 1960. The Soviets also developed a defense network against strategic bombers, including a ring of early-warning radars—dubbed the Tall King system by NATO, deployed starting in 1959—that could pick up incoming American planes at a distance of 300 miles, which gave them about a half hour to scramble interceptors.[13]

With the pendulum swinging back to defense, interest in counteracting radar revived in the US. A review at the end of World War II by the Army Air Forces Scientific Advisory Group had struck a pessimistic tone. The study, completed in 1946, was better known as the von Kármán report after the group's chairman, Theodore von Kármán, a pioneering aeronautical scientist who had come to the US from Hungary in 1930 to lead Caltech's aeronautical laboratory. The report included a volume on radar, written by several leaders of the American wartime radar effort. It declared that an airplane had too complicated a shape to reduce its radar cross section, a measure of how big an airplane looks to a radar and therefore how easy it is to detect; it is expressed in terms of area, such as square feet. The report concluded, "*We cannot foresee any means by which aircraft can be made invisible to radar.*"[14]

The Air Force nevertheless supported a small research program into what makes radar waves bounce back from a plane. It sounds simple, but it was in fact a fiendishly difficult problem. The radar signal returned from an airplane varies hugely, on the order of a million times, depending on the frequency and polarization of the radar wave and on the airplane's angle to the radar beam—for instance, whether it is viewed head-on, or from the side, or somewhere in between; or whether the plane is level or banking away from the radar beam, exposing more of the airplane's bottom, or toward it, exposing the top.

Scientists and engineers at Wright-Patterson Air Force Base began a systematic exploration of how to measure radar return experimentally, model it theoretically, and reduce it in practice. The research focused on two main paths to reducing the radar cross section: changing the shape of the aircraft, and changing the material it was made out of. For the first, shaping, the von Kármán report's judgment still held: airplane shapes were just too complicated, and theoretical models of radar scattering were stymied by the complexity of the calculations, at least until more powerful computers arrived. Experimental measurements, made using a scale model of the plane mounted on a pole on a radar range, were meanwhile plagued by false returns—from the ground, or distant objects, or the pole—or by large but mysterious differences between similar models. Trial-and-error measurements on the radar test range did offer some insights. For instance, certain features, such as engine inlets or cockpit canopies, contributed an outsized share of radar echo, essentially causing spikes in the signal.[15]

Since shaping seemed a dead end, Air Force engineers instead focused on developing radar-absorbing materials, or RAM, a continuation of the World War II effort on antiradar coatings or paints. By the late 1950s they had some promising candidates. They coated a T-33 jet trainer with an inch of one such substance and sent it up for a test flight. The test pilot was Virgil "Gus" Grissom, who went on to become one of the Mercury Seven astronauts. The thick layer of RAM helped with radar visibility but played havoc with the plane's aerodynamics. William Bahret, the lead engineer, later recalled the radio conversation on the first flight with Grissom. As the plane lurched around the sky, Grissom radioed back, "Bahret, how the hell do I land this thing?" Bahret replied, "Very carefully, Gus."[16]

That was not the end of the experiments, but it did not exactly foster enthusiasm in the Air Force. There was a more general resistance as well. Few Air Force program managers at the time had a technical background, and not surprisingly they thought in traditional aeronautical terms when it came to aircraft performance. So when they planned new aircraft, they asked for ones that could fly, say, twice as far or twice as fast. Now a few engineers were telling them to think about something called "radar cross section." As Bahret recalled, "They weren't too anxious to have some jerk from the laboratory come along and say, 'Well, boys, now we have to do this.'...There wasn't a lot of dancing in the streets over the prospect of having to incorporate this sort of thing."[17]

Although this effort made few inroads with the Air Force, it did provide an important theoretical and experimental basis for later developments. This was in part thanks to work done at two heartland institutions known more for their rivalry on the football field than for their contributions to Cold War technology, the University of Michigan and Ohio State University, each of which had a major hand in radar research.[18]

The University of Michigan's program centered on Willow Run, the former Ford plant that had cranked out B-24s by the thousands during World War II. After the war the government sold the surplus plant for a dollar to the University of Michigan, whose Ann Arbor campus was about fifteen miles away, and it became the Willow Run Research Center, with radar as a major focus. (In 1972, after campus protests against classified military research during the Vietnam War, the university spun it off as a nonprofit lab and renamed it the Environmental Research Institute of Michigan.)[19] Led by Keeve "Kip" Siegel, Willow Run issued a series of "Studies in Radar Cross Sections" in the 1950s, culminating in a summary report in 1959, "A Theoretical Method for the Calculation of the Radar Cross Sections of Aircraft and Missiles." The report laid out the Michigan approach to the problem: first, model the radar reflection from simple shapes, such as cylinders, cones, wedges, and rectangular flat plates; then treat an airplane as a collection of such shapes to approximate roughly the radar return.[20]

Meanwhile, Ohio State created its Antenna Laboratory in 1941 and used it during the Cold War to pursue theory and experiments involving the scattering of radar waves from objects. By the late 1960s it had over a hundred on staff, including a couple dozen professors, and was renamed the ElectroScience Lab. The Ohio State group took on the computation problem, developing numerical techniques and computer codes to solve the complex calculations. In the mid-1960s it also offered short courses on scattering theory; attendees included several participants in the later Stealth story.[21]

The laboratories at Ohio State and Michigan provided a theoretical foundation but no immediate technological fix to the radar problem. American strategic bombers relied either on speed and altitude, as with the B-47 and B-58, or on electronic countermeasures, as with the B-52. Those countermeasures could be simple, such as emitting metallic chaff, or complicated, such as frequency-sweeping jammers. Another approach was to saturate the defense, overwhelming a radar with decoy targets; some B-52s in the 1960s began carrying one such decoy called a Quail, a cruise missile with radar reflectors that gave it the signature of a B-52. Fighter and attack aircraft also had to deal with radar, but the Air Force's Tactical Air Command was staffed by fighter pilots who relied on speed, maneuverability, and surprise to evade radar-guided defenses. Their attitude, as one Air Force officer recalled it: "They didn't need jamming pods to defeat the missiles, they would outfly them—no sweat!"[22]

No sweat…until American planes started dropping from the skies over North Vietnam. Soviet-made SA-2s decimated American planes at high altitudes, and when the US shifted to low-altitude raids, shoulder-fired SA-7s proved surprisingly effective. Electronic countermeasures helped but often required support aircraft to fly alongside; over North Vietnam, the US averaged a ratio of four radar-jamming aircraft to every strike aircraft. And the Air Force still lost planes at an alarming rate, including eleven B-52s shot down over one four-day stretch in December 1972 during Operation Linebacker II, also known as the Christmas Bombings—a loss rate comparable to the 8th Air Force over Germany in 1943. The 1973 Arab-Israeli War confirmed the lesson, as Soviet-built radar systems dealt high losses to the Israeli Air Force, downing over a hundred aircraft in eighteen days. Radar-guided anti-aircraft missiles were making strike aircraft intolerably vulnerable. The advantage had shifted decisively to the defense.[23]

———

Even as Soviet air defenses increasingly imperiled aircraft, US military strategy was putting greater emphasis on strike aircraft. As the US and the Soviet Union built up arsenals of nuclear-tipped missiles through the 1960s, it became increasingly clear that a thermonuclear war would mean civilizational suicide—a strategic conundrum captured by the term "mutual assured destruction," or MAD. Meanwhile, the US had relied on smaller, tactical nuclear weapons to counter the Soviet advantage in conventional arms. American planners assumed that the Soviets would flood the plains of Western Europe with a hundred tank and infantry divisions. NATO ground forces might be able to halt the initial attack but would be overwhelmed by the following waves.[24]

This was the challenge facing American and NATO strategists by the 1970s. Soviet doctrine itself offered a possible solution. To avoid concentrations of troops, which provided tempting targets for tactical nuclear weapons, the Soviets had developed the concept of echelons, with attacking forces arrayed in depth—basically making the battle front not a line on the map but rather a box.[25] Thus the battle would consist not of a single all-out charge but of a series of attacks in waves as the echelons moved forward. American planners asked, What if you could strike the back of the box—that is, leapfrog the first, daunting wave of the attack, and instead catch the Soviets unaware at the rear, attacking their second echelon before they attacked you?

But a leapfrog maneuver, as any schoolkid knows, dangerously exposes one's underside. For American aircraft to strike the rear echelons, they had first to get over the ramparts of Soviet air defense without getting caught. In short, the US needed an airplane that Soviet radars couldn't see. That raised a question: How small a radar footprint would an airplane need to avoid detection?

An extensive CIA program in the 1960s provided the answer by mapping the precise capability of Soviet radars. It first addressed the long-range, early-warning radars, including the recently constructed Tall Kings, which defended against spy planes as well as nuclear-armed strategic bombers targeting sites within the Soviet Union itself. The question was how to get information on radars that lay beyond the horizon, out of the line of sight. (Such radars worked by bouncing their radio waves off the ionosphere.) Eugene Poteat, a young engineer newly arrived in the CIA's science and technology directorate from his previous job at Bell Labs, recalled that astronomers had been using radar to study the moon's surface, and had the inspiration to use the moon as a radar reflector. The CIA could simply aim radar receivers at the moon to pick up the reflected signals from Soviet early-warning antennas. These data, supplemented by spy planes carrying radar receivers, mapped the location and strength of the Tall Kings and found that their low-altitude coverage was better than expected.

The US, however, still needed to know the resolution of Soviet radars—that is, how small a radar cross section American aircraft would need in order to avoid them. The answer came from another bit of ingenuity dubbed Project Palladium. American spy planes would receive a Soviet radar signal and feed it into a variable delay to create an aircraft of any apparent size, speed, and location—and then beam that signal back to the Soviet radar receiver. The process, in effect, conjured a ghost aircraft on Soviet radar screens. The CIA then had the National Security Agency (NSA) monitor the communications of the Soviet radar sites, whose reactions revealed when they could detect the ghost aircraft.

The CIA used the Cuban Missile Crisis as a Palladium experiment. CIA planes first generated a false signal to mimic an American aircraft attacking Cuba; then a Navy submarine off the coast surfaced and released, at set intervals, metallic balloons of carefully calibrated sizes. The Soviets, as expected, activated a nearby SA-2 radar to track the ghost aircraft, and the radar then reported seeing the mysterious spheres near the target. The NSA-intercepted communications revealed just how small a sphere the SA-2 site could detect—which gave an estimate of the radar cross section needed by US airplanes.

The experiment seems reckless in retrospect. What if the SA-2 site had fired at the nonexistent aircraft in the midst of the most dangerous crisis of the Cold War? Indeed, the Cubans scrambled interceptors to meet the phantom "attacking" aircraft, and the Cuban planes were soon circling over the submarine, which had to dive quickly to safety. But the gambit nevertheless yielded what the Americans needed to know.[26]

The laws of physics, however, presented a basic obstacle to invisible airplanes. The radar equation states that the cross section varies with the fourth power of the distance. Say that a Soviet early-warning radar could pick up an American aircraft at 200 miles, which gave the Soviets twenty minutes to alert their antiaircraft missile batteries and scramble interceptors. Cutting the detection distance in half, to 100 miles, required cutting the radar signature not by 2 but by 2^4, or 16. And that still gave the Soviets ten minutes, plenty of time. What the US really needed was to drop the distance by a factor of 10, giving the Soviets only a couple of minutes to react. And that meant cutting the radar signature by a factor of 10^4, or 10,000.[27]

An airplane that was physically 10,000 times smaller would be the size of a gnat. If anything, American planes at the time were getting bigger: the F-15, which was just entering flight test in the early 1970s, was almost twice the length and three times the wing area of a P-51 Mustang, its predecessor three decades earlier. In the late 1960s a group in the Air Force known as the Fighter Mafia pushed for the Lightweight Fighter, a smaller, single-engine plane that became the F-16, but they were motivated by the need for a maneuverable, dogfighting aircraft, not by interest in a smaller radar cross section.[28]

To engineers, cutting the radar cross section by 10,000 seemed a ludicrous goal. Engineers usually think in terms of incremental advances of a few percent; to make something twice as good is revolutionary. Stealth aimed for something 10,000 times as good. Consider an analogy: if we could make a car with 10,000 times the gas mileage, you could get 300,000 miles per gallon; that is, a car you could drive twelve times around the world on a single gallon of gas. That was the level of advance the Stealth program demanded.[29] It was not enough to deter some technological visionaries on the nation's far coast from attempting it.

CHAPTER TWO

TOMORROWLAND

The solution to the problem of radar cross section came from aircraft firms in Southern California, and only in Southern California.

Why was Stealth invented in Southern California? For one, because that's where the aircraft industry was. The region had been the epicenter of American aviation going back to the 1910 Los Angeles Air Meet, the first international aviation event held in the US. But that just brings up another question: Why did the industry concentrate in Southern California?

This was not inevitable. The Wright brothers, after all, were based in Dayton, Ohio, and many other American cities and regions over the years were home to aircraft and then aerospace firms: Buffalo (Curtiss), Detroit (Ford), Seattle (Boeing), Wichita (Stearman), Long Island (Grumman, Republic), St. Louis (McDonnell), Dallas (Chance Vought). None, however, boasted the concentration of Southern California, whose roster of aircraft firms included Douglas, Lockheed, Northrop, Hughes, North American, and Consolidated-Vultee (later known as Convair). Of the top five aircraft producers in World War II, four were in Southern California, three in LA.[1]

Most people assume this was just because of the weather. Southern California sunshine allows year-round flying and made outdoor construction of large aircraft possible in the early days. But many other places in the United States have nice weather, the California coast is often socked in by fog, and almost all aerospace work is conducted indoors. A host of other factors, besides the weather, attracted early flyers to Southern California.

One was real estate. Hard to believe amid today's suburban sprawl and skyrocketing real estate prices, but a century ago Southern California had bountiful open space and cheap land for airfields and aircraft plants. In addition, city boosters—from newspaper publishers to real-estate developers to Hollywood moguls—seized on aviation as the technological wave of the future. The real-estate magnate Henry Huntington helped raise money for the 1910 Los Angeles Aviation Meet; Harry Chandler, the *LA Times* publisher (and real-estate baron in his own right), helped Donald Douglas raise capital for his airplane firm. One local businessman proclaimed in 1926, "There is going to be a Detroit of the aircraft industry. Why not here in Los Angeles?"[2]

Then there were the local universities that supplied research, testing facilities, and, most importantly, the scientists and engineers who went out and populated the aircraft firms: most notably Caltech, which boasted one of the first and finest aeronautical engineering programs in the country, eventually followed by UCLA, USC, Cal State Long Beach, and others.[3] Several key actors in Stealth studied or worked at Caltech, UCLA, and USC. Open-shop labor provided another inducement; Southern California aircraft plants only began to be unionized in the 1930s, and even then their growing contributions to national defense constrained union activity.[4]

Then, once a few firms located in the region, they and their followers enjoyed the benefits of what economists call agglomeration. The firms in the area could tap a network of close-tolerance machine shops, electronics fabricators, and other specialized suppliers, along with a specialized, skilled workforce.[5] Engineers could bounce from firm to firm, accumulating experience and spreading ideas. Notable examples included Jack Northrop, who worked for Douglas and then Lockheed before striking out on his own, and, later, a few key figures for Stealth. Cold War defense work encouraged such flightiness—as a contract at one company wound down, its engineers would start looking for the next contract ramping up at another firm—and helped coin a moniker for these mobile engineers: "aero braceros."[6]

A final, less tangible factor was a regional culture of expansive imagination and entrepreneurialism. Southern California had long attracted iconoclasts, visionaries, and dreamers, nourishing a culture of risk-taking and boundary-pushing. The émigré architect Richard Neutra, who arrived in 1925, found "a people who were more 'mentally footloose' than those elsewhere." In Southern California, Neutra wrote, "one can do almost anything that comes to mind and is good fun."[7] Carey McWilliams, the perceptive early chronicler of Southern California, described the region in 1946 as "a great laboratory of experimentation."[8]

———

As that laboratory remobilized to wage the Cold War, the vast influx of people and federal funding launched Southern California into the economic stratosphere. The US military funneled $50 billion into California between 1952 and 1962, a bonanza that produced what some historians have described as perhaps the greatest growth in prosperity in modern history.[9] The space race then ignited a second stage of growth, boosting the local economy into orbit. Many local aircraft firms, including Lockheed and Northrop, made the transition from aero to space, joined by a bevy of upstarts: Aerojet, Rocketdyne, Autonetics, Aeronutronics—their very names radiating Space Age enthusiasm.[10]

Southern California intensified its hold on the national imagination as a land of limitless possibility. As the writer Matt Warshaw described the era, "Los Angeles would try anything: it inhaled people, and exhaled ideas and trends." At the end of 1969, just a few years before the invention of Stealth, a *Time* magazine cover story, titled "California: A State of Excitement," declared California "virtually a nation unto itself." The *Time* writers rhapsodized, "This El Dorado is the mirror of America as it will become, or at least the hothouse for its most rousing fads, fashions, trends and ideas. . . . California is billed as a now scene. But the fact is, everyone living here has one foot in now and another in tomorrow. Here, you get the feeling, is the authentic international dateline. Here the future begins." Just two years earlier, the writer Wallace Stegner had famously declared that California was like the rest of America, only more so. He added, less famously, "This is indeed where the future will be made."[11]

The rest of Stegner's essay, however, made a plea for the past, for tradition and stability—because aerospace wasn't the only thing happening in

California in the 1960s. Another development, of course, was the counterculture.

There are two iconic images of 1960s California. One is the long-haired, tie-dyed hippie; the other is the aerospace engineer, in short-sleeved white button-down, skinny dark tie, and crew cut, with pocket protector and slide rule. The images seem orthogonal: the hippie a free spirit, flipping the bird to authority and denouncing the military-industrial complex; the aerospace engineer dedicated, conservative, and patriotic. On one side, romantic hedonism, turning on and dropping out; on the other, rocket-science rationality and can-do discipline. Norman Mailer saw it that way; after the moon landing, he mocked the hippies: "You've been drunk all summer . . . and *they* have taken the moon."[12]

But the realms of the hippie and the engineer were not completely opposed. Some of the "Sixties" infiltrated aerospace—and the Stealth program.[13] Now, no one would ever mistake Kelly Johnson for Timothy Leary, or aerospace industry offices for Haight-Ashbury. Aerospace engineers were not antigovernment, they still trusted people over thirty, and security clearances deterred drug use. Still, these engineers were most decidedly freethinkers, who would readily question authority if they thought the engineering facts were on their side. Consider the words of a former military test pilot who came to the Skunk Works to fly the first Stealth prototypes:

> I must admit I was kind of surprised when I got to the Skunk Works....I was surprised at the level of patriotism and how hard those people worked for the airplane. Rag-tag militia. I mean, you talk about beards and mustaches and long hair and tie-dyed shirts and all those things....Tearaways. Free thinkers. Oh, yeah. Yep. And it's encouraged.[14]

The region's risk-tolerant, freethinking climate may help explain why Stealth emerged there. In the boom years of the 1950s and 1960s, as billions of federal dollars poured into Southern California, the hothouse atmosphere nourished countless intersections between aerospace and the broader culture. The LA architects William Pereira and Albert Martin Jr. rendered Space Age aesthetics in glass and steel for aerospace companies, in what has been described as "aerospace modernism."[15] In art, Robert Irwin worked with Lockheed and NASA engineers, exploring how the sensory deprivation of anechoic chambers or of astronauts in orbit affected aesthetic perception, while the Art and Technology movement sought to forge collaboration between leading artists such as Robert Rauschenberg and engineers at local aerospace firms.[16] In literature, aerospace not only helped make LA a capital of science fiction; it also gave Thomas Pynchon his start (as a technical writer for Boeing), and he filled his books with aerospace allusions—including *Gravity's Rainbow*, which he wrote in the late 1960s and early 1970s while living in Manhattan Beach, a beachside bedroom community for aerospace engineers from nearby TRW and Northrop.[17]

Aerospace engineers also helped create Southern California's vaunted leisure culture. A Caltech engineering student and Douglas Aircraft employee, Bob Simmons, made the crucial innovations in surfboard design that led to surfing's postwar boom; a RAND aeronautical engineer, James Drake, invented the windsurfer (his report announced that "boredom is completely eliminated"); another aerospace engineer, Tom Morey, brought wave-riding to the masses with the boogie board.[18]

Aerospace engineering, in short, was deeply interwoven into the culture of Southern California. The engineers themselves would likely deny that their aircraft reflect the surrounding culture. The laws of physics or engineering are the same everywhere; airplanes of a given era often resemble each other no matter where they're built, because their designs reflect not particular cultural whims but universal laws of nature. But technologies can reflect the place of their production. Soviet aircraft and rockets, for example, often displayed a characteristic gigantism, seeking to impress through sheer size; the Tupolev ANT-20 of the 1930s boasted eight engines and a 200-foot wingspan, far larger than any American plane.[19]

We have no concrete example of a cultural influence on Stealth design—no airfoil or engine inlet modeled on a surfboard. But we do have a tantalizing suggestion.

———

The exemplar of postwar Southern California culture, of course, was Walt Disney, whose Disneyland opened in 1955. Disneyland repackaged small-town midwestern America for the sprawling postwar aerospace suburbs, presenting a sanitized, nostalgic Main Street. That backward-looking ethos hid a forward-looking embrace of technology. As the historian Eric Avila has noted, Disney represented an essential paradox, "using technical innovations to represent traditional values."[20] Disney captured the blue-sky technological sensibility in his trademark, "Imagineering."

Some of Disney's technical innovations came from California's defense industry. Disney hired Stanford Research Institute, a defense-oriented think tank, to choose the park's site and plan its layout, and Disneyland's robot animatronics, for instance in the Enchanted Tiki Room, were controlled by a magnetic tape system originally developed for the Polaris submarine missile, for which Disney licensed the patent.[21] Another quintessential Californian, Ray Bradbury, in a 1965 article titled "The Machine-Tooled Happyland," marveled at these animatronics and called Disney and his park the "prime movers of our age."[22] One of Disneyland's main attractions, Tomorrowland, symbolized faith in aerospace, especially its centerpiece ride, the Rocket to the Moon. A later Tomorrowland exhibit, the Carousel of Progress, opened in 1967 under the sponsorship of General Electric, which would soon build the engines for both the F-117 and B-2.

There was, in fact, a more direct Disney connection to Stealth. It came in the person of Richard Scherrer, who combined Disneyland and aerospace with another typically California pursuit, hot rods. Scherrer was born and raised in Seattle; his father spent time in prison for his role as a driver and mechanic for rumrunners and apparently passed on his mechanical ability to his son. Scherrer, like many other future engineers, built model airplanes as a youth, and in junior high school he had a job running a punch press making parts of model planes. That job led eventually to shop-floor jobs at Boeing, in between stints at the University of Washington. He apparently also inherited his father's love of fast cars; he dropped out of college at one point "due to some foolish expenses," he recalled, "including a 1938 Lincoln-Zephyr V-12

Coupe." He eventually graduated in 1942 with a degree in aeronautical engineering and went to work for the Ames Research Center, a lab run by the National Advisory Committee for Aeronautics (the forerunner to NASA) in Mountain View, south of San Francisco.[23]

In the early 1950s Scherrer was working at Ames and goofing around with hot rods—this was, after all, the hot-rod heyday later celebrated by the Beach Boys and "American Graffiti." It is no accident that hot-rods became a particular symbol of California just at the time the aerospace industry took off. Many California hot-rodders were young aerospace engineers who spent their weekends tinkering in garages with custom camshafts and exhaust manifolds.[24] One of them was Scherrer, who was building a sports car with some buddies and looking around for a place to do the welding. He found it at the Arrow Development Company, a machine shop near Ames in Mountain View, so he started hanging around the shop while working on his car.

The Arrow shop was run by Ed Morgan and Karl Bacon, a couple of mechanical geniuses of a type common to midcentury America; they could seemingly fix or build anything. In the early 1950s they had gotten a job making some playground equipment, which led to work on a merry-go-round, then a miniature train ride, and eventually to a contract from Disneyland making the cars for Mr. Toad's Wild Ride. That led to a long association with Disney, for whom they built some of the canonical early Disneyland rides.[25]

Bacon and Morgan recognized a kindred spirit in the young Scherrer and recruited him to help with the engineering on the Disney jobs. Scherrer agreed, moonlighting at Arrow for several years while working his regular job at Ames, trying to keep his Ames bosses in the dark despite mysterious phone calls. His Disney projects at Arrow included the Tea Cups, Dumbo the Flying Elephant, the Matterhorn, and the Flying Saucers.[26]

Scherrer continued consulting for Arrow even after he took a new job in 1959 with Lockheed. The engineer who helped build the Flying Saucers for Disney's Tomorrowland would, less than twenty years later, help invent Stealth aircraft. In fact, Scherrer was the only major designer to work on Stealth at both Lockheed and Northrop, on both the

F-117 and the B-2. Most engineers would say there is no connection. Engineering is purely about optimizing a machine for a particular function—whether that function is maximizing the fun on an amusement park ride or minimizing the radar signature of an airplane. But if engineers can help Dumbo take to the air, perhaps so, too, can they make some other far-out, blue-sky contraptions fly. And that was not the last connection between Disneyland and Stealth.

————

Disney provided an antidote to another vision of Los Angeles, one that was not clean, controlled, and conservative but rather disorderly, dirty, and dangerous. Southern California had long toggled between two opposing visions of the place. On the one hand, there was the sunshine state of palm trees and beaches, extraordinary technological creativity, and economic opportunity; on the other hand, a dark dystopia where the powerful exploited the underprivileged and plundered the environment, and violence lurked in the shadows. The wonderful world of Disney against the cynicism of *Chinatown*. In short, sunshine versus noir.[27]

As much as Disney tried to banish this darker vision of California, it survived—and resurfaced just as Stealth was germinating. Southern California in the early 1970s no longer had the heady buzz of the space race. Even as astronauts were stepping onto the moon, delivered by rockets and spacecraft made in California, the aerospace economy had stalled, like a rocket motor at apogee. It soon entered a tailspin, with a flaming trail of pink slips.

The downsizing actually started in the late 1960s, as NASA began ramping down from Apollo and the cost of the Vietnam War ate into new weapons development. *Aviation Week*, the industry's barometer, declared 1970 "the gloomiest year in decades," and the decline only steepened, finally bottoming out in 1972. From 1967 to 1972 LA aerospace firms shed over fifty thousand jobs, a third of the aerospace workforce.[28]

Layoffs and cutbacks caused resentment to percolate through Southern California, amplifying the effects of a national recession and providing a rude awakening to the region after two decades of affluence. To economic woes one could add traffic on the freeways, smog in the air, racial tension, drug abuse, and a general hangover of anxiety. Antimilitary attitudes prompted by the Vietnam War further stressed the region's defense industry. The turmoil reached even the suburban sanctuary of Disneyland, where in summer 1970 a group of three hundred antiwar protesters overran security and raised a Viet Cong flag on Tom Sawyer's Island.[29]

Far from the utopian visions of just a few years earlier, Los Angeles was becoming synonymous with dystopia, soon represented in movies such as *Blade Runner* and *The Terminator*. A 1972 book entitled *California: The Vanishing Dream* identified a "crisis" in the Golden State.[30] In 1977 *Time* magazine, retreating from its previous sunny outlook, asked in a headline, "Whatever happened to California?" The article answered, "Everyone agrees that the California of the '60s, a mystical land of abundance and affluence, vanished some time in the '70s.... California has clearly lost the magic it once had."[31]

———

California had only misplaced the magic, not lost it altogether. Southern California had long gotten used to the boom-and-bust cycles of aerospace: the golden age of Lindbergh and Earhart gave way to the Great Depression, and World War II's vast mobilization evaporated after the war's end. The early 1970s were indeed dark days for Southern California, but sunny days soon returned—in part because, amid the desperation, a handful of engineers thought they knew how to build an airplane with a radar signature ten thousand times smaller than that of existing planes. And those enterprising engineers worked in two firms based about twenty miles apart across the LA basin. In a land of make-believe, if you believe it, you can make it.[32]

CHAPTER THREE

BREEDING INVISIBLE RABBITS

The initial push for Stealth came from the Advanced Research Projects Agency, known by its acronym, ARPA. As its name suggested, the agency was designed to pursue far-out ideas, ones with uncertain and distant payoffs, beyond the short-term horizons of the military services. Created by Congress and President Dwight D. Eisenhower in 1958, amid the national alarm after Sputnik, ARPA provided a focal point for the nation's missile projects, at the time scattered among the various services. When NASA and the Air Force took over much of the missile work, ARPA shifted toward general long-term, high-risk technologies. In the 1960s, for instance, it supported research on missile defense, particle beams, and a distributed computer network known as ARPANET, forerunner of the internet.[1]

ARPA reported to the director of defense research and engineering, better known as the DDR&E, a post created at the same time as ARPA and for the same reason: to promote advanced military R&D, coordinating efforts among the various services. In 1969 David Packard, the cofounder of Hewlett-Packard and Nixon's deputy secretary of defense, bolstered the DDR&E office as part of a broader effort to improve military technology. The office recruited a small staff of engineers and applied scientists from industry and government labs and gave them latitude to find and push new ideas.[2]

In the early 1970s ARPA became DARPA when "Defense" was added to its name. It had already started thinking of the future of military technology. Together with the Defense Nuclear Agency, DARPA convened a series of seminars on long-range R&D, or LRRD, from 1973 to 1975. The LRRD workshops started as a high-level, informal,

classified discussion of nuclear strategy but soon undertook a fundamental reconsideration of conventional weapons, for both technological and strategic reasons. Computers and sensors were getting smaller,
faster, and cheaper, making it possible to identify and then strike targets accurately, and the indiscriminate nature of nuclear weapons, with
colossal collateral damage, alarmed strategists. Precision conventional
weapons, combined with survivable delivery systems, might allow the
US to counter a Soviet attack on Western Europe without using nuclear
weapons.[3]

This fertile environment for technology and strategy encouraged the
search for such survivable delivery systems—airplanes that would be
invisible to the radars of Soviet air defenses.

————

The laws of physics made radar reduction seem impossible. Inspiration
that it might be possible came from the world of model airplanes, a
world that has played an underappreciated role in aviation history.
Model planes served as an entry point in the early to mid-twentieth
century for many budding aerospace engineers, a number of whom cut
their aeronautical teeth as youth on balsa-wood, rubber-band-powered
model aircraft, customizing airfoils and shaving off ounces with razor
blades. Some further honed their skills in contests, the simplest one
based on time aloft from a single windup of the rubber band, another
called Combat, where two wire-controlled planes trailing long ribbons
sought to buzz off each other's ribbon with their propeller. Several engineers who later worked on Stealth at Lockheed and Northrop built
and flew model planes as kids.[4]

And some of these model-plane enthusiasts maintained an interest
into their adult years. One of them was the DDR&E from 1965 to
1973, the physicist John S. Foster, better known as Johnny, who in his
free time liked to build and fly radio-controlled model planes with his
son. Foster's hobby had a direct influence on the origins of Stealth. At
the time the Vietnam War was revealing the Army's paramount need
for ground reconnaissance. Foster wondered whether a big model
plane, equipped with a camera and sensors, and taking advantage of

new miniature electronics for a lightweight radio control, might help. The result was the miniature remotely piloted vehicle, or Mini-RPV. In effect, the RPVs were the predecessors of today's camera-bearing drones (or UAVs, as some know them). An early model built by Philco-Ford in 1972 was a propeller-driven, fixed-gear airplane that looked like a boxy, scaled-down Cessna, with a 12-foot wingspan, a weight of about 70 pounds, and a price tag of $10,000, almost all of that for high-tech stability and control electronics. The weight included a pay-load of cameras, infrared sensors, or laser target designators.[5]

Engineers soon discovered a surprising side benefit: the Mini-RPV's relatively small size, together with its plastic material and judicious shaping, made it much less visible to radar. DARPA commissioned a couple of "observable-optimized" Mini-RPV models—one a rounded delta wing with twin canted-in tails from Teledyne Ryan, the other from McDonnell Douglas with a V-tail—and found they could achieve radar cross sections orders of magnitude below those of conventional tactical military aircraft, in the .005-.01 square meter range, or as low as half a square foot, about as big across as the book you're read-ing. The F-15, by comparison, had a cross section of about 25 square meters—roughly 5,000 times greater than the lowest value obtained by the Mini-RPV. Now they were getting somewhere.[6]

ARPA tested one such Mini-RPV model against a captured Soviet ZSU-23, a radar-guided, 23-millimeter antiaircraft gun that had proved devastating against Israeli planes in the 1973 Arab-Israeli War. In the test, the gun crew tried in vain to find and track the RPV on their radar screens. As the story goes, a frustrated gunner finally switched off the radar, saying that he could aim better with his optical sight. In a 1974 article about the Mini-RPV, DARPA program managers introduced a term for this radar-evading capability: "stealth."[7]

These results set two men in particular to thinking. A piloted military aircraft, carrying weapons and fuel, would of course be bigger than the Mini-RPV. But what if you took the concept demonstrated by the Mini-RPV, of low radar cross section, and pushed it? If you pushed to the limit, could you make an airplane essentially invisible to radar?

One of the two men was William Elsner, an engineer at Wright-Patterson Air Force Base outside Dayton, where the Air Force Aeronautical Systems Division oversaw the development and acquisition of new airplanes and weapons systems. In order for the Air Force to know what it needed and whether its contractors were providing it, Wright-Patt, as it was called, had its own extensive engineering staff. Elsner was one of them, in the Air Force RPV program. He used crutches because of a childhood bout with polio; low-key and quiet, open and friendly, Elsner was widely admired and respected within an engineering fraternity circumscribed by military secrecy.[8]

The other man was Ken Perko of DARPA. A big, genial engineer, Perko had worked in the Air Force RPV office at Wright-Patt and thus knew Elsner and the Mini-RPV results. In June 1974 Kent Kresa, a DARPA manager working on the Mini-RPVs, hired Perko for DARPA's Tactical Technology Office. It was an inspired choice. Perko was a master string-puller, one of those bureaucratic entrepreneurs who knows how to work the system to get things done.[9]

Elsner and Perko became the true believers in Stealth on the government side. They took the Mini-RPV results and pushed the idea of radar invisibility in a combat aircraft. They would be the key initial middlemen between the world of strategy and politics on the one hand and technology on the other, the midlevel program managers who saw Stealth's potential, got the funding to explore it, and then oversaw its development.

Perko and Elsner had support from above. In 1973 Johnny Foster stepped down as DDR&E; his replacement was Malcolm Currie, a PhD in engineering physics from Berkeley who had gone to work at Hughes and risen to direct the Hughes Research Labs. Currie brought in a new DARPA director, George Heilmeier, a PhD in electronics from Princeton who had worked at RCA, where he helped invent liquid crystal displays in the 1960s, a major advance in consumer technology. Both Currie and Heilmeier had a research background, but both also came from industrial labs where the goal of R&D was a working device. The nation, after all, was still at war. At DDR&E and DARPA, they looked for ideas that would lead to practical military technology.[10]

In 1974 Currie asked Robert Moore, a deputy in DARPA's Tactical Technology Office, if he had any good ideas for new programs. Moore told Currie about the idea of an airplane invisible to radar, which he had heard about from Perko, who had recently arrived at DARPA and was working for Moore. Currie was interested and had money to support good ideas, so Perko tapped that fund for $200,000 to support an initial round of studies.[11]

Further inspiration came from Charles Myers, who had joined the DDR&E air warfare group the previous year. Myers had been a World War II bomber pilot, then a Navy test pilot, and in the late 1960s had been one of the Fighter Mafia backing the Lightweight Fighter, the future F-16. Myers had also developed an interest in an aircraft that could defeat radar, and through Moore he learned of Perko's Mini-RPV approach. Myers provided not only interest in the project but also a name for it: Harvey, after the 1950 film starring James Stewart, about a man whose best friend is a six-foot-tall invisible rabbit.[12]

Perko asked five aircraft firms to submit proposals for Project Harvey, for an aircraft with a low radar cross section. Fairchild and Grumman had no interest, and General Dynamics responded with a plan that relied on electronic countermeasures, or ECM, defeating radar by active electronic jamming. Only Northrop and McDonnell Douglas responded with promising proposals involving shaping and materials, so each got a $100,000 contract in late 1974 to conduct further studies. DARPA ran the contracts through the RPV office at Wright-Patt, which meant that Elsner was the lead Air Force engineer on the project, working with Perko at DARPA.[13] If the initial studies looked promising, DARPA would pursue a bigger program—but that meant getting Air Force support.

The Air Force brass at first did not welcome Stealth with open arms. The service had an entrenched commitment to ECM, and to the ECM community Stealth represented a diversion—or even a threat, siphoning off funds that might otherwise support its programs. ECM represented a relatively mature technology, about three decades'-worth, going back to the "Battle of the Beams" in World War II, a much safer bet than some engineers proposing a ten-thousand-fold reduction in radar cross section. What one Northrop scientist described as "electropolitics" helps explain why he and his colleagues feared that Stealth would be stifled in its cradle.[14]

The Air Force not only had to overcome resistance from its ECM community; at the time it was focused on building the F-16, the Lightweight Fighter backed by the rebellious Fighter Mafia, and Air Force leaders were not keen to take on another outsider-backed project that challenged established elements of the defense community. Engineers in general had a name for this tendency: they called it "NIH syndrome," for "not invented here." Currie arranged a breakfast meeting with the Air Force chief of staff, General David Jones (known, inevitably, as Davy), where he pledged to back Jones on the F-16 if Jones would support Stealth. Currie then arranged for Perko and Heilmeier to brief Jones and Lieutenant General Alton Slay, Jones's deputy for R&D. Slay was skeptical, but at the end of the briefing Currie asked Jones for his thoughts, and Jones, holding up his end of the bargain, replied, "I don't see how we can turn away from this." Slay fell into line, and the Air Force was on board for Stealth.[15]

Perko and Elsner now had to see if Northrop and McDonnell Douglas could produce actual designs. One firm Perko had not invited to the initial dance was Lockheed, which had been out of the fighter aircraft business for over a decade and to some eyes had lost its cutting edge. Most of its recent work was on decidedly unsexy patrol and transport aircraft along with the L-1011, a big passenger airliner. In fact Lockheed's Skunk Works had built several spy planes for the CIA that included early forays into Stealth. The problem was that the spy planes were so highly classified, at a level known as a Special Access Program, that few people—not Perko, in any event—knew about them. A Lockheed engineer, however, got wind of Project Harvey, which at the time was classified merely at the Confidential level, the lowest level of clearance, and he alerted Lockheed management to the program. Lockheed got permission from the CIA to reveal its Stealth experience to DARPA, but they were too late: DARPA had already awarded all the available money to Northrop and McDonnell Douglas. Lockheed managers responded, in effect, that they would do it for nothing, and the company entered the contest using its own money.[16]

In their initial design proposals Lockheed and Northrop seemed to take a similar approach and McDonnell Douglas an alternate path. When radar waves encounter a surface they are reflected back, and some of the reflected waves can make their way back to an adversary's radar antenna. If the surface has straight edges, the radar waves bounce back perpendicularly, as if from a mirror, so you get a spike, like a glint of light, in one direction. If the surface has curved edges, you get a smaller return but in all directions. The Lockheed and Northrop philosophy was that it was better to have one single spike and then make that spike go the wrong way, away from the radar antenna. The McDonnell Douglas approach was to avoid a spike altogether and scatter the reflection in many directions. So Lockheed's and Northrop's designs, looked at from above, had straight edges along the fuselage and wings; the McDonnell Douglas outline, viewed from above, had continuous curves, with the fuselage flowing into the wing edges.[17]

The similarities between Lockheed and Northrop's design, however, obscured a fundamental difference. The two firms agreed that the edges should be straight. But what about everything in between?

In spring 1975 DARPA had identified a particular radar cross section as the threshold for Stealth, a number below which an airplane would be effectively invisible to radar. In August DARPA asked the three firms to propose an aircraft design to achieve that number. Lockheed and Northrop submitted designs that, according to computer models of radar scattering, met the number. McDonnell Douglas's design could not; it proposed to make up the difference with ECM. That eliminated them. In November 1975 DARPA awarded contracts of about $1.5 million each to Lockheed and Northrop to enter the next round of what was now called the Experimental Survivable Testbed program, or XST. In Phase I the two firms would have four months to design and build a full-scale model to test against an actual radar. Whichever firm achieved a lower radar cross section would win Phase I and proceed to Phase II, building and flying two prototype aircraft based on the Phase I design. In short, the XST contest would determine who built the first Stealth airplane.[18]

CHAPTER FOUR

LOCKHEED

TIN SHED IN A HURRICANE

In 1912 Allan and Malcolm Loughead, brothers who were self-taught mechanics, started an aircraft business in San Francisco. They first built seaplanes for sightseeing on the bay, moved to Santa Barbara and then Hollywood, and finally, in 1928, settled in Burbank. Along the way the firm went through several rounds of failure and reorganization, driving Malcolm out of the business; meanwhile Allan, tired of being called "Lug-head," Americanized the company's spelling to match its Scottish pronunciation. Yet another collapse eventually drove Allan out as well, and when a group of investors bought the company in bankruptcy court in 1932, all that remained of the founding brothers was the name on the letterhead.[1]

Lockheed's new owners started with a small plant in Burbank and intended to stay relatively small, thinking they might someday reach a few thousand employees. In the late 1930s tensions in Europe started military contracts flowing, and then World War II unleashed a flood. Lockheed swelled to ninety-four thousand employees working in three shifts around the clock, each shift change sweeping a vast tide of human labor in and out of the Burbank plant. Lockheed was not unique in this respect; other Southern California aircraft firms, such as Douglas and North American, reached similar sizes, and like the workforces of those other firms, Lockheed's included a substantial number of women, true to the image of "Rosie the Riveter." The wartime Lockheed line turned out Hudson bombers, Lodestar transports, and Ventura and Harpoon patrol bombers, along with almost three thousand B-17 bombers based on Boeing's design and ten thousand of Lockheed's P-38 Lightning, a twin-engine fighter with distinctive twin booms and tails.

When the war ended, the aircraft industry entered a nosedive. Lockheed slashed staff to 14,500 within a couple of years, but the emerging Cold War soon brought a new wave of defense contracts. By the mid-1950s Lockheed was the third-largest aircraft firm in the US, and it bolstered its position by launching into the military side of the Space Age. Most notably, Lockheed built the Polaris submarine missile and the Corona spy satellites, the former providing a survivable third leg to the nuclear deterrent, the latter providing detailed information about the Soviet Union.

Lockheed from its reincarnation in 1932 was run by a series of financiers, not engineers. Aircraft was, after all, a business, one that required knowledge not only of airflows and propulsion, but also of stock issues, loans for plant expansion and operating capital, and shareholders and a board of directors. The financial acumen of Lockheed's managers balanced the technological enthusiasm of engineering staff with a keen eye for the bottom line.[2]

That keen eye had reason for concern in the early 1970s. The aerospace drawdown hit Lockheed especially hard, putting the company on the verge of bankruptcy and leading to thousands of layoffs. The company had bet big on the L-1011, a technologically advanced commercial airliner, only to see the project hit political and technical snags and hemorrhage billions of dollars. A $250 million loan guarantee from the government rescued Lockheed from imminent collapse; nevertheless, by 1975 Lockheed stock had fallen to less than $3.75 a share, a third of its value a dozen years earlier. In February 1976 the chairman of Lockheed's board, Dan Haughton, and its vice chair and president, Carl Kotchian, resigned, under additional fire for a bribery scandal involving foreign sales.[3]

The financial woes made Lockheed wary of investments in risky new technologies. Amid these stormy seas, however, there was a secret island of creative iconoclasts, which offered some hope for Lockheed's entry into Stealth.

———

The island's ruler was an engineer named Clarence L. Johnson. Though of Swedish heritage he was known universally as Kelly, a nickname bestowed by childhood classmates after he won a schoolyard brawl; they decided that a tough Irish name suited him better than Clarence. Kelly was fixated on flight from an early age, drawing remarkably accurate pictures of airplanes as a young boy and even more sophisticated renderings as a freshman engineering student at the University of Michigan. In 1933 Lockheed hired Johnson fresh off his master's degree in aeronautical engineering, also from Michigan; he was thus part of the shift in the aircraft business from the self-taught tinkerers of the early air age to university-trained engineers from the new departments of aeronautical engineering.[4]

One of Kelly's first acts in his new job was to tell his superiors that their latest airplane design stank. Lockheed had sent a model of the plane to Michigan for testing in its wind tunnels, and Kelly had seen the data and concluded that the plane was unstable. The Lockheed engineers said to the cheeky new hire, in effect: OK, hotshot, how should we fix it? Kelly went back to the wind tunnel and found an elegant solution, replacing the single tail with twin tails for better control. The twin tails became a hallmark of that generation of Lockheed planes, including the P-38 Lightning. Hall Hibbard, who was Lockheed's chief designer and no slouch himself, exclaimed, "That damned Swede can actually *see* air."[5]

In addition to admiration for his engineering acumen, Kelly acquired a reputation for impatience, aversion to bureaucracy, and a temper. As he rose into management, he regularly blew up at underlings and fired them on the spot—and as quickly forgot about it, so that after a point fired staffers didn't bother cleaning out their desks; they just kept their head down at work for a couple of days.

During World War II Lockheed assigned Kelly a small group to develop the XP-80, the first operational American jet fighter, for the Army Air Forces, the predecessor to the Air Force. He had total authority over every phase of the work, from staffing and purchasing to production and testing. This allowed Kelly to shortcut the usual detailed procedures needed for mass production by low-skilled employees, and the group designed and built the XP-80 in a nearly miraculous 143 days. He took the lessons from that experience to heart.

Lockheed kept Kelly's group intact at the end of the war, operating as a largely independent fiefdom within Lockheed. Officially known as Lockheed Advanced Development Programs, or ADP, the outfit acquired a nickname: the Skunk Works. The name came from the L'il Abner comic strip, one of whose characters brewed liquor in a pungent outdoor still, which he called the "Skonk Works." Kelly's group early on endured a bad stench from a nearby factory, and one of them jokingly answered the phone one day with the greeting "Skonk Works!" Kelly was not amused, but the name stuck, and Lockheed eventually trademarked it—with the proper spelling, to appease the cartoonist's lawyers.

Brilliant and blunt, Kelly ran the Skunk Works by a set of principles that boiled down to using a small team of very good people and granting them space to work. Kelly summarized his approach thusly: "Be quick, be quiet, be on time." Or, as he put it in another axiom, "Keep it simple, stupid"—what he called the KISS principle.[6] The Skunk Works applied the streamlined approach to a series of cutting-edge aircraft, starting with the F-104 jet fighter, which first flew in 1956, and then the celebrated U-2 and SR-71 spy planes. The strict secrecy around the spy planes helped Kelly keep government oversight—and accompanying bureaucracy—at bay, building advanced aircraft quickly and on budget. The secret projects also sealed off the Skunk Works from the rest of Lockheed, which meant the Skunk Works built up its own capability for manufacturing and supporting aircraft after deployment, both of which would prove crucial when it came to Stealth.

In the early 1970s, as Lockheed entered the Stealth competition, the Skunk Works was itself in transition. Kelly, its founder and motive force for three decades, planned to retire at the end of 1974 and hand the reins to his hand-picked successor, Ben Rich. As a young Skunk Works engineer, Rich had helped design the propulsion system on the SR-71, one of the most daunting of that airplane's many technical challenges. At Mach 3, each engine inlet funneled air into the voracious turbojets at a rate of 100,000 cubic feet of air per second, a volume equivalent to the amount of water flowing over Niagara Falls. At that rate supersonic shock waves developed in the inlets, blocking the flow of air and stalling the plane. Rich applied a complex combination of aerodynamic and thermodynamic theory to design a variable cone-shaped inlet, with the cones moving in or out depending on the speed, accommodating the shock waves yet still delivering the huge volume of air to the engines.[7]

Rich's engineering skills, and his energy and ambition, caught Kelly's eye, and Kelly had taken him under his wing. In other ways, however, Rich brought a different style to the Skunk Works. Though Kelly was known to play a prank or two, his general demeanor was brusque and intimidating, backed up by a linebacker's physique. Rich was slight in stature and an incorrigible raconteur, with an ever-present twinkle in his eye and a smile on his lips, often preceded by one of his apparently boundless store of jokes. As one CIA program manager put it, "Kelly ruled by his bad temper. Ben Rich rules with those damned bad jokes." Rich also contrasted with Kelly in his willingness to play the political game, and his jovial schmoozing worked wonders with Pentagon officials and military brass. Kelly's my-way-or-the-highway attitude had gotten technical results, but it had also rubbed a number of Air Force officers the wrong way. That helps explain why the Skunk Works in the early 1970s had no major new project in the offing—which made the Stealth contest all the more important.[8]

Rich, however, almost wasn't around to run the Skunk Works' Stealth project. He was nearly on the other side. In 1972 Northrop offered him a job—and a substantial raise—to run their entry in the lightweight fighter competition. He was ready to take the offer, but Kelly talked him out of it at the last minute, in part through a promise that Rich would take over the Skunk Works when Kelly retired in three years.[9]

By the mid-1970s, then, the Skunk Works had developed a formidable reputation for blue-sky, boundary-pushing aircraft—and a matching confidence in its own abilities. Some of the experience would contribute to its development of Stealth. Some of the self-confidence would not.

———

The experience came on the U-2 and SR-71. The CIA knew how much the spy plane overflights enraged the Soviets, and also knew that Soviet radars had managed to track the high-flying U-2. The Soviets just couldn't reach the spy plane with their missiles...yet. In 1957, three years before the Soviets shot down U-2 pilot Francis Gary Powers with a radar-guided missile, the CIA undertook Project Rainbow to reduce the U-2's radar signature. Skunk Works engineers coated the bottom of the fuselage with a fiberglass honeycomb covered with a graphite-bearing layer, developed with the help of radar experts at MIT's Lincoln Lab. The quarter-inch-thick radar-absorbing material indeed absorbed radar waves, but only in certain wavelengths. It also acted as an insulator, trapping engine heat in the fuselage. On a test flight in April 1957 the heat buildup caused an engine flameout, and the pilot died in the crash.

They then tried another approach, stringing copper-plated wire with ferrite beads around the fuselage and tail, so that the plane looked like it had flown through a wire fence. The gain in radar protection again came at a steep cost: all that dangling wire increased the airplane's weight and drag, cutting its operating altitude by 5,000 feet and its range by 20 percent; the planes were dubbed "dirty birds." Since the whole point of the U-2 was high-altitude flight and long range, Kelly scotched the radar treatment.[10]

The U-2 taught the Skunk Works a vital lesson: techniques to reduce radar cross section could not be retrofitted onto an existing aircraft. For the successor to the U-2, the Skunk Works engineers had the opportunity to incorporate a low radar cross section from the outset, in the design phase. For this follow-on, Kelly first sketched a U-2 variant, which he called, coincidentally, the B-2. Instead of a cylindrical fuselage, it had an upper fuselage that sloped inward to deflect radar energy, and the lower fuselage blended smoothly into the wing bottoms. Other brainstorming Skunk Works engineers sketched more outlandish concepts, including a flying wing and a "Batplane," a blended wing-body with curved leading and trailing edges. Kelly also considered making an airframe out of fiberglass or plastic so it would be transparent to radar, similar to the way some early aviators had tried transparent wing or fuselage materials to make planes harder to see from the ground. But that just meant the radar reflected from the guts of the plane, starting with the metal engine.[11]

Some of these concepts looked like they might shed radar, but they were aerodynamically unstable and never got off the drawing board. Kelly therefore went a different direction: if an airplane flew fast enough, and high enough, it might zip through a radar beam too quickly to detect. Some of the Lincoln Lab radar experts thought that he was more interested in pushing the aerodynamic envelope than in addressing the radar signature—and moreover that he was not interested in ideas offered from the outside the Skunk Works. Kelly "showed no interest at all," as one of them put it, "in minimizing the radar cross section of any successor to the U-2." Not for the last time.[12]

In Kelly's defense, Skunk Works engineers had looked at radars and concluded that likely advances in technology in coming years would render *any* aircraft detectable, even ones with reduced radar cross section. That is, they believed that radars would improve faster than airplanes could. Kelly argued further, with some reason, that the CIA's hugely demanding requirements for speed, altitude, and range for the new spy plane (something like Mach 3, 90,000 feet, and 2,000 miles) could *not* be met by a design that also incorporated radar-dodging features; the CIA couldn't have its cake and eat it too. The CIA eventually in effect agreed and reduced the requirements, especially for altitude, for the final version. Finally, Kelly no doubt had an unspoken reason for his attitude toward radar cross section: on the U-2 he had seen a test pilot crash and die in the attempt to reduce it.[13]

There was one person taking radar cross section seriously: the country's commander in chief. The Soviets' ability to detect and track the U-2 made President Eisenhower very nervous. Even if the Soviets couldn't yet shoot it down, their knowledge of overflights raised tensions and the threat of nuclear war. As Ike observed, how would Americans react if they knew that Soviets were conducting regular flights over the US? He was thus pressing hard on the CIA either to make a spy plane undetectable or stop the flights altogether.[14]

To get Kelly's attention, the CIA brought in Convair to compete with Lockheed for the next-generation spy plane—and the agency let Kelly know that Convair had the inside track. He got the message. The final iteration of Lockheed's design incorporated several features to reduce

FIGURE 4.1
Lockheed's A-12 model on the radar test range at Area 51.
Source: Lockheed Martin Skunk Works.

the radar visibility, including a gently rounded top and bottom of the fuselage, and chines from the nose to the wings, with the chines as well as the wings blending into the fuselage to avoid radar-reflecting corners. (A chine on an airplane is a horizontal surface sticking out from a length of the fuselage, something like an extended stubby wing.) The twin tails were also canted inward 15 degrees to avoid reflections directly to the side. This was the famous A-12, better known by its offshoot, the SR-71 Blackbird, whose design—finalized by 1960—is still revered by aircraft aficionados for its sleek appearance; it just looks fast. An SR-71 today sits front and center in the Udvar-Hazy branch of the Smithsonian's National Air and Space Museum.[15]

The chines and the canted tails, however, were for aerodynamics as well as to deflect radar: the chines provided added lift and stability, and the canted tails similarly provided better airflow and control. When it came to reducing the radar signature, more attention went to materials than to shaping—that is, to coating vulnerable surfaces with radar-absorbing material rather than changing their shape. Much systematic effort went into developing that material, which was an asbestos honeycomb loaded with graphite, with the exact composition tuned to absorb specific frequencies of Soviet radars. The leading edges of the chines and wings were major sources of radar return and thus needed the radar-absorbing treatment; so were the engine inlets and exhaust outlets, where radar waves tended to bounce around and resonate as if in a radar echo chamber. (On the SR-71 one can see the distinctive sawtooth pattern of the radar-absorbing material around several edges, analogous to the cone-shaped pattern that damps sound in an anechoic chamber.) For the exhaust problem, Skunk Works engineer Ed Lovick came up with the idea to add cesium salt to the jet fuel; the cesium ionized the exhaust gas, creating a plasma plume to absorb radar and shield the exhaust ducts.[16]

Thus, although the A-12 and SR-71 included some radar-reducing features, the design was dictated primarily by aerodynamics, and most of the radar reduction came from materials. And while the radar-deflecting techniques worked—the A-12's radar cross section was 1/20th that of the B-47 bomber, for example, an airplane of similar length—the Skunk Works still expected that Soviet radars would detect the A-12 but not be able to track it because of its high speed.[17] In short, the A-12 and SR-71 ultimately relied on speed, not stealth, to survive.

The Skunk Works' experience on these planes nevertheless proved crucial fifteen years later, when the CIA allowed Lockheed to reveal the classified work to DARPA and Lockheed won a late entry in the initial Stealth contest. Some of this experience, especially with radar-absorbing materials, proved useful in the contest itself as well. But Lockheed's Stealth design also relied on new ideas, a number of them drawn from outside the Skunk Works. And one of them came from way, way outside the Skunk Works, from a most unlikely source: an obscure physicist in the Soviet Union itself.

Pyotr Ufimtsev was born in 1931 in a town called Ust-Charyshskaya Pristan, in the Altaiskii Krai region on the southern Siberian steppe. A small but bustling port on the Ob River, it had about ten thousand inhabitants. Ufimtsev's childhood was far from idyllic. Stalin's reign of terror was sweeping the country, and when Ufimtsev was three his father was arrested on undisclosed charges and sent to the gulag. Young Pyotr was allowed to say goodbye to his father, not knowing it was the last time he would see him; his father would die in prison, leaving his mother to raise three sons and two daughters. Then World War II descended, and Pyotr's two brothers went off to the front, where they were killed. Since the collective farms sent everything to the army, the remaining family members barely had enough food to survive. The end of the war brought little respite; two years later, life in the town remained extremely grim.

Despite these severe hardships (or perhaps because of them), Ufimtsev had a cheerful personality, though it hid a toughness common to the people who live in Siberia. In earlier times, when migrants arrived to settle in his village, the residents first gave them a test: they were presented with a stack of felled trees and given one day to build a house out of them. (Ufimtsev's grandparents upon their arrival had been given another Herculean trial—to clean out, in a single night, the building used for skinning animals.)

This toughness manifested in perseverance, which Ufimtsev channeled into math and science. One evening in the third grade, stumped by a math homework problem, he stayed up until three in the morning to solve it. He benefited from the Soviet education system, which held small village schools to the same standards as those in Moscow, especially in math and science. He benefited further from a physics teacher at his high school, who, impressed by an essay Ufimtsev wrote on Faraday's laws of electromagnetism, gave him his old college physics textbook as a gift.

One day in his first year of high school, Ufimtsev was picking weeds in the communal garden with his mother. She asked him what he planned to do with his life—presumably something other than picking weeds in a Siberian potato patch. He replied that he wanted to go to university to study math and physics and then, for a career, "to solve physical problems with mathematical methods." Seventy years later, he recalled with a laugh: "And it was done."[18]

Hardship launched him on his career path. He went first to university at Almaty, in Kazakhstan—the choice dictated by his lack of winter clothes, which turned his gaze south to warmer climes. He then transferred to the university at Odessa, again because of privation: he was losing his eyesight, which he ascribed to postwar malnutrition, and the doctors in Almaty recommended he seek care at the renowned eye institute there. In his final year of study toward his master's degree at Odessa, in 1954, a recruiter from a Moscow defense institute came to the physics department and promised Ufimtsev a job upon graduation.

The institute was the Central Research Institute for Radio Engineering, the Defense Ministry's center for radar research. For a young physicist interested in electromagnetism and optics, it was a dream job. Founded during the war, the institute boasted a stellar staff, including such luminary physicists as Vladimir Fock, who had made major contributions to quantum mechanics and general relativity.[19] Much of the institute's work was secret, which to the young Ufimtsev suggested that his father had not been guilty of whatever had condemned him to the gulag. Otherwise Pyotr never would have been trusted with a security clearance.

Ufimtsev took up the problem of diffraction, a topic of long interest to students of nature (including Isaac Newton, for one) that concerns how waves—whether water, sound, or light—behave around the edges of an object. People often think of physics in the twentieth century as exclusively concerned with the exotic new topics of quantum theory and nuclear physics, but older fields such as electromagnetism and optics continued as active research areas, with renewed relevance thanks to technologies such as radar. The great German physicist Arnold Sommerfeld, for example, best known for his work in quantum and atomic theory, wrote a chapter on diffraction theory for an advanced textbook in the 1920s.[20]

Ufimtsev ran across Sommerfeld's paper, and it sparked a basic insight. Illuminate a flat surface or plate with light, or a radar beam, and according to the laws of optics it will reflect at a particular angle. One can treat the beam as individual rays that reflect from the surface or refract around the edges; alternatively, one can—as Ufimtsev did—treat the beam as electromagnetic waves that strike a surface and create currents along the surface, and the currents then radiate electromagnetic waves back out into space. The problem comes when you consider something besides an infinite plate—that is, a finite surface with edges. Physicists knew that an edge actually gave a stronger scattering than the rest of the plate, but they struggled to explain why. In the 1950s Joseph Keller, a mathematician at New York University, developed a so-called geometrical theory of diffraction, but Keller's theory failed in certain crucial regions around objects.[21]

Ufimtsev's breakthrough was to separate the surface currents into uniform and nonuniform components. The uniform current was the same as that expected on a flat surface by standard physical optics. The nonuniform current was what appeared at irregularities in the surface: edges, tips, cracks, or curves. Ufimtsev called these nonuniform components "fringe currents," since they appeared along the edges of bodies. By showing how to calculate the fringe currents and the radiation they generated, he accounted for the diffracted waves in the missing region. He published his theory in a 1962 report—in Russian, of course—whose title translated as "Method of Edge Waves in the Physical Theory of Diffraction." (The research had helped earn him his PhD degree in 1959, which in turn won him a promotion to senior scientist at the institute.) The name he chose for his theory was apt: the *physical* theory of diffraction dealt with real-world features like curves and cracks; Keller's competing *geometrical* theory was based on idealized rays.[22]

Ufimtsev recalled that he was not driven by Cold War ideology. As he saw it, the Great Patriotic War—World War II—had been a real war, an existential threat to the Soviet Union. The Cold War, by comparison, was merely a competition. And that competition included science, which, in his eyes, was akin to a race anyway, as much against his Soviet colleagues as against Americans. In other words, Ufimtsev's motivation in his research was not to defend the fatherland against the American imperialists; it was to understand how waves behaved—and to do so better and sooner than anyone else did. That's why he kept close tabs on American research, including Keller's: to make sure he was in the lead. What mattered to him was the knowledge, not what was made out of it.

That attitude perhaps made it easier for him to accept what the Soviet military did with his theory. Namely, nothing. His institute didn't see enough military value in it to classify it as secret. The theory seemed fairly abstract to begin with, and it furthermore concentrated on radar diffraction for simple shapes like cylinders and cones (what a mathematician calls a "body of revolution"). But the shapes, in fact, betrayed a practical interest within his institute—not in aircraft but rather in *missiles*, which are, after all, made of cylinders and cones. In particular, the theory addressed what was called the "reentry vehicle": the cone-shaped nuclear warhead, like a diabolically destructive dunce cap, that the missile lobbed on a ballistic trajectory toward the other side of the world. Each side had radars to detect the incoming warheads, which mostly just let you know when you would be vaporized in a nuclear holocaust. But in the early 1960s each side also had high hopes for missile defense, and hence much interest in how radar waves scattered off cone-shaped warheads.[23]

Even after Ufimtsev and his institute tried applying the theory to airplanes, in effect pursuing the concept of Stealth, the Soviet military showed no interest. On the contrary, they met outright resistance. The aircraft design bureaus insisted that aircraft design was a matter of aerodynamics, not electromagnetism—and that aeronautical engineers, not physicists, designed planes. Thus the aircraft designers' standard response to Ufimtsev: "Go away." And word came down to Ufimtsev's institute to stop working along such lines. It was not the last time aeronautical engineers dismissed the input of radar physicists.[24]

Ufimtsev, for his part, shrugged and returned to his equations. He was completely unaware that his theory had sparked a revolution in the other camp. Early in the Cold War the US government had recognized a need to translate the proliferating Soviet technical literature. This involved both wholesale translating of Soviet scientific journals, cover to cover, and translating particular articles or reports on demand.[25] The

Air Force had a Foreign Technology Division at Wright-Patterson Air Force Base dedicated to this effort, with both computer and human translators.

The effort paid off. Stan Locus, a senior member of Northrop's radar group, had become something of a guru to the younger members thanks to a back-to-basics philosophy, an insistence on working from first principles. To this one might add cosmopolitanism and persistence. Locus was in the habit of browsing translated Soviet journals. He ran across an article by Ufimtsev that seemed interesting and urged Northrop's resident diffraction theorist, Kenneth Mitzner, to read it. Mitzner put him off for several weeks, thinking the Soviet work would just rehash existing American theory, but Locus kept nagging him. Mitzner finally gave in and read the report. As he put it, "the whole world changed. My eyes opened: 'oh, this is what we need.'" Ufimtsev's article cited his longer 1962 report, so the Air Force, at Northrop's request, ran it through a computer translator in 1971. The machine translation was spotty but serviceable—and the most important part, the equations, was in the universal language of mathematics.[26]

Ufimtsev's nonuniform currents filled the crucial gap in existing theory about radar scattering. No American scientist had ever met him, but the Soviet physicist, known only as a name and theory, became a legendary figure in Stealth design rooms. Northrop's team liked to interrupt their work with choruses of "Go Ufimtsev!" to the tune of "On, Wisconsin!"[27]

To the US intelligence community, meanwhile, Ufimtsev's name became equally mythical, but as a source of concern. They already knew that Soviet physicists and mathematicians were top-notch. Here was a crucial advance made in 1962, and the US only translated it in 1971. The Soviets had about a decade's head start. How far ahead were they now?[28]

———

Lockheed did not yet know about Ufimtsev when it learned about Project Harvey, sometime around the end of 1974. In February 1975, soon after getting the Skunk Works into the Stealth competition, Ed

Martin, the head of science and engineering for all of Lockheed's California operations, assigned an engineer from Lockheed's advanced design office to the Skunk Works to tackle the design job. That engineer was Richard Scherrer.

When we last left Scherrer he was working at the National Advisory Committee for Aeronautics' Ames laboratory in Mountain View and moonlighting at the Arrow Corporation making rides for Disneyland, in between fiddling with his own hot rods. In 1959 Scherrer left Ames for a job in advanced design at Lockheed, where he worked on submarine patrol aircraft and the L-1011 airliner. Before leaving Ames, however, he had worked on wind tunnel tests of supersonic airfoils made out of flat panels, so that when viewed from the side the airfoil looked a double wedge of cheese instead of a curve. The wedge-shaped airfoil offered advantages at supersonic speeds, often in combination with a delta-wing planform (the plane's outline when viewed from above).[29]

Meanwhile, Skunk Works engineers had toyed with flat plates for a different reason. Experiments during the radar-reduction efforts on the U-2 and SR-71 had shown that when a flat plate was large compared to radar wavelength—say, more than 25 wavelengths wide—it would simply act like a mirror, sending all the radar energy off in one direction. For a wavelength of 2 centimeters, that meant the flat plate needed to be at least 20 inches across. (Two centimeters was the wavelength of the Soviet "Gun Dish" radar in the ZSU-23 antiaircraft system, the one used in the original Mini-RPV tests that inspired the Stealth program.) The spy planes had ultimately not used this insight, owing to the aerodynamic demands of the speed and range requirements, but a few of the engineers had made mental note of it.[30]

When he got to the Skunk Works in early 1975, Scherrer learned about these radar results and combined them with his earlier experience with flat-plate airfoils at Ames. What if you built an airplane, Scherrer asked, only out of flat plates? If the plates were angled in the right direction, they might reflect radar energy *away* from the radar receiver. And the Ames research showed that it might work aerodynamically. But how to angle the plates?

The answer came from the head of the Skunk Works computation group, Denys Overholser, a young engineer from a town called Dallas—the one in Oregon, west of Salem, and definitely not Texas-sized. A youth spent roaming the western Oregon woods made Overholser a lifelong outdoorsman, and he had the compact but strong physique of a former college wrestler and some of the same tenacity, doggedly grappling with a problem until he had attained some leverage over it. A smart but indifferent student, he graduated from Oregon State in 1962 with degrees in electrical engineering and math and then took a job working on missiles at Boeing. Like other aerospace firms, Boeing at the time was struggling to integrate computers into aircraft design, as commercial digital computers grew ever more powerful. The problem was that design engineers had trouble communicating their needs to the computer programmers, and vice versa. Boeing decided that it needed a mediator, someone to translate between the two realms, and Overholser got the job. He knew engineering, but he also knew electrical engineering and math, so Boeing sent him for training in computer programming.[31]

In 1964 Overholser left Boeing for Lockheed's Skunk Works, which for similar reasons had formed a small computing group, consisting of a few people, under mathematician Bill Schroeder. The group did not pursue radar cross section calculations at the time, instead taking up myriad programming problems from the computer-controlled machining of titanium to the dispersal of pressure waves in hydraulic tubes. By 1975, after Schroeder had retired, Overholser was running the computer group. He had over a decade of experience with computers but was still only in his midthirties. As Ben Rich put it, "Most of our [Skunk Works] veterans used slide rules that were older than Denys." Then as now, it was the youngsters who knew computers.[32]

Overholser entered the Stealth project by way of sheer coincidence. He happened to occupy the office next to Warren Gilmour, head of operations research at the Skunk Works. Gilmour had gotten the job for the Harvey project of studying the Soviet radar system and determining how stealthy an airplane needed to be to avoid it. In April 1975 Gilmour decided to ask his office neighbor for help. That brought Overholser, an avid bow hunter, into the hunt for invisible rabbits.[33]

Overholser, too, had discussed with Schroeder the idea of using flat plates to deflect radar, and Scherrer now asked him to write a computer program to predict the radar cross section of a given arrangement of flat plates. Overholser asked him when he needed the program. The next month, Scherrer replied. Overholser, incredulous, said that it would take more like six months at least. Maybe he could code it faster, he added, but it would take the combined effort of the whole computer group, then about half a dozen people, with unlimited overtime, and it would also require bringing back Schroeder as a consultant. Scherrer knew that Lockheed was a late entry into the Harvey competition, and that the design team would need a few months of working with a finished code in order to meet DARPA's deadlines. So Scherrer got the extra effort approved, and Overholser and his team launched into a heroic effort, working ninety-hour weeks to crank out the code in the FORTRAN programming language. As a salaried manager, Overholser didn't get overtime pay. However, at the end of one month he had a finished code in hand, called ECHO.[34]

Scherrer meanwhile began figuring out how to build a flyable airplane out of a bunch of flat plates, and he, too, called in some help, including Ed Lovick, who had worked on the U-2 and SR-71; Dick Cantrell, an aerodynamicist; and Kenneth Watson, like Scherrer from advanced design, who helped build a flyable airplane, with everything it needed inside, out of the external configuration Scherrer and Overholser provided.[35]

ECHO worked on the principle that radar waves induced electrical currents on the surface of a metallic object, and that those currents then determined the scattered radiation. ECHO calculated the induced electrical currents on a particular surface and then performed a complicated integral over the entire surface to arrive at the total radar scattering. The output was a computer plot showing the radar cross section from various viewing angles—say, from nose-on, or 45 degrees from the nose, or side-on—and various radar frequencies. At this point it did so using only standard physical optics, not the refinement provided by Ufimtsev's theory. The standard theory, as we know, failed to account for currents along the edges, but Lockheed's designers negated those currents with the special radar-absorbing materials Lockheed had developed for the SR-71's edges.[36]

Above all, ECHO could not handle curved surfaces or curved edges.[37] Like a man looking for his lost keys under a streetlight, Lockheed's engineers knew they could calculate what happened when radar waves hit flat surfaces, so they designed a plane with flat surfaces. Lockheed's program thus highlighted the growing role of computers in aircraft design—not just for aerodynamics but also in modeling the behavior of radar waves around airplane surfaces.

Scherrer and Overholser developed a working pattern. At the end of each day Scherrer gave Overholser a new configuration of flat plates. Overholser and his programmers entered the configuration into a deck of punch cards that evening and fed the deck into the computer. The computer chewed on the numbers overnight and the next morning spit out a plot showing how well the design worked from a radar standpoint. Scherrer then took the results and spent the ensuing day tweaking the design, trying to reconcile the radar cross section with aerodynamics and other demands of aircraft design, such as making room for the engine, fuel, pilot, and so on. At the end of that day Scherrer sent the tweaked design back to Overholser for another round through the computer.

By about May 1975, after several weeks of these iterations, Scherrer and Overholser had evolved a design composed entirely of flat triangular panels, an odd, wingless and tailless contraption that looked more like a UFO than an airplane. It had a flattened diamond shape whether viewed from the front, back, side, or top, prompting skeptical wags in the Skunk Works to christen it the Hopeless Diamond. According to ECHO, the diamond would appear to radar about the size of a ball bearing—as Overholser joked to Rich, it wouldn't even look as big as an eagle, more like "an eagle's eyeball."[38]

The eagle's eyeball was based only on ECHO's estimate, however, which in turn rested on theoretical assumptions about radar scattering. The true test came a month later, around June 1975, when Skunk Works engineers put the Hopeless Diamond on the radar range to see if theory matched experiment. The tests at both an indoor and then a larger

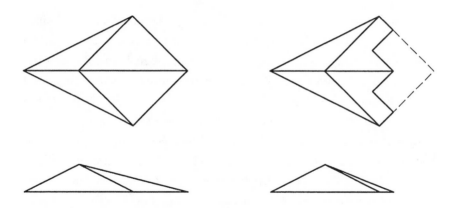

FIGURE 4.2

Basic outline of the Hopeless Diamond, on the left, in plan (top) and side view (bottom). On the right is the modified XST design, with notched tail, which dramatically improved aerodynamic performance with little penalty in radar cross section. The XST provided the basis for the Have Blue design.
Source: Alan Brown.

outdoor range confirmed the estimate: the measured radar cross section, and the overall pattern of scattered radar waves, matched ECHO's prediction. The computer program worked—and made it possible to design an airplane astonishingly undetectable by radar.[39]

———

These results have fed a popular version of Stealth's origins, with Stealth celebrated as a triumph of the fabled Skunk Works tradition. Scherrer later called it the "Big Bang" version of the story: after the flash of initial insight to use flat panels, "Stealth creation only took a nanosecond and has been expanding ever since."[40] This version not only fails to include the Northrop side of the Stealth story; it also ignores determined resistance within the Skunk Works to Scherrer and Overholser's faceted design. Far from a triumph of the Skunk Works design philosophy, Stealth in fact required a *revolt* against it.

The invention of Stealth occurred as much in spite of the Skunk Works as because of it. For starters, crucial funding for Lockheed's XST entry came from outside the Skunk Works. For the key radar test in June 1975, Scherrer and Overholser needed $25,000 to build an exact scale model of the Hopeless Diamond design. Recall that since Lockheed had been left out of the initial solicitation, it had entered the contest using only internal company funding. Ben Rich had an advisory board of senior Skunk Works engineers to review such substantial budget requests, and the committee rejected the proposal: given that the design likely wouldn't work, it wasn't worth the cost. Ed Martin, who was outside the Skunk Works in Lockheed's general aircraft division, asked Scherrer one question: "Will it work?" Scherrer replied, with bravado, "Hell, yes!" Martin then went to Andrew Baker, who was also outside the Skunk Works as head of Lockheed's long-range planning—and thus in control of discretionary funding. Baker had once worked on a similar problem of electromagnetic scattering from flat plates when he was a grad student in physics, and he had also worked on radar systems in the Army and then at Bell Labs. He saw the promise in the idea and ponied up the money for the crucial radar test that validated the concept. Years later, Baker concluded that the project "would not have been started if it had been left alone in the Skunk Works."[41]

Not only did the money come from outside the Skunk Works; so did several key people. In addition to Scherrer, Leo Celniker, who had been Scherrer's boss in advanced design in the general aircraft division, joined the project in summer 1975 as chief engineer. Another outsider was Robert Loschke, a flight-control system design whiz who would prove crucial to making the faceted design fly. Celniker in turn brought in Alan Brown, who like Scherrer had worked under Celniker in advanced design outside the Skunk Works. A wry, unassuming English engineer, Brown was a man of hidden talents, singing in musical theater and making his own musical instruments, in addition to having an interest in model airplanes. Thanks to his expertise in both aerodynamics and electromagnetism, Brown soon became the deputy program manager for Lockheed's XST design and, after that, program manager for the F-117, and thus a key figure for Stealth at Lockheed.[42]

Brown likened his arrival in the Skunk Works to an outsider walking into a small town in Maine: "You know, if your great-grandfather didn't live there, you were in trouble." The outsiders had to overcome native prejudices. Skunk Works engineers had won their formidable reputation by building aerodynamic airplanes. Brown had another saying, a twist on the old saw "Nothing succeeds like success." Brown's version ran, "Nothing fails like success." Like generals fighting the last war, Skunk Works veterans wanted to keep doing what had worked for them in the past. In essence, they wanted to make a stealthier SR-71. In particular, they insisted on using the D-21 Tagboard drone as the basis for Lockheed's Stealth entry. The D-21 was a small knockoff of the A-12/SR-71; like its forebears it incorporated some radar reduction, but its design was driven primarily by the demands of high-speed, high-altitude flight—over Mach 3 at 90,000 feet. Thus the old Skunk Work hands told Scherrer that "it was impossible to improve on the D-21."[43]

All of which explains why Scherrer hung a 20-foot-wide banner in the Skunk Works design room that summer of 1975. The banner played on the Pogo cartoon by Walt Kelly, with a number of Skunk Works engineers caricatured as Pogo characters and, in bold foot-high letters, the caption: "We has met the enemy...and they is us."[44]

One opponent was Ed Baldwin, who had started in the Skunk Works in 1944, designing the P-80 jet fighter, and had then been a principal designer of the U-2 and SR-71. A gruff and grizzled sort, Baldwin was the source of the "Hopeless Diamond" jibe. In Rich's words, Baldwin was "crusty as a pumpernickel"; Scherrer called him "the most abrasive cynic that I have ever known." At Scherrer's first meeting in the Skunk Works, as he was being introduced around to his new colleagues, Baldwin welcomed him by turning to Ed Martin and asking, "Why do we need *him*?" Martin replied coolly, "His win-loss ratio is better than yours," adding that the Skunk Works hadn't flown a new plane in several years and "needed new blood."[45]

The resistance, however, came from the top. Kelly Johnson, despite his retirement, was still a regular presence in the Skunk Works, and he opposed the faceted approach from the outset. Kelly had stopped speaking to "that dumb shit Scherrer," as he called the newcomer to others; when they passed each other in the hallway Kelly would only nod and keep walking. (To be fair, Kelly was often all business, and he cut an intimidating figure; Scherrer may not have been the only Skunk

FIGURE 4.3

The eagles and the mouse. The mouse, Scherrer,
is holding a faceted panel behind his back.
Source: Richard Scherrer.

to get the silent treatment.) Ben Rich, at least at first, listened to Kelly, since Rich sided with his advisory board and rejected the request for funding of the radar test.[46]

At one point in the program Ed Martin presented Scherrer with a cartoon of several menacing eagles, giant talons outstretched, swooping down on a small mouse. The mouse had one hand behind its back holding a faceted panel. Its other hand was held out toward the eagles in defiance, with middle finger raised. The eagles were Kelly Johnson, Ben Rich, and Ed Baldwin. The mouse was Scherrer.[47]

Ben Rich, to his credit, soon came around. DARPA had insisted on cost sharing for the XST program. For each contractor, DARPA would provide one-third of the funding, the Air Force another third, and the company itself had to contribute one-third. DARPA realized it could not ask either the Air Force or the companies to bear all the risk of a novel technology, but it also wanted the other two parties to have some skin in the game. Rich persuaded Lockheed management to agree to the cost sharing, despite the company's dire financial outlook at just that time. Lockheed would eventually cover about $10 million in costs on the two phases of the XST program from internal funds.[48]

After DARPA picked Lockheed and Northrop as winners of the initial round in November 1975, it gave them four months to refine their designs in Phase I of the XST contest. Although the Skunk Works had offered resistance to Stealth, with a contract in hand it now offered several advantages, starting with its engineering experience. As Scherrer and Overholser's design team grew, the group of mostly outsiders was joined by several Skunk Works veterans—including Baldwin, who applied his long experience to the design of the aft fuselage, which had two hot jet engines inside it. The Hopeless Diamond sprouted wings and tails: a delta wing, with the wings highly raked backward at 72 degrees, and twin tails steeply canted inward.[49]

The Skunk Works experience with radar-absorbing materials also helped, especially along the sharp leading edges and the engine inlets and exhaust outlets. Alan Brown in particular solved the problem of the engine inlets, where radar tended to bounce around and resonate, in effect turning the airplane into a radar harmonica. The problem was to keep radar waves out of the inlet but still allow air into the engines. Brown's solution was a honeycomb grid over the inlet, consisting of long fiberglass tubes, several inches long and spaced about a half inch apart, wide enough to funnel air to the engine but small enough— about half the shortest radar wavelength expected—to block radar waves. Any waves that did get through met a heavy layer of carbon-loaded, radar-absorbing material. Some stray radar waves might get in, but they wouldn't get back out.[50]

But for most of the airplane, especially the exterior, the key advance was not materials but rather geometry. As Overholser put it, the most important factors for shedding radar were "shape, shape, shape, and materials."[51] And the key to the shaping was the flat facets. Though the refined design now resembled an airplane more than the Hopeless Diamond did, it still disturbed the sensibilities of the Skunk Works veterans. Shouting matches echoed down the hallways of the Skunk Works, and when Kelly saw the first three-dimensional drawings of the new design, he said it would never get off the ground; the airplane, he scoffed, looked like "a tin shed after a hurricane."[52]

The resistance continued to frustrate Scherrer. In August 1976 he suffered a stroke, which he attributed to the stress caused by Skunk Works intransigence. The stroke left him paralyzed on his right side, and he could barely talk or stand. A year of intensive physical therapy gradually restored his speech and mobility, though by that time the XST contest was resolved. Scherrer still had a role to play in Stealth's next act, but even decades later emotions remained raw.

The competition, however, was not only within Lockheed. The whole point of XST's first phase was to see whether Lockheed's flat facets could indeed shed radar waves—and, most importantly, do so better than the other team's design. Because Northrop's engineers were proving that there was one more than one way to skin an invisible rabbit.

CHAPTER FIVE

NORTHROP

SEEING THE WAVES

The histories of Lockheed and its competitor for Stealth were intertwined, and from the earliest days of aviation. John K. Northrop, better known as Jack, was born in New Jersey in 1895 but raised in Santa Barbara. Shy and, in his words, "a loner," Northrop was entranced by flight after seeing a biplane for the first time as a teenager. After graduating from high school in 1913 he had stints as a mechanic and draftsman at a couple small firms, then in 1916 took a job as an engineer for Loughead Aircraft, which had just moved to Santa Barbara.

Like the Loughead brothers and many others in the first generation of airplane builders, Northrop was a self-taught tinkerer with mechanical gifts. He worked first on seaplanes and then, in 1919, designed the S-1 Sport biplane, an aircraft long on technical innovation and short on a market. When the Loughead firm collapsed in 1920, Northrop worked construction for a few years before going to work for Douglas Aircraft in Santa Monica, and then in 1927 he rejoined Lockheed (the firm having since Americanized its name). That year Northrop helped design the Lockheed Vega, a fast but rugged plane that was flown by Amelia Earhart, Wiley Post, and other famous flyers and set speed and endurance records. The Vega cemented Lockheed's reputation for innovative, high-performance aircraft, and Northrop's reputation as a brilliant designer.[1]

Jack Northrop typified early aviation in another respect: the business was not for the faint of heart, or those seeking stability. Between 1928 and 1938 he worked for several different aircraft firms, including a couple that carried his name but were run by outside investors. But he continued to turn out innovative designs, and finally in 1939 he struck out on his own to form Northrop Aircraft, leasing 72 acres of farmland in Hawthorne, California, several miles southwest of downtown Los Angeles and a couple of miles from the coast. As president of the firm Northrop oversaw a total staff of six.[2]

As with Lockheed, World War II brought a flood of contracts to Northrop, including one for the P-61 Black Widow, a night fighter that was the first airplane designed around one of the new radar systems. Northrop built almost seven hundred P-61s and in total over a thousand planes for the war effort. The firm soon had ten thousand employees—a fraction of the ninety-four thousand at Lockheed, but also a far cry from the six employees of 1939, and more than enough to fill the Hawthorne site.[3]

The company had already begun to pursue its founder's fixation. Aircraft designers had long recognized that, since an airplane's wing was the source of lift, an all-wing aircraft—one with no fuselage or tail—would maximize lift and minimize drag. To Jack Northrop, an idealist as well as an iconoclast, the flying wing represented the purest and most efficient form of flight, and he had formed his company with the express purpose of pursuing it. He started designing flying wings in the late 1920s, and his first true flying wing, the N-1M, flew in 1940. A prototype for a larger bomber, the N-1M, nicknamed the Jeep, was 17 feet long and 38 feet wide, with drooping wingtips and twin pusher propellers on the back of the wing. The small plane, painted bright yellow, looked something like a boomerang; it now sits on display at the Smithsonian's National Air and Space Museum.[4]

Northrop soon scaled up the flying wing. In 1941, as the Battle of Britain raged but before the US entered the war, the Air Force requested a bomber capable of flying 10,000 miles with a 10,000-pound payload. The range would allow American planes to reach Germany if Britain fell. Northrop won the contract with the XB-35, a flying wing with a 172-foot span. The airplane encountered development and production problems and did not fly until 1946, too late for the war; of the 270 originally planned, only 15 XB-35s were built. Northrop meanwhile converted the propulsion system from propellers to jets in the YB-49 flying wing, which flew in 1947. Despite a horrific crash in flight test

FIGURE 5.1

A Northrop YB-49 in flight.

Source: courtesy of Northrop Grumman Corporation.

the following year—both outer wing sections broke off, killing the five-man crew—the Air Force ordered thirty of the aircraft.[5]

The Air Force soon changed its mind, however, and canceled the contract. The flying wing's demise remains a matter of controversy and conspiracy. In a 1979 interview, Jack Northrop recounted that in a meeting in July 1948 the secretary of the Air Force, Stuart Symington, demanded that Northrop merge with Convair, which was building the B-36, the main competitor to Northrop's B-35 and B-49 bombers. Symington apparently wanted to thin the aviation-industry herd. Northrop asked Symington what alternatives he had to a merger, and Symington replied, according to Northrop, "Alternatives? You'll be goddamned sorry if you don't." (Northrop's board chairman at the time corroborated this story in his own 1979 interview.) In Northrop's account, when his firm failed to merge with Convair, Symington took the money allocated for the flying wings and gave it to Convair to build more B-36s.[6]

There are less nefarious explanations for the cancellation, including the fact that Northrop's flying wings couldn't carry the atomic
bomb—at the time the most important payload in the American arsenal. President Truman's budget cuts had forced the Air Force to slash
funding, and the YB-49, which could not compete with the B-36 on
range and payload, took the hit.[7] The upshot, however, was that the
surviving flying wings were eventually scrapped, and an embittered
Jack Northrop retired from Northrop in 1952, walking away at the
age of fifty-seven from the aviation field that had fascinated him since
childhood.

Nevertheless, Northrop and his firm remained identified with the
flying wing. In the 1970s paleontologists discovered fossils of a pterosaur, a flying dinosaur from 65 million years ago with a 50-foot wingspan, the largest flying animal yet known. They named the new species
Quetzalcoatlus northropi.[8]

––––––

Through the 1950s Northrop Aircraft had a succession of leaders until
Thomas V. Jones took the helm at the end of the decade. Jones was
born in 1920 in Pomona, at the time a belt of orange groves about 25
miles east of downtown LA. He earned his undergraduate degree in
aeronautical engineering at Stanford in 1942, in time to join the war
effort at Douglas Aircraft, designing dive bombers. The wartime experience reinforced a philosophy derived in part from his accountant
father: although the military customer often asked for the highest performance—bigger, faster, more complex—the better solution was often
something simpler and cheaper, which meant you could build them
quicker and build more of them for the same cost.

Jones stayed at Douglas through the war. In 1946 he joined a group
of prominent American aeronautical engineers who went to Brazil,
teaching aeronautics and advising Brazil's Air Ministry on how to build
its aviation business. It was the first of several moves that revealed
a contrarian streak in Jones. After a few years in Brazil he returned
to California to take a job at the RAND Corporation, the Air Force
think tank. At RAND he did cost-benefit analyses of transport aircraft,

showing the trade-offs between various designs in terms of cost, range, speed, and payload—and in the process showing that an airlift could be used not just in emergencies (the recent Berlin Airlift being the prime example) but as a primary strategy, by allowing the US to keep a smaller garrison army in Western Europe and reinforce it quickly with stateside troops in case of war.

In 1953 Jones left RAND for Northrop. His Air Force contacts warned him that Northrop was foundering and that the Air Force might let the firm go under to reduce the number of contractors supported by the government. Jones welcomed the challenge and wanted to be at a smaller firm where he might have a greater say in management, rather than be a small fish at one of the bigger companies. He rose rapidly and in 1959, when Whitley Collins died, became Northrop's president. He was not yet forty years old. The following year he was named CEO, and in 1963 he became chairman of the board; he thus held all three top positions in the company by his early forties, a remarkably young age. In 1961 *Time* magazine put a dapper-looking Jones—"a trimly handsome man," the accompanying article gushed—on its cover as "the bright young star of the aerospace industry."[9]

The *Time* article included a photo of Jones relaxing by his backyard pool with his wife and young kids, a sunny portrait of California vim and vigor. Jones was charming and worldly, fluent in Portuguese and a collector of Burgundy vintages, fine cigars, and modern art. He also acquired a reputation as a maverick, with a taste for risk. Like the earlier generation of aviation executives, including Jack Northrop himself, Jones was not content to wait for the military to request an airplane; he wanted to design a new airplane and *then* sell the military on it. In the early 1950s Northrop had developed a lightweight supersonic trainer that became the T-38. Jones backed development of the F-5 fighter based on the same design, even though the military had no plans for it and no contract was in the offing.

When Northrop failed to interest the US Air Force or Navy in it, the firm turned to foreign markets, selling F-5s to Iran, South Korea, the Philippines, Turkey, Greece, Taiwan, Norway, Spain, and Canada. Jones himself often led the pitch; a natural salesman, he traveled tirelessly, marketing the F-5 to foreign leaders. Along the way he hob-nobbed with Dutch and Saudi royalty and counted the shah of Iran and Madame Chiang Kai-shek as friends; parties at his Bel-Air mansion attracted passels of foreign dignitaries, and his office walls were lined with Persian rugs and other treasures from his travels.[10]

These foreign sales transformed Northrop's image. The firm had a celebrated heritage for innovative thinking, derived from its founder, but it lost out on the competitions that led to the "Century series" of fighters (the F-100 to the F-106, designed by North American, McDonnell, Convair, Lockheed, and Republic), the F-16 (General Dynamics), and the A-10 (Fairchild). No longer seen as an advanced fighter/attack aircraft house, Northrop instead became known for no-frills, high-volume military planes like the F-5 and T-38, selling well over two thousand F-5s overseas and over one thousand of the T-38, known as the Volkswagen Beetle of airplanes. Lockheed CEO Robert Gross, whose firm cultivated a reputation for innovative, and expensive, boundary-pushing aircraft, mocked Northrop's philosophy as "cheap airplanes for barefoot nations."[11]

Foreign sales also landed Northrop, and Jones, in legal trouble. In the 1960s the US government controlled foreign sales, but the Nixon administration relaxed federal oversight and let friendly governments deal directly with aerospace firms, a development Jones applauded in his 1974 annual report to shareholders. The result of this laissez-faire approach was a surge in foreign arms deals in the early 1970s—and a surge in bribery scandals in the aircraft industry, as managers from American firms curried favor with foreign governments in bids to win big contracts.[12] One such scandal, as we know, ensnared Lockheed, but Northrop's greater reliance on foreign sales ensured its entanglement as well. In the early 1970s the federal government accused Northrop of paying $30 million to foreign officials in order to land F-5 sales, and Jones and the company's leaders faced a battery of investigations by the Securities and Exchange Commission, congressional committees, grand juries, and Northrop's internal auditors. Jones finally signed a consent decree with the SEC in 1975, promising to end foreign payoffs. Jones had just pled guilty in 1974 to a felony charge of making illegal campaign contributions of $150,000 to President Nixon's 1972 reelection campaign, in violation of a law prohibiting such donations by government contractors.[13]

The scandals tarnished Jones's image, but the foreign sales meant that Northrop could afford to invest in new projects. For 1975, the year of the XST competition, Northrop reported sales of almost $1 billion, earnings of $25 million, and a backlog of orders totaling over $1 billion, with much of the profit and the backlog from F-5 orders. The numbers were unprecedented (in 1960, for example, when Jones became CEO, its sales were $234 million, earnings $7.7 million, and backlog $309 million)—enough to persuade the company's board to overlook the controversies and stick with Jones. Although Northrop brought in a new president in 1976 in order to settle a shareholder lawsuit over the scandal, Jones remained as chairman and CEO. He and the company, the *Los Angeles Times* reported, "appear to be weathering a storm of controversy and adverse publicity quite well."[14]

Northrop's bargain-basement image made it an underdog in the Stealth competition. Nevertheless, Jones—a youthful fifty-five years old—was still very much in the game. And with stacks of chips at his elbow, he could afford to push some onto the table for Stealth, in the belief that Northrop's designers could come up with a winning hand.

———

The money for Northrop's Stealth entry came from overseas. The ideas came from even further out. Jones had early pushed Northrop to enter the space business, through guidance electronics and sensors, to the point that Northrop had dropped "Aircraft" from the company name.[15] In fact, Northrop had entered the Space Age even before Jones arrived—and in the process started on a path to Stealth.

A common misperception is that Stealth developed entirely out of the aircraft world—from places like the Skunk Works, which only built airplanes. Another is that there are two separate engineering realms in the aerospace world: conventional aircraft on the one hand, and strategic missiles and spacecraft on the other. The term "aerospace" itself emerged in the 1950s, but instead of suggesting a seamless link between the two realms it could appear just as a cynical marketing ploy, a word invented so that aircraft firms could get into the space business and Air Force generals add outer space to their mission.[16] In the case of Stealth, however, there were indeed connections, as crucial contributions to the aircraft came out of work on strategic missiles.

In the 1950s Northrop was building the Snark, a first-generation cruise missile that Jack Northrop himself named after Lewis Carroll's imaginary creature. The Snark is mostly remembered today for a series of failures in its early test launches from Cape Canaveral, which led wags to jibe that the ocean off the Cape was "Snark-infested waters." When Northrop engineers finally got the Snark to fly, however, they were surprised to find that the tracking radar lost the missile. They had to put a special reflector on the missile on later launches just so they

FIGURE 5.2

The radar-evading Snark missile. The scooplike engine inlet on the bottom was a major source of the radar return.

Source: courtesy of Northrop Grumman Corporation.

could track it. They determined that the Snark, about 1/10th the size of a B-52 bomber, had perhaps 1/20th the radar signature. In a 1959 interview, Thomas Jones declared that the Snark was "almost impossible to detect. It has very few 'corners'—the right angle surfaces that bounce radar signals back."[17]

Northrop engineers began to think about why radar missed the Snark—and how they might turn that to advantage. They started experimenting on the radar test range, and they found that much of the radar return—what little there was of it—came from the scoop-shaped engine inlet on the Snark's bottom. Since the inlet magnified the return, engineers tried to damp the reflection by lining the inlet with conical baffles, something like the inside of an egg carton. These empirical, trial-and-error tricks helped reduce the small radar signature even more, but the engineers wanted a deeper understanding, so in the early 1960s Northrop formed a group to study the basic interaction of radar waves with surfaces.

The head of this group was Moe Star. A New York native, Star had learned radar electronics courtesy of the US Army during World War II and then earned a degree in electronics through the GI Bill from Brooklyn Polytechnic, whose Microwave Institute had made it an early center for radar electronics.[18] Star landed at Northrop in 1960 and set about hiring young theorists from schools strong in radar and electromagnetic theory, including Hugh Heath from UCLA; Fred Oshiro, another Brooklyn Poly grad, who worked as a radar antenna specialist at Lockheed until 1964; and Ken Mitzner, a Caltech PhD whom Oshiro had met at an Ohio State radar seminar. Oshiro also brought in Stan Locus, who was a bit older; an experimentalist as well as a theorist, he had a knack for finding simple solutions to complex problems.[19]

Jones at first supported the group through Northrop's internal discretionary money (called Independent R&D, or IR&D), and later with funding from the Air Force and US Army Missile Command.[20] The support by both the Air Force and Army reveals that after the Snark cruise missiles provided the initial inspiration for Northrop's radar work, ballistic missiles—not aircraft—became the primary motivation. For one thing, missiles were easier to understand than aircraft: the existing theories estimated radar cross section from a collection of basic shapes, like cylinders or cones, so that missiles presented a much simpler calculation than aircraft.[21] For another, missiles assumed a higher priority. With the advent of intercontinental ballistic missiles on both sides of the Cold War in the late 1950s, detecting and tracking missiles and their payloads—and conversely understanding how one's own missiles and warheads might avoid radar detection—became increasingly urgent.

The Air Force especially wanted to reduce radar cross sections on reentry vehicles, the conical housings on the tops of missiles that carried nuclear weapons and protected them when they reentered the earth's atmosphere. The first attempts at cutting radar signature were on the Titan reentry vehicle, followed by more concerted efforts in the mid-1960s on the Mark 12 reentry vehicle used on later versions of the Minuteman. The Defense Department in the 1960s had a major program, called Advanced Ballistic Re-Entry Systems (ABRES), to study the behavior of reentry vehicles, including their radar signature. These efforts included not just radar-absorbent materials but also some of the first attempts at shaping—that is, using the geometry of the vehicle to deflect radar waves away from it. By the time of the Mark 12, built by General Electric and first deployed in 1970, reentry vehicles had evolved from short, squat, egg-shaped objects to longer, pointier cones, like a dunce cap but with a rounded base. The program capitalized on important contributions from Britain, which had studied the radar problem so that its comparatively limited arsenal of warhead-bearing missiles would evade Soviet missile defenses.[22]

While the Air Force oversaw ballistic missile programs, the Army had primary responsibility for missile defense. Existing defense systems relied on radar to detect incoming reentry vehicles and try to shoot them down before they hit American soil. It had become clear that the Soviets might spoof a missile-defense system by adding lightweight decoys, such as inflatable balloons shaped like a conical warhead, to a missile's payload, and the US wanted to use radar to distinguish between heavy warheads and lightweight decoys. A 1965 report from Moe Star's group noted that the military had "an acute interest in reflectivity signature for vehicle identification," what was known as "discrimination."[23]

Star's team, called the Electronic Systems Research Group, started with the results of the Michigan and Ohio State radar programs. Instead of seeking exact analytical solutions to the integral equations for radar scattering, they sought approximate numerical solutions. For instance, they approximated a curved surface as a series of very small straight lines, assumed the electromagnetic current was constant over each line segment, and then calculated the scattering.[24] This approach was especially amenable to computers, and the Northrop group began developing a library of computer codes known as GENSCAT, for "general scattering," to predict radar cross section for a given shape and a given radar wave (say, with a certain frequency, polarization, and angle of incidence). GENSCAT was analogous to Lockheed's ECHO, but Northrop's group developed it earlier and over a longer period.

Star's radar group provided a crucial theoretical foundation for Northrop's entry into Stealth. Lockheed did not have a comparable theory group.[25] By the time of Project Harvey in 1974 Northrop had over ten years of experience studying radar scattering and calculating cross sections, with that expertise expressed in a series of reports and, more importantly, embodied in a group of smart and seasoned theorists. A Northrop report in 1971 touting the firm's achievements in cutting-edge research declared, "Perhaps one of the best recent examples is in Radar Cross Sections."[26] The group had also already incorporated Ufimtsev's diffraction theory, before Denys Overholser at Lockheed revised the ECHO code to include it. Northrop's Stan Locus, after all, was the one who first stumbled across Ufimtsev's articles and requested a translation of his longer report, thus making it available to other companies, including Lockheed.

Missiles and missile defense made one more contribution to Northrop's radar group. It arrived a year before Project Harvey, in the person of John Cashen. Cashen grew up in West Orange, New Jersey, just outside Newark, where he had a youthful interest in model planes, graduating from the basic rubber-band-powered models to radio control. His favorite design was a customized flying wing, built from his own design. He also got into ham radio, which led him into electronics. After a stint in the Army following high school, he trained as a radio technician at vocational school and landed a job at Bell Labs, but he continued his education in night school, eventually earning an engineering degree from the New Jersey Institute of Technology. In the early 1960s Bell Labs had a contract to build the Safeguard missile defense system, and Cashen worked on how to detect incoming reentry vehicles with radar—in particular, how radar waves interacted with the hot gas and plasma surrounding the reentry vehicle, thanks to the friction-generated heat as it traced its fiery path through the atmosphere.[27]

Cashen went to California in 1965 on a work-study program at Hughes, working at the company while studying at UCLA for his PhD in electrical engineering, with a concentration in electromagnetics. At Hughes he continued to work on radar phenomenology for the Hardsite missile defense system, studying how to discriminate between warheads and decoys and how radar waves interacted with reentry vehicles. All of this required an immersion in existing theories of radar scattering, such as that of the Michigan school, calculating radar cross section by summing up the scattering from a collection of simple shapes. The ABM Treaty of 1972 put an end to the missile-defense work, and Cashen briefly applied his experience on a proposed follow-on to the short-range attack missile, or SRAM, a surface-to-air missile armed with a nuclear warhead; his job was to help reduce the SRAM's radar cross section.

Hughes then lost that program, and Cashen found himself adrift. After working briefly on infrared systems, he took a job at Northrop working on lasers, but that program also soon petered out. In the fall of 1973 Cashen was about to join the growing ranks of unemployed engineers when he heard that Moe Star's group needed someone to work on radar cross section. He jumped at the chance.

As a result of all of his work on missile defense, Cashen had received a thorough grounding in radar scattering and radar cross sections. And he knew what many aircraft designers did not know because of classification: that radar-scattering theory had already been applied to actual airborne craft, including the Mark 12 reentry vehicle and the SRAM

missile—and, further, that those vehicles had achieved remarkable reduction in radar cross section not through radar-absorbing material
but from the shape of the vehicle itself. In short, the first Stealth aircraft
weren't airplanes; they were missiles and reentry vehicles.[28]

––––––

Cashen was an ebullient personality and, like Ben Rich, a natural sto-
ryteller. He also had relentless drive and ambition and was a fierce
competitor, and he threw himself into the Stealth competition against
Lockheed with relish. As he put it, his enemy wasn't the Soviets; "personally, my enemy was Ben Rich." Rich liked Cashen's attitude and
reciprocated it.[29]

At times, though, Cashen may have thought his enemy was closer
at hand, in his own program. Northrop engineer Irv Waaland was the
son of Norwegian immigrants and grew up in Brooklyn during the
Depression. After a stint in the Army Air Corps following World War II,
he attended New York University on the GI Bill, got his degree in aeronautical engineering in 1953, then took a job at Grumman on Long
Island. At Grumman he helped design a series of aircraft, including
the XF10F, Gulfstream I, F-11, E-2, F-111, and F-14, but after twenty
years he moved to Northrop, in part because he felt that Grumman
had grown too bureaucratic, in part because his wife had tired of New
York winters. He arrived at Northrop in 1974 as an aerodynamicist in
advanced design, just in time to join the XST program.[30]

The affable Waaland had a genial grin that hid a steely resolve,
backed by his extensive experience designing airplanes. He knew every
trick that aerodynamicists used to make air go precisely where they
wanted it, from foils and flaps and air fences to slots and strakes and
spoilers. While the theorists in Moe Star's radar group were learning
how to think like a radar wave, Waaland could think like an air mol-
ecule, visualizing how air flowed at very high speed over a given shape,
streaming this way or that or spinning into vortices.

By 1975 Northrop's radar group had long experience calculating radar
cross sections, but they had not yet tried to apply that knowledge to a
specific aircraft. The XST design now had to combine the work of Moe

Star's group with that of people who knew how to design an airplane. And that brought in Waaland, as chief engineer. The manager of the XST program, Mo Hesse, moved Cashen and the radar group out from under Waaland and put them directly under himself. The move signaled the importance of radar cross section in the design but also made Cashen and Waaland, in essence, co-chief engineers—and direct competitors.

The competition stemmed from the difference in disciplines, between Waaland's aerodynamics and Cashen's radar physics. Waaland naturally wanted to preserve the aerodynamics, while Cashen prioritized radar cross section. The differences were also philosophical: Cashen came from an academic environment (including the research-oriented Bell Labs and Hughes) and inclined to seminar-style discussions; Waaland's approach was more in line with traditional aerospace firms, straightforward and to the point. And it was ultimately a clash of personalities, Cashen with a restless mind, Waaland orderly and methodical. But they had one thing in common, besides their devotion to the job: neither was a shrinking violet.

All of this added up to arguments that were, in Cashen's words, "legendary." Waaland recalls them as "shouting matches," and other Northrop engineers saw the two as like oil and water: fine separately, but immiscible. Each recognized the other's ability and intelligence, but not always in the heat of the moment. They were, one colleague said, "like a married couple that should have gotten divorced."[31]

Any engineering design involves compromises, whether the trade-off is between cost and performance or between different measures of performance (such as speed versus maneuverability or range for an aircraft). As at Lockheed, finding middle ground at Northrop in pursuit of Stealth at times devolved into heated battles. And, as at Lockheed, it was finally made clear at Northrop that whenever the radar cross section and aerodynamics performance conflicted on the XST, any compromise would favor radar.[32] But having Waaland as chief engineer gave aerodynamics a strong voice in the design—stronger than at Lockheed.

From the physics of electromagnetic waves, the best shape to avoid radar is a flat plate. But an airplane can't be a two-dimensional plate; it needs volume in order to carry the engines, fuel, weapons, and pilots.

There are two ways to add volume: with flat surfaces or curved surfaces. Lockheed's solution was to use flat surfaces. Northrop's was to use curves. And as birds and the Wright brothers knew, the best shape for flying is a curve. It turned out that in some cases, curves could also help dodge radar.

Northrop's engineers started with flat facets, for the same reason as Lockheed's: because a computer could model them. But at the junctions where the facets met, the sharp angles not only produced vortices and drag in the aerodynamics; they also threatened to reflect radar waves. So the designers introduced curves to blend one facet into another. Northrop's design had several features to benefit aerodynamics: a rounded underbelly; less sweep on the wings; and a curved airfoil over the wing, in addition to rounded leading and trailing edges. The wingtips were also rounded, viewed from above. Northrop engineers learned that when radar waves hit the wing, instead of reflecting they would follow the curve a certain distance and then separate from it, similar to the way a wing sheds airflow.

Although GENSCAT provided an early guide for Northrop's Stealth design, Northrop's radar group relied more on what they called phenomenology—or, highly informed intuition. Cashen called it "seeing the waves": the ability to look at a surface and understand how a radar wave would interact with it, informed by the ten-plus years of experience that Northrop's radar group had spent immersed in the subject. A corollary was an empirical, cut-and-try approach, testing models on the radar range, tweaking the design, then testing again to see how it worked.

For example, they tried curves of different radii on the wing's leading edge to see which one shed radar the best. Stan Locus had the simple inspiration to drive a nail into the model on the test stand. If the radar reached the nail, it would reflect and light up like a beacon on the radar screen. When the nail showed up on the radar, they pried it out and hammered it in again, this time a bit farther back around the curve; when they reached the point where it didn't show up on radar, they knew how well that particular curve performed. Running through the same exercise with several different curves gave them a way to determine which one best shed radar.[33]

The end result was a diamond-shaped delta wing. Like Lockheed's, it had a faceted canopy, just aft of the pointed nose, and twin vertical tails, canted inward and steeply raked. The similarities ended there. Instead of twin engine inlets tucked into the side of the fuselage, above the wings, Northrop's had a single inlet looming behind the cockpit on top of the fuselage, like a big blower scoop on the hood on a muscle car. And unlike Lockheed's highly swept wings, extending back beyond the tail, Northrop's wings flared wider, giving the plane a broad, stubby look. More prominent still were the curves. Northrop's model had curves where the delta wing blended into the fuselage, at the wingtips and across the belly, at the leading and trailing edges of the wings and tails, and around the top edges of the engine inlet, tapering from the inlet to the tail.

The role of computers presented a key difference between the two competitors. Although both Lockheed and Northrop had in-house codes, Lockheed relied more heavily on computers, while Northrop retained a role for physicists' intuition, "seeing the waves." Thus Lockheed's accounts of Stealth tend to feature computer programs, while Northrop's involve modeling clay. There is a parallel here to the two American labs involved in designing nuclear weapons, Los Alamos and Livermore. Los Alamos relied more on designers' intuition, Livermore more on computer codes.[34] In this case, the different approaches manifested in the airplane designs: one based on flat facets, the other on curves.

The irony is that in the late 1940s Northrop had pioneered the development of electronic computers, including the first one to use the stored-program principle. Northrop's computing group spun off over a dozen early computing firms. Northrop pursued these computers with the goal of building a computer small enough to guide aircraft and missiles, starting with the Snark. But it did not apply them extensively to aircraft design.[35]

And that points to a second difference between Lockheed and Northrop in the XST contest: Northrop didn't use computer-controlled fly-by-wire, sticking instead to standard flight controls. Cashen, for one, thought that Northrop made a mistake by not incorporating flight-control computers—they could have devised a stealthier design had

FULL-SCALE RCS MODEL AT RATSCAT

FIGURE 5.3

Northrop's full-scale XST model on the radar range at RATSCAT.
Source: courtesy of Northrop Grumman Corporation.

they used fly-by-wire. Robert Loschke, Lockheed's flight-controls whiz, agreed.[36] But one could also argue that not using fly-by-wire was part and parcel of Northrop's overall approach, favoring phenomenology over computers, and including aerodynamics alongside radar in the design. Thanks to its curves, the resulting aircraft was aerodynamically

FIGURE 5.4

Artist's conception of Northrop's XST design.

Source: courtesy of Northrop Grumman Corporation.

stable in all three axes: pitch, roll, and yaw. Northrop didn't need computers to help fly the plane, because the plane flew fine on its own.[37]

And Northrop's engineers didn't need computers to help them design it—at least to the degree Lockheed did—because they thought they had a winning design in hand.

CHAPTER SIX

SHOWDOWN AT RATSCAT

After Lockheed and Northrop submitted their designs in the fall of
1975, DARPA had to choose the winner. In most competitions for new
planes, the competing designs engaged in a fly-off, to see which one best
met the specifications. "Fly it before you buy it," as the Air Force saying
went. In the case of the XST, DARPA had a "pole-off," with the radar
cross section of each design determined through a model mounted on a
pole at a radar test range. The aircraft would be judged solely on their
radar signature; DARPA wouldn't even bother flying them yet.

The pole-off occurred at a remote spot in the desert in south-central
New Mexico known as the Tularosa Basin. During World War II the
US government had appropriated vast tracts of the basin's desert and
grasslands for bombing and gunnery ranges, and they provided the test
site for the first nuclear bomb in July 1945. After the war the basin's
vast empty spaces became the initial home of the US space program,
since missileers could launch their experiments dozens or hundreds
of miles downrange without fear of hitting someone. The US Army
sent Wernher von Braun and other captured German engineers there
in 1945 to test their V-2 rockets, and over the ensuing decades the
military fired tens of thousands of missiles over the desert scrub, pock-
marking the landscape with impact craters and spent rocket casings.
What became known as the White Sands Missile Range eventually
encompassed over 3,000 square miles, a space bigger than the state of
Delaware.[1]

In the early 1960s the White Sands range got a new facility, the Radar
Target Scatter Site, known initially by the unfortunate acronym RAT
SCAT (later shortened to the less obviously scatological RATSCAT).

It was set up by the Air Force Space Surveillance and Instrumentation Branch, suggesting an initial orientation toward space vehicles rather than airplanes. RATSCAT consisted of several sets of radar antennas up to 30 feet in diameter spread around a central pole that held a test model. The antennas could generate radar of various frequencies, polarizations, and directions and then detect the radar waves scattered from the model. The pole had to get the model high enough off the desert floor to avoid backscatter from the ground; it was originally made of Styrofoam, a nonconducting surface that scattered few radar waves.[2]

A crucial problem was that both Lockheed and Northrop's airplane models promised cross sections far below what RATSCAT or any other test range could measure. Substantial effort thus went into improving test ranges, to lower the background radar clutter to the point where the test range radars could measure the model cross sections. In particular the Styrofoam pole reflected far more radar than the model, so Lockheed supplied a stealthy pole designed by Denys Overholser and Richard Scherrer, something like a long angled knife blade sticking out of the desert floor.[3]

RATSCAT lay just northwest of White Sands National Monument. Gypsum, the white mineral that gives the place its name, usually dissolves in rainwater and is carried away by streams and rivers, but the Tularosa Basin has no outlet to the sea, allowing the gypsum to accumulate as sand. Trapped runoff from nearby mountains sometimes filled the plain; one such event was dubbed Lake Oshiro, after Northrop's radar engineer. Groundwater could affect the radar tests: Scherrer once recorded scattering from a target over the course of an entire day and found that it varied by several decibels, which he eventually traced to the tidal rise and fall of the underground water table. The gypsum also undermined security. When some Skunk Works engineers checked into a local hotel after visiting the site, the clerk at the desk exclaimed, "Oh! You're the guys working at RATSCAT!" Wondering who had blown their cover, they looked around the lobby . . . and saw their trail of white footprints.[4]

The surreal landscape entranced engineers. The wind blowing across the desert floor made the white sand look like flowing water, and coyotes roamed at night under the big radar dishes.[5]

———

The remarkable surroundings offered a distraction, but the two teams kept their eyes on the prize. They all recognized the stakes: a head start on a revolutionary technology, one that might underpin the next generation of American military aircraft. Engineers on each side thus geared up for a showdown in the western desert, armed not with lethal six-shooters but with radar beams aimed at bizarre airplane models.

Despite the intense competition, all of these men—and both engineering teams were all men at this point—had one crucial thing in common: they were all technical problem-solvers who spoke the language of physics and math. They realized that they constituted an exclusive fraternity within American aerospace, working on utterly novel and unique aircraft. And "fraternity" is the right word. It was a world of salty language, ego, and towel-snapping banter.

That realization underpinned a willingness to work hard: sixty- to eighty-hour weeks, often, to meet the demanding schedule. One consequence of the Cold War was the remarkable dedication demonstrated by these engineers, despite the toll it took on them personally—and on their loved ones. Engineers rarely saw their families; there was a common saying in the aerospace business that major projects generated a divorce for anyone who was fully involved in them. During the XST competition John Cashen was consuming coffee by the potful and cigarettes by the pack, and still burning out from the stress.[6]

It helped that many of the engineers were relatively young. The more senior of them (Alan Brown, Irv Waaland, Cashen) were in their middle to late forties. It required a tricky balance: they had to be old enough to know what they were doing but young enough to welcome innovation—and to work very hard. The dean of Berkeley's engineering school once summed up the challenge: "Development engineering work is a tough way for an engineer or scientist to make a living. It is a young man's type of work, requiring discontent with the past and unbounded optimism for improvement. Uncertainty is their constant companion. Age brings a desire for stability, an impatience with constant change, and a weakening of the imagination and creative urge."[7]

The price was apparent. Cashen recalled, "Young men became old very quickly."[8] Waaland ended up with shingles, and Scherrer, as we know, had a stroke just after the competition.[9] So why did they do it? Why subject themselves to the workload and the stress? Part of it, of course, was career advancement: do a good job, and the company would reward you with better status and pay. There was also patriotism, fueled by the fear that without Stealth, Americans might soon be speaking Russian. For some of them, however, the main competition was not the Soviets but rather their engineering colleagues at the other firm. As Cashen put it, "It's just like we were playing with the best in the Super Bowl every year."[10]

Above all, though, was the technical challenge, the chance to tackle daunting engineering problems and solve them. In short, it was fun. Cashen's assistant, Maggy Rivas, recalled, "It was so wonderful to see people doing what they loved. . . . Everybody was doing it for the love of the job." Cashen added, "It's very smart people doing things in half the time with great urgency and loving it. Absolutely loving it and in a way loving the people they work with. There was a certain, if not love, certainly respect. . . . And we knew we were making aviation history."[11]

Some might ask what is fun about designing better ways to wage war. However, that's how these engineers viewed it. In this respect they resembled the scientists and engineers who built the atomic bomb at Los Alamos in World War II. Whatever their subsequent views of nuclear weapons, they recalled their wartime work as an intense, almost magical experience of intellectual creativity and dedicated teamwork, enhanced by being thrown together in a remote and desolate landscape.[12]

———

In March 1976 the engineering teams from Lockheed and Northrop trooped out to RATSCAT with their models. The full-scale models were made of either plywood or foam and fiberglass, coated with conductive silver paint to mimic the radar behavior of a metal plane.[13] Over the course of several weeks the local RATSCAT engineers suspended the models on the knife-blade pole high above the desert floor, zapped them with various radar beams, and measured the radar waves that bounced back. During one test Lockheed's radar signature bloomed by about 50 percent. It turned out a flock of birds had lit on Lockheed's model and proceeded to do what birds do, and the bird turds blew up the signature.[14]

The two teams were kept strictly sequestered. They shared a hangar with a divider down the middle, so they knew the competition was close at hand but couldn't see them; they couldn't watch the other team's tests or see its model.[15] Even after DARPA declared the winner, program managers kept the two teams compartmentalized. DARPA didn't try to take good ideas from the loser and ask the winner to incorporate them. It was an all-or-nothing contest.[16]

There was some gamesmanship. Northrop, for example, knew that Lockheed had an advantage in radar-absorbing materials owing to its experience on the SR-71. Northrop had no access to Lockheed's side of the hangar, but Cashen had the Northrop shop techs surreptitiously scour the ground outside the hangar when they went out for a cigarette break, looking for fragments that might have flaked off Lockheed's model on its way to the test pole. Northrop's crew picked up tidbits of any black material and put them in a baggie, and Cashen sent the samples back to Hawthorne for analysis. (They found that it was similar to Northrop's formula but produced with better quality control than Northrop's off-the-shelf commercial supplier could provide.)[17]

Accounts of Stealth's development hinge on the concept of radar cross section. This is usually expressed as a single number: the cross-sectional area of a sphere with an equivalent radar cross section to that of the aircraft, given in square meters. For example, a nonstealthy plane might have a cross section given as 10 square meters, meaning that of a sphere that would yield the same radar return. (During Pentagon briefings, Ben Rich liked to take a ball bearing the same size as the radar cross section of Lockheed's Stealth design and roll it across the table to impress the military brass with how small it was.)[18]

The seeming simplicity of the number, however, concealed how it was actually measured. First of all, it depended on whether the radar looked at the front of the plane or the side or rear. Most radar measurements put the model on the pole and rotated it through 360 degrees while illuminating it with the radar. The resulting plot, or graph, showed the scattered radar signal as a function of the viewing angle, with 0 degrees looking straight on at the nose; 180 degrees, at the tail; and 90 and 270 degrees, directly from the side. For an ideal plane the plot would be symmetric (that is, the one for 0–180 degrees would mirror-image that of 180–360 degrees), but for a real plane they often displayed some asymmetry. The radar signal, displayed on the vertical axis, was given in decibels, which is a logarithmic scale. Like the Richter scale for earthquakes, it is based on multiples of 10 relative to a reference value. So 10 decibels is 10 times the radar signal of 0 decibels, 20 decibels is 100 times greater than 0 decibels, 30 decibels is 1,000 times greater, and so on. Radar engineers used the logarithmic decibel scale to cover the dynamic range of signals, with some being a million times greater than others. That also meant that a change of only a few decibels could mean a substantial difference in the actual radar signal.

A particular test on the range thus yielded a graph, but only for a particular frequency of radar waves. For a different frequency the graph would look different. Facets, for example, didn't work as well for low frequencies as for high ones and showed more spikes in the signal. The graph also changed for different polarization of the radar waves. Finally, it changed if the radar was not exactly level with the airplane—say, if it was looking up at it from below at a 20-degree angle, or looking down from 30 degrees.

All of this meant that a radar cross section was not really a single number. Or, rather, although it was often presented as a number, that number in fact represented only a single measurement. For example, the 7/16-inch ball bearing that Lockheed engineers rolled across briefing tables represented only the cross section of their XST design when viewed nose-on and level and for a particular radar frequency.[19] The overall cross section represented a collection of numbers, and the way the numbers were combined reflected a number of assumptions about the viewing angle, the frequency and polarization, and so on. And that had fundamental implications for the Stealth pole-off competition.

To set the rules of the contest, DARPA hired an engineering consultant named Nikander (better known as Nick) Damaskos, who came up with a numerical formula that gave varying weight to the numbers, depending on how the model reflected radar at different frequencies, polarizations, and viewing angles. At the end of the pole-off, each team would take the results they got for each of these different measurements and plug them into Damaskos's magic formula, and the formula would spit out a single number. The team with the lowest number would win the contest.[20]

First was the issue of radar frequency. Generally, big early warning systems like the Tall Kings used lower frequency, while antiaircraft radars used higher frequencies to provide the resolution needed for precise tracking and targeting. The Damaskos criteria called for testing in several frequency bands over this range, from about 200 MHz, for the Tall Kings, up to 10 GHz. Lockheed focused its design on the higher frequencies and decided to take its chances at the lower bands, in part because it had not yet tested its radar-absorbing edge treatment at low frequencies. The decision paid off; Lockheed indeed won at high frequencies, and the difference at lower frequencies was not enough to sway the outcome.[21]

The second, more contentious issue was viewing direction. Neither team had worried much about a radar beam hitting the plane from the side, and Damaskos's formula likewise discounted it; if an antiaircraft radar saw a plane from the side, the plane would be moving too fast to track. So that left the front and the back. Damaskos's formula defined the nose and tail sectors as anything within 45 degrees of the airplane's centerline, either forward or aft. Viewed from above, the pattern looked something like the outline of a butterfly, with a 90-degree wedge to the front and a similar wedge to the back.

Northrop immediately protested. Radar would light up most attacking aircraft, speeding toward enemy territory, from the front. Northrop's engineers had thus designed their plane assuming a wider radar threat in the front, 60 degrees from centerline, or a 120-degree wedge in all. They similarly assumed that radar hitting the back of the plane was a lower priority, since that meant the airplane was speeding away from the antiaircraft site and therefore presented a harder target to hit. So for the rear of the plane Northrop designed around a zone only 35 degrees from centerline, meaning a 70-degree wedge. Basically, Northrop's butterfly was much bigger in the front than the back; Damaskos's wedges were equal.[22]

Northrop already had suspicions about Damaskos's neutrality, because he had helped the CIA analyze the radar cross section of Lockheed's SR-71. There may not have been a conspiracy, but the criteria did apparently originate with Lockheed. Scherrer had asked Overholser to come up with the target levels for Lockheed's design— that is, what numbers was the design trying to achieve, and how were they measured? Overholser had split the 360-degree azimuth into four quadrants, each 90 degrees, and averaged the cross section over each quadrant (again, with a different value depending on the radar's frequency, polarization, and elevation angle). Scherrer then passed these numbers to Perko at DARPA, who apparently conveyed them to Damaskos, who incorporated the quadrants into his formula.[23]

As soon as Northrop's team learned about the criteria, they guessed that they were cooked. Because of the narrow wedge they assumed for the back of their model, they had tolerated a big spike in the radar signal just outside their 35-degree zone. Damaskos's wider wedge would catch the spike. Waaland lamented, "We had a fat ass—the way they were measuring it." Northrop could only have corrected its rear-end problem by tearing down the whole design and rebuilding it, and there was no time for that. Northrop engineers protested they'd been snookered, but DARPA stuck with Damaskos's formula. Waaland recognized, "That essentially killed us." Cashen, whose survivability analysis underpinned Northrop's approach, admitted, "I was outgamed, all right?"[24]

Damaskos's formula worked in one sense, however, by revealing the basic differences in the two approaches. Since ECHO could not handle rounded edges, Lockheed had used a sharp wing leading edge. A sharp leading edge can produce vortices in the airflow, which can lead to a stall on unswept wings. A stall means there is not enough airflow to sustain lift, so the airplane will stop flying and fall. For high-sweep wings, on the other hand, the vortices run along the wing edge and can actually help produce lift. So Lockheed had a highly swept wing, which happened to minimize radar return from the back of the plane. Lockheed's reliance on ECHO thus partly manifested in its good radar performance under Damaskos's criteria. Northrop meanwhile had less sweep on the wings because of its pursuit of better aerodynamic performance. The cost was a radar spike to the rear of the plane. Northrop could have compensated for its rear-end problem with flight controls, but it had shunned fly-by-wire in favor of pure aerodynamic stability. And it paid the price.

In April 1976, after several weeks of testing at RATSCAT, the two teams went to Washington to present their results to DARPA. Both made their case the same day, with Northrop's walking into the briefing room just as Lockheed's was walking out. DARPA intended to declare the winner the following day. The night before the announcement Perko hosted a party for both teams. It was not the most relaxed gathering, and not even the sociable Perko, well liked on both sides, could break the ice.[25] The next day DARPA announced the winner of the XST competition. Lockheed won.

CHAPTER SEVEN

HAVE BLUE AND THE F-117A

Having won the shootout, Lockheed earned the right to build two prototype airplanes and show that its winning design would in fact fly. This joint Air Force/DARPA program was to produce an airplane code-named Have Blue. If Have Blue flew right, then the Air Force might give a production contract for a substantial quantity of Stealth aircraft, meaning hundreds of millions of dollars were at stake. The catch, though, was in the flying. Kelly Johnson knew a thing or two about airplanes, and his critique of Lockheed's Stealth design—"that damn thing will never get off the ground"—was not entirely unfounded. To get the damn thing in the air, the new guard turned again to computers—this time not to design the plane but to help fly it.

———

From the earliest days of aviation there has been a debate over the importance of pilots: Were they simple machine drivers or expert and independent professionals? Test pilots over the years consistently argued that they were no mere chauffeurs or, worse, passive passengers but pilots who should have control over the aircraft. The advent of faster and more responsive jet aircraft after World War II, however, began testing the limits of human reflexes, and at the same time, the emergence of electronic computers presented a potential aid to human pilots—and perhaps even an alternative to them.

The pilots won the argument. Engineers began using computers to help fly planes—but only to help. The Mach-6 X-15, which first flew in 1959, had a computer to help translate the pilot's control-stick motions into suitable actions from the control surfaces, but the computer would not fly the plane itself. Similarly, the Mercury Seven astronauts, all of whom had been test pilots, insisted that they have the ability to fly their space vehicles. The Apollo flight computer was designed not to exert autonomous control but rather to augment the astronaut's actions, as Neil Armstrong famously demonstrated when he took over the controls to land the *Eagle* on the moon. It did not hurt that American politicians at the height of the Cold War liked to compare heroic, individualistic American pilots to the supposed automatons of the Soviet space program. Test pilots were the cowboys of the twentieth century, from X-15 pilot "Cowboy" Joe Walker to Tom Cruise in *Top Gun* (call sign: Maverick).[1]

Today's drone aircraft have diverged from the tradition favoring skilled pilots over computers. In 1976, Lockheed's Stealth flight controls continued in the older tradition of augmenting, not replacing, the pilot in the cockpit, employing fly-by-wire. This meant that the computer mediated between the pilot and the control surfaces, so that the surfaces—like the wing flaps and tail rudders—no longer responded directly, and mechanically, to the pilot's commands. If the pilot wanted the plane to do something—say, pitch up a certain amount, or roll a certain angle to one side—he would move the stick the appropriate amount, and the flight-control computer, knowing the airplane's performance and its current speed and attitude, decided which control surface to move and how much to move it. Have Blue needed fly-by-wire because it was unstable in all three axes: pitch, roll, and yaw. (Pitch means rotating around a lateral axis, moving the nose up or down; roll means moving around a longitudinal axis, tipping the wings up or down; and yaw means moving about a vertical axis, moving the nose left or right.) This instability could lead to cross-axis coupling: if the pilot tried to change the pitch, the aircraft could go out of control in roll or yaw. As far as the pilot was concerned, fly-by-wire gave the same end result: if he asked the airplane to roll 5 degrees to the right, the airplane ended up rolling 5 degrees right.[2]

Unlike Apollo's digital computer, however, which had programmable microelectronics, the Air Force had developed an *analog* flight-control system and deployed it on the F-16, which had first flown two years before Have Blue.[3] To save time and money, Have Blue used the F-16 flight-control computer, which was already flight-qualified through testing for vibration, stress, heat, and so on. So instead of building a computer, Lockheed engineers had to devise new control laws for various aspects of flight—say, to control the pitch, roll, or yaw. These laws merged the pilot's actions with aerodynamic data from a system of sensors and issued instant corrections to the control surfaces.

Have Blue's computer had four channels and was a characteristically American design in that it was democratic: three channels voted on every action, with the fourth as backup. For example, if channel one gave a reading of 2 volts, channel two said 2.5 volts, and channel three said 3 volts, the system would go with 2.5 volts. If one channel diverged from the others by some specified amount—say, by reading 10 volts in this example—the system would kick that one out and bring in the standby channel.

Each channel consisted of seven circuit boards, each measuring about nine inches by twelve inches. The computer as a whole, comprising twenty-eight circuit boards, was about twenty-four inches long, fifteen inches wide, and twelve inches high and weighed about fifty pounds. These weren't programmable semiconductor chips; they were analog circuits consisting of both microchips and discrete electronic components like transistors, all hardwired on a circuit board. That meant engineers made changes in the flight controls not by rewriting the software code but rather by physically rewiring the circuit boards. For example, to make a change in the pitch-control law, an engineer would pull out the board for pitch control on each of the four channels, pull out a transistor and put in a new one with the needed spec on each of the four boards, solder the new transistor into place, slide each board back into its slot, and then test the board and the voting system to make sure it all worked and that the new component didn't mess up any of the other controls. Fine-tuning the control laws meant endless, painstaking iterations of this process.[4]

Stealth thus marked a double challenge to aircraft design tradition: first from electromagnetics experts, and second from fly-by-wire. Since the golden age of flight fifty years earlier, aeronautical engineers had dominated aircraft design, fine-tuning airfoils in wind tunnels and crafting ever-sleeker aerodynamic forms. By the 1970s electrical engineers had entered the picture, armed not with blueprints but rather with computer codes and circuit diagrams. As the engineers themselves put it, the coneheads were taking over from the tin-benders.[5]

———

Along with the rise of flight-control systems was the concurrent emergence of the control systems engineer, usually coming out of electrical engineering, speaking a language of feedback loops and frequency responses.[6] Lockheed's lead flight-controls engineer was Bob Loschke. A native Oklahoman, in 1976 Loschke was not yet forty years old and slight, quiet, and methodical. He had triple degrees in aeronautical, electrical, and control-systems engineering, and his patient problem-solving was already earning him a reputation as an engineer's engineer.[7]

A corollary to the rise of fly-by-wire was a dependence on flight simulators. The X-15, an early example of fly-by-wire, was also, not by coincidence, one of the first aircraft to make extensive use of a flight simulator, and the Apollo astronauts—who after all could not log actual hours in space learning to fly the lunar modules—logged countless hours in simulators.[8] So, too, for Stealth. Working the kinks out of the flight controls—seeing if the airplane would respond correctly if the pilot applied, say, a certain roll or pitch rate to the stick—was a trial-and-error process. There were plenty of anomalies in the system, and Loschke and his colleagues did not want to lose real airplanes, not to mention pilots, finding them. Have Blue's two test pilots thus logged far more time in simulators, probably over a thousand hours, than they would later spend flying the actual plane. And that simulator time was as crucial to the program as the actual test flights.[9]

The mild-mannered Loschke betrayed a fiendish side by designing simulator sequences with the deliberate goal of tripping up test pilots. For instance, he would start with a task, such as landing the airplane in a 20-knot crosswind, and then throw in an engine failure on top of that. In particular Loschke was trying to find situations that might produce a so-called pilot-induced oscillation. A PIO is a latent feature of flight controls, a result of using computers that react quicker than humans. A PIO could occur when the computer detected a certain motion and acted to correct it, while the pilot, a split second behind, also acted to correct it, leading to an overcorrection; the computer, followed quickly by the pilot, then would overcorrect in the opposite direction, and so on, each correction greater than the previous in a feedback loop, eventually pushing the plane out of control in a matter of seconds. Years later, in April 1992, a test flight of the stealthy YF-22 (a successor to the Have Blue design) got into such an oscillation a hundred feet above the runway, pitching violently down and then up before slamming down and skidding 8,000 feet on its belly, trailing flame and destroying the plane. The pilot thankfully walked away from it.[10]

Fly-by-wire presented potential pitfalls in such feedback loops, but also advantages. To save money, Have Blue's design team used an off-the-shelf landing gear, which turned out to flex a bit under the weight of the aircraft. When it was rolling down the runway and the pilot applied the brakes, the gear would bend slightly. The computer would sense the torque and shift a rudder to correct for it, which would turn the airplane's nose. If the nose started swinging, the airplane could veer off the runway and crash. Because of the fly-by-wire system, engineers could address a problem in the airplane by simply tweaking the electronics. They still had to pull out a circuit board and solder in a new component, but it was far easier than breaking down and rebuilding an airframe or, in this case, replacing the landing gear.

The revelations in the simulator led to some design changes in the Have Blue airframe. The designers found that the elevons, the flaps on the back of the wings, were too small to control the plane's tendency to pitch its nose up in certain situations. So they put hinges on the trailing edge of the exhaust deck, at the very back center of the plane. When needed this new flap would flop down to keep the airplane's nose pitched downward. It was a big flap, sticking straight off the airplane's tail. They called it the platypus.[11]

The simulator also helped teach the pilots about the strange bird they were going to fly. Have Blue's inherent instability meant that the fly-by-wire system sometimes sent counterintuitive commands to the control systems, sending rudders or elevons the opposite direction they would move for a given maneuver on most other planes. For instance, in a regular plane, if a pilot wanted to slow the plane down he would pull back on the power, and to stay in trim the elevons on the trailing edge of the wing would shift up to keep the plane from pitching down as it slowed. Have Blue, however, had a natural tendency to pitch up when the pilot slowed down, so the flight controls shifted the elevons *down*. The flight simulator had indicators showing the pilot where the control surfaces actually were, and test pilot Bill Park saw the elevons going the opposite way from any airplane he'd ever flown. He asked Loschke, "Bob, are they really going to do that?" Loschke said, "Yep." Park sighed. "I don't want to know."[12]

———

It is one thing to conceive a new technology, another thing to build it. Consider nuclear weapons. Scientists around the world recognized in 1939 that a nuclear weapon was possible, but it took the US and its allies a vast effort, over several years of World War II, to actually build one. Some countries still haven't managed it. Similarly for Stealth: even after physicists showed that Stealth was possible, and design engineers had an aircraft plotted on blueprints, the manufacturing engineers still had to turn those equations and blueprints into hardware.

The popular image of the aerospace engineer is the design engineer hunched over his slide rule or computer. But there is another side of aerospace: the shop floor, where machinists, assembly workers, and manufacturing engineers practiced what Wernher von Braun liked to call "dirty-hands engineering."[13] And those workers were by far the largest group in the Skunk Works. Perhaps a quarter of the total staff were design engineers, plus smaller groups for finance, security, administration, and so on. Well over half were in manufacturing, perhaps two-thirds when big projects were in production.

The shop floor was a different world from the offices and desks of design engineering: a place of drop hammers, rivet guns, hydraulic presses, autoclaves, and lathes instead of slide rules and French curves; high school diplomas instead of advanced degrees; ethnic diversity instead of an all-white culture; blue collar instead of white collar. But it was as important as a source of innovation.

One of the Skunk Works' strengths was its integration of design and production engineering, keeping both in constant contact and interplay. Designers and production worked in the same building, so that the people building something could trot upstairs and talk to the people who designed it, telling them when their designs couldn't be built, or couldn't be built for the allotted cost. Some American businesses have learned a lesson about the benefits of integrating design and production, after offshoring of manufacturing severed the connection. As an industrial designer at General Electric recently put it, "There is an inherent understanding that moves out when you move the manufacturing out. And you can never get it back."[14]

The ingenuity of Have Blue's designers would have gone for naught had the shop-floor workers not matched it. How to make the flat faceted surfaces? Do you cast them, machine them, form them? How do you ensure structural integrity of the surface? How do you achieve the unprecedented tolerances required, since any dimples or gaps could reflect radar? Until Have Blue, airplanes had usually been built from the inside out: first the skeleton and then the external skin. Since the surface requirements were crucial, Have Blue was built in a sense from the outside in.

Then there were the temperamental materials involved, many of which changed characteristics at different temperature, pressure, humidity. As one shop-floor worker put it, it was as if they had a metabolism—they were more like a living, breathing animal than an inert hunk of metal.[15]

For example, to absorb radar waves the leading edges of the wings and tails used a fiberglass honeycomb loaded with a conductive ferrite mixture. The ferrite was graded in density so that the electrical resistance at the edge was low and the resistance at the back was highest, matching the resistance of the metal structure. It was difficult enough to form a standard leading-edge airfoil with enough precision to satisfy the aerodynamic requirements. Doing it with these new materials was far harder. It meant setting down layers of ferrite-loaded fiberglass with the weave for each layer in a particular orientation, and then forming the whole thing in a die, matching the tolerances not only for the dimensions but also for the gradation in density.[16]

The ferrite-loaded fiberglass on the edges was intended to absorb low-frequency radar at the edges. Meanwhile, all of the faceted surfaces were covered with a rubberized ferrite-loaded coating, about 30/1000s of an inch thick, to absorb high-frequency radar. The manufacturing team had to apply this top rubbery layer to the plane like wallpaper, which proved to be a headache. As any paperhanger could tell you, if the surface is not perfectly clean the coating will peel away from it.[17]

Have Blue's airframe was mostly aluminum, except for titanium around the engine. Titanium, first used in an aircraft by the Skunk Works on the SR-71 in the early 1960s, introduced its own problems. Kelly Johnson once said that even if you gave the blueprints of the SR-71 to the Soviets they couldn't replicate the aircraft; they wouldn't have the technology to cut, shape, and weld titanium. (The US, however, had to rely for a time on the Soviets for titanium ore before developing its own sources.)[18] Forming titanium required heating it in a furnace to 1,400°F, then keeping it hot while forming it with a hydraulic press located inside the furnace itself. The so-called hot shed required different skills than the regular machine shop. Most of all it required patience, since it took a while to form parts at high temperature.[19]

The job of overseeing Have Blue manufacturing fell to Robert Murphy, a lean, energetic man, forty-seven years old at the time. Murphy had fallen in love with airplanes as a young teen in upstate New York during World War II and enlisted in the Air Force straight out of high school (he was only seventeen, but he talked his mother into signing the papers). He trained as a mechanic and was sent straight from boot camp to work on planes during the Berlin Airlift. When he got out of the service in the early 1950s he and a buddy drove cross-country to California, because that's where the aircraft business was. He got a job at Lockheed and soon landed in the Skunk Works, armed only with a high school diploma, surrounded by engineers with graduate degrees. He nevertheless gained a reputation as a genius for his knack for devising elegant solutions to the knottiest engineering problems. He worked as a flight-test mechanic first on the XF-104 and then on the U-2, and by age twenty-five Murphy was a supervisor, managing men decades his senior. After stints stationed with the U-2 program in Japan—he met his wife there; she was working for the CIA—and Turkey, Kelly Johnson put him in charge of final assembly and flight-test operations on the SR-71 in Palmdale, at the ripe age of thirty-four.[20]

Murphy was known as someone who got things done and brooked no excuses. The Skunk Works gave people like that room to work; Johnson was famous for telling workers simply what needed to be done, not how to do it, and then leaving them to figure it out. Have Blue gave ample opportunity to exercise initiative. By 1977 Murphy was deputy director of Skunk Works operations, which included everything aside from design engineering and contracts. Blunt and salty-tongued, Murphy had a sense of humor, which helped take the sting out of demanding assignments for those working under him. And however much he asked of his team, he asked more of himself, up at 5 a.m. every morning and in the shop soon after.

There was another major difference between the design offices and the shop floor at the Skunk Works: the shop-floor workers were unionized. That fact almost derailed Have Blue. In October 1977, two months before the target date for Have Blue's first flight, Lockheed's machinists—including those in the Skunk Works—went on strike.[21] Lockheed's contracts manager wanted to ask the Air Force to slip the flight deadline one day for every day of the walkout. Murphy did not budge: the flight would not slip, he insisted, "One. Hundred. Percent."

Murphy split his production managers into two teams, and they went to work themselves on the plane, each team working a twelve-hour shift, seven days a week. Even design engineers were pressed into service, though some were handier than others. Test pilots watched nervously as design engineers, some of whom didn't know a jig from a jigsaw, took up tools and went to work on the airplane. The plane flew on time.[22]

———

The test flights occurred at a place that didn't appear on any maps. About twenty years earlier Kelly Johnson had gone looking for a place to test the U-2 and settled on Groom Lake, which is actually no lake but rather a dry salt flat in the southern Nevada desert, about midway between Las Vegas and Tonopah. Johnson chose it for the same reason that Muroc Dry Lake in California's Mojave Desert had become a flight-test center in the 1930s: the dry lakebed provided a perfectly flat and hard landing surface if an aircraft couldn't make it to the runway in an emergency. And the US government already owned the land: it lay on a corner of the Nevada Test Site, where the US tested nuclear weapons in the early Cold War. In the days of aboveground nuclear testing, Groom Lake got regular dustings of fallout. The test site had been laid out in a numbered grid, which led to the more familiar name for the airfield: Area 51. Johnson puckishly called it Paradise Ranch, to sell employees on working there; Lockheed staff came to call it simply "the Ranch." The airspace above the site acquired a more evocative name: Dreamland.[23]

Area 51 at the time had not yet achieved notoriety among conspiracy theorists as the home of cryogenically preserved aliens from UFOs, which linked the base in the public imagination to Roswell, New Mexico. (Indeed, the later revelation that the first Stealth flights took place there would contribute to Area 51's mystique.) Reality was more mundane. Groom Lake combined the dull routine of a military base with the dry, dusty desolation of the Nevada desert. The bare-bones base housing—first trailers and later cheap dorms—gave the site a ramshackle, low-rent vibe, complete with tumbleweeds.

Like its California cousin, however, the Groom Lake test program broke the military monotony with remarkable exploits involving the most boundary-pushing high technology the nation possessed. Literally, high technology: first the U-2, designed to cruise at 70,000 feet, out of reach of antiaircraft missiles; then the A-12 and its close cousin the SR-71 Blackbird, which flew not only high but fast. Very fast: its evasive strategy was simply to outrun missiles, flying at Mach 3.2, fast enough to get from Los Angeles to Washington, DC, in about an hour. These exploits included hair-raising close calls for the pilots, some of whom survived engine flameouts and inverted flat spins; several others did not.[24]

The longest-serving pilot at Groom Lake by the mid-1970s, and the pilot tabbed to test-fly Have Blue, was the aforementioned Bill Park. A native of Charleston, South Carolina, Park enlisted in the Army Air Corps at the end of World War II, flew over a hundred missions in Korea in the F-80, an aircraft designed by the Skunk Works, and then joined Lockheed in 1957 as a test pilot. Park was a legendary flyer. He landed a U-2 on an aircraft carrier and was the first to fly the A-12 at Mach 3. On one test flight of the A-12, as the plane was coming in to land, 500 feet above the lakebed, it started rolling over and didn't stop. The ground crew watched in horror as the plane augered into the lakebed in a giant ball of flame. They assumed Park was a goner and were soon stunned to see him calmly stroll up with his parachute bundled in his arms—he had punched out at 200 feet, and his chute had opened a split second before his feet hit the ground. It was not his last close call there.[25]

The test pilot business required extraordinary tolerance for danger, but these pilots were no daredevils. As one F-117 test pilot put it, "I don't think you'll find any of us that are complete set-your-hair-on-fire-and-let's-go kind of guys. We're pretty methodical, risk-averse guys."[26] The younger ones, especially, represented a gradual shift within the test pilot fraternity, from barnstormers to engineers, from cowboys to calculators—in short, from Chuck Yeager to Neil Armstrong.[27] Many of these younger pilots had advanced engineering degrees, which helped in two ways: they had a solid technical understanding of the aircraft, and they took an engineer's rational approach to risk, analyzing and minimizing it.

That's not to say they were dull. Dry, maybe. Park in particular had a sardonic side. On one U-2 flight, the engine had fuel problems and he had to dead-stick the plane back to the base, barely clearing a fence at the end of the runway. Ben Rich raced out to meet him and asked, "What happened?" Park replied, "I don't know. I just got here myself."[28]

But they knew how to have fun. They worked hard and played hard; the base eventually had a basketball court and softball field, and some of them pursued their fascination with model planes by flying radio-controlled models. And they partied hard. Just as Edwards Air Force

Base had the Happy Bottom Riding Club, the notorious saloon run by Pancho Barnes and made famous in *The Right Stuff*, Area 51 had its own bar, Sam's Place, named after Sam Mitchell, a CIA employee and early Area 51 base commander. Although Sam's was the main watering hole, Lockheed engineers later started their own private bar in their dorm, in Building 79. They called it the Conehead Bar, in honor of the control-system engineers, and on the bar's logo they included the hexadecimal number 4F, which translated to 79 in decimals. They had a name for their hangar, too: since they were housed at the south end of Area 51 airfield, they dubbed it Baja Groom Lake.[29] The Conehead Bar, one pilot recalled, saw some raucous nights, including "knock-down, drag 'em outs. . . . Just boys being boys."[30]

The hijinks hid a personal toll. In addition to the stress of working long hours at Area 51 to meet deadlines, the program strained marriages and families. Every Monday morning Have Blue's engineers and test pilots left their Burbank-area homes for the week, disappearing to a place they could not reveal. (Most of them to this day, four decades later, refuse to say where the test flights occurred.) Some would return home on weekends, while others stayed away for weeks at a time when schedules got tight. Lockheed gave their spouses a special phone number to call if there was an emergency at home; the voice that answered would convey a message. And the company also provided extra pay for the out-of-town work. Still, it is small wonder that some workers quit the project, deciding the strain on their personal relationships was not worth the reward.[31]

Have Blue first flew on December 1, 1977, twenty months after Lockheed won the contract, with Park in the cockpit. (Park insisted on a bonus for flying such an unstable plane, and Ben Rich agreed to it.) Test flights usually occurred just after sunrise, before the base's regular workforce arrived for the day, to avoid arousing curiosity, and if any Soviet satellites were known to be passing overhead the airplane stayed in the hangar.

Ad hoc engineering continued right up to the finish line. Seventy-two hours before the first flight, the crew was running some final engine tests and found that the engine was overheating the fuselage. Murphy

Have Blue takes off on a test flight with Ken Dyson as pilot. This is the
second test aircraft, without the long air-data boom.
Source: Ben Rich papers, The Huntington Library.

decided to make an impromptu heat shield; he spied a steel cabinet
in the corner of the hangar and, figuring that "steel is steel," cut the cabinet into small panels. That was not his last improvisation on Have
Blue.[32]

Broomsticks loom large in the history of American aviation. Many
know the story of Chuck Yeager's 1947 flight to break the sound barrier, when his flight engineer jury-rigged a cockpit door handle with a
sawed-off broom. For Have Blue's maiden flight thirty years later Bill
Park was in the cockpit on the runway, as Lockheed and Air Force
brass arrived for the occasion. There was a problem, though, with fuel
migrating from the fuselage tanks to the wings. Bob Murphy hooked
up a fuel pump to fix it, but the fuel tank burped an air bubble and
blew the cap into the tank. "Oh, shit." The cap was sitting on a narrow
ledge at the top of the tank, but Murphy couldn't get his hand through

the opening. Park kept asking, "What's going on back there?" Murphy, to Park: "No sweat!" He spotted a push broom nearby and grabbed it—the broom handle just fit, Murphy snagged the cap, and he called to Park: start the engines.[33]

The first flight was uneventful, but subsequent flights revealed design and production problems. The platypus, for example, took the full heat of the engine exhaust over its upper surface, so the top would get hot while the bottom surface stayed cool; thanks to differential expansion the platypus curled up like a potato chip, which in turn blew up the radar signature. Structural engineers tried several different redesigns, testing each iteration under high-power quartz heat lamps, before arriving at a solution that stayed flat.[34]

The test flights also revealed a problem with the brakes. To save money the Skunk Works had skimped on Have Blue's brakes, and the first plane had a drag chute to help it slow down. Nevertheless, at the end of every rollout after landing, the ground crew found the brakes were literally red-hot and glowing. The crew had to station big fans at the end of the runway and run them out to the plane to cool off the brakes before they caught fire.[35]

The brake problem led to one of the closest calls. On one flight in May 1978 Park tried to bleed off speed before landing in order to spare the brakes. Just before touchdown, he slowed the plane too much and the flight controls dropped it onto the runway. The jolt bounced the plane back into the air, and Park instinctively hit the gas to circle around for another pass. The impact, however, bent one of the landing gears, and when Park retracted the gear it got stuck inside the wheel well. He tried to jar the gear loose with high-g turns and then with hard touch-and-go landings on the remaining good gear—to no avail. The test pilots had previously discussed just this situation and agreed that they would eject if only one landing gear deployed, since a plane landing with one gear would likely roll up into a ball of metal. By then the plane was running out of fuel, and Park, out of options, finally ejected. The force of the ejection knocked him out on the canopy, he broke a leg when he hit the ground, and he ended up facedown and unconscious, suffocating on a mouthful of dirt.[36]

For every previous Have Blue flight, a helicopter had been airborne with a medic on board in case disaster struck. Earlier that morning the base commander had come up to Park and told him that he was canceling the helicopter; he needed the medic back on the base, and after five months and thirty-six test flights Have Blue seemed to pose no risk. Park insisted that he wanted the helicopter airborne, and the base commander gave in. It probably saved Park's life. When the medic reached him he was turning blue. They cleared his airways and got him to a hospital, but it was his last flight.[37]

Ken Dyson then took over. He had flown in Vietnam before becoming a test pilot and was the logical replacement for Park, having flown some of the sorties on the first airplane. Dyson was tall and had to scrunch down to fit in Have Blue's tight cockpit, and even then his head banged on the canopy; he had a flight mechanic put rubber coating on his helmet to keep it from scratching the glass.

The second of the two Have Blue prototypes had just arrived when the first one crashed, so there was no gap in the flight program. The second airplane, though, differed a bit from the first. The first was intended to test flyability, not radar performance, so it had a 6-foot-long boom protruding from its nose to collect air data, plus the box for the drag chute on the back. The second airplane lacked the boom and also lacked the box for the chute (like the first, it had three very short, low-signature air-pressure probes plus eight flush-mounted static pressure ports). Also, the first airplane had been built by production managers, aided by some design engineers, during the strike; for the second plane the regular shop-floor crew was back from the strike, and to Dyson the tolerances seemed a bit tighter.[38]

By July 1979 Dyson had flown the second plane more than fifty times against ground-to-air and air-to-air radar systems, all of them confirming Have Blue's stealthiness to radar. On one of the last scheduled flights in the program Dyson lost hydraulic pressure in the flight controls, which meant the airplane suddenly became, indeed, little more than a tin shed in the air. The plane pitched down violently, giving Dyson about negative-six g's, then pitched back up, then down again. Dyson managed to eject safely, and as he dangled from his parachute

FIGURE 7.2

Have Blue in flight, viewed from below. The retractable antenna at center right is in the extended position. The slight gap in the landing gear doors, less than a quarter inch, was caused by differential pressure from altitude changes. The gap increased the nose-on radar cross section by a factor of three and sparked a redesign for the F-117.

Source: Lockheed Martin Skunk Works.

he watched the plane drill into the desert floor in a ball of flame. The force of the ejection gave him compression fractures of three vertebrae. Still Dyson was not done flying Stealth aircraft. He did, however, have to come up with a cover story for his family: he told his daughter that he got hurt climbing a ladder to get into the cockpit.[39]

With the second and last airplane reduced, like the first, to smoldering wreckage, no Have Blues survived to end up in museums. They had served their purpose, proving the airplane's design envelope—it could fly at Mach 0.8 and as high as 45,000 feet, though it usually flew below 30,000 feet to avoid contrails—and its flight-control electronics.[40] In short, it demonstrated that the tin shed could indeed fly, and evade radar while it did.

There was no guarantee that the Air Force would follow Have Blue with a mass-production contract, and the test flights might have been the end of it—an impressive demonstration, nothing more—but for one more factor. The advent of Stealth in 1977 and 1978 coincided with the arrival of a remarkable team of defense policymakers, extraordinarily qualified to evaluate a technology such as Stealth. It may not be surprising that President Carter, a former engineering officer in the nuclear Navy, should assemble a technically competent team in the Defense Department upon his inauguration in January 1977. But the breadth and depth of that team's scientific expertise remains singular. It started with Defense Secretary Harold Brown, who had a PhD in physics from Columbia and had just served several years as president of Caltech. Brown was the first PhD scientist to be defense secretary. Pentagon staffers were soon startled to find him double-checking their technical assessments, leaving derivations of technical equations running down the margins of memos.[41]

For undersecretary of defense for research and engineering (commonly known as the DDR&E) Brown chose William Perry, a math PhD and cofounder of Electromagnetic Systems Laboratory, a defense electronics firm in Silicon Valley. Perry was therefore well acquainted with the potential of new digital technologies. The undersecretary of the Air Force, Hans Mark, was a physics PhD from MIT and had directed NASA's Ames center, the same lab where a young Richard Scherrer had worked before joining Lockheed. Perry meanwhile had hired a special assistant, a young Air Force officer named Paul Kaminski, who had a PhD from Stanford in aeronautics and astronautics. This tree full of owls then found a roost for General Lew Allen, who had a PhD in nuclear physics and whom Carter appointed Air Force chief of staff in July 1978. Allen was the first chief of staff who rose to the position through the technical branches of the Air Force, rather than as a command or combat pilot, and rumor had it that his appointment gave Curtis LeMay, the hard-line former chief of staff, a heart attack.[42]

Finding PhD scientists and engineers in some of these positions, such as DDR&E, was not uncommon. What was unusual—in fact, unique in American history—was to have them all over the place, from the

Secretary of Defense to the Air Force chief of staff. This formidable team of scientists and engineers unsurprisingly embraced the concept of using technology to offset Soviet advantages in conventional weapons, such as numbers of soldiers, tanks, and planes. The US had previously relied on nuclear weapons to counter this Soviet advantage, but by the mid-1970s the Soviets had achieved nuclear parity. With the Soviets drawing even in nuclear weapons, and remaining far ahead in conventional weapons, the US turned to technology as an asymmetric way to level the strategic field. Brown and Perry in particular pushed this new "offset" strategy and made Stealth a centerpiece, finding funds to push it, fast, even if that meant raiding other projects.[43]

After a careful evaluation by Kaminski, the DDR&E office concluded that Stealth was in fact a breakthrough. Kaminski's report noted the possibility that Stealth might not work as well in the field—rain and sand and dirt might degrade its performance, as would having maintenance performed by Air Force mechanics instead of Lockheed technicians. However, the report pointed out, Stealth would also enjoy an advantage in practice: it could dodge the strongest Soviet defenses by careful choice of routes, and could further foil Soviet radars by choosing routes full of clutter, features in the terrain that would provide false returns in the radar signal.[44]

Perry passed Kaminski's recommendation to the Air Force, but not before considering one more option: to shut down Stealth, for fear that an American program would reveal to the Soviets what was possible, and that they would then use it to penetrate US defenses. Perry, however, decided it was better to race the Soviets in high technology than to hold back—better, that is, to play offense than defense. And since the Soviets had invested far more in air defenses than the US had, they didn't need Stealth as much as Americans did.[45]

In November 1978 the Air Force gave the Skunk Works a production contract under a new program called Senior Trend, with the Air Force now the sole agency in charge. The aircraft themselves were called the YF-117A for the development version for flight test and the F-117A for the production version. The airplane got the "F" designation instead of "A," for attack, or "B," for bomber, even though it wasn't a true fighter, since it wasn't designed for air-to-air combat but rather for air-to-ground bombing missions. As Alan Brown recalled, the Air Force general in charge of Tactical Air Command declared, "I'm having my top fighter pilots flying this airplane and none of them is going to be asked to fly an 'A' or worse yet a 'B' airplane. . . . So make it an 'F.'" (The same general, when briefed on the extensive research Lockheed had done on visual camouflage for the airplane, asked, "The airplane is going to fly at night, isn't it?" Brown replied, "Yes." "Well, paint the god-damn thing black." Lockheed's paint engineer, when informed of this edict after countless hours of work on paint schemes, protested, "You can't do this!")[46]

Since Stealth seemed like a "silver bullet" for America's Cold War arsenal, the Air Force wanted it quickly and planned a production run modeled on the SR-71: build a small number of planes, but build them fast. The Skunk Works would build five YF-117As and fifty-nine F-117As; the schedule called for first flight in twenty-two months and deployment in fifty-one months, by December 1982. The streamlined schedule was matched by the management approach. The initial contract was only seventy pages, and Lockheed and Air Force managers replaced paperwork with daily phone calls and frequent visits by Air Force managers, some of whom took up full-time residence at the Skunk Works during critical stages.[47]

The Air Force initially asked Lockheed to study both a "small fighter" option (the size of the F-15, which was 64 feet long with a 43-foot wingspan) and a "large fighter" (B-58 size, 97 feet long, 57-foot wingspan), and the contract settled on the "small" option.[48] One reason for the choice: since the combat version had to carry weapons and fuel for long-range missions, even the "small fighter" version was about a third larger than Have Blue and presented enough of a challenge to scale up. Have Blue was approximately 47 feet long and 8 feet tall, with a 23-foot wingspan; the F-117A came in at 66 feet long and 13 feet tall, with a 43-foot wingspan. There were several other design changes from Have Blue, the most obvious being the tails. Lockheed engineers found that the inward canted tails on Have Blue trapped exhaust heat, leading to a huge infrared target, so on the F-117 they switched to outward

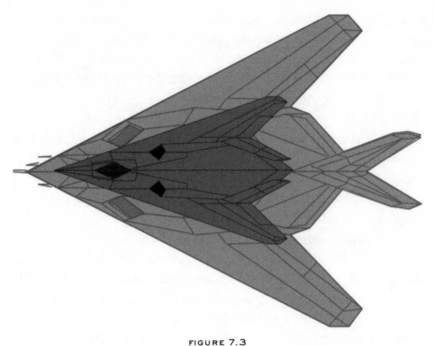

FIGURE 7.3

The relative sizes of Have Blue (smaller, dark gray figure)
and the F-117 (larger, light gray figure).
Source: Alan Brown.

canted tails in a V-shape and moved them aft, which cleaned up the infrared signature at only a small cost in radar cross section.[49]

Have Blue had taken eighteen months to build. Ben Rich had agreed to build the first YF-117—far bigger and more complicated than Have Blue—in twenty-two months. He soon regretted it, as the design caused problems in production. Outside forces also conspired against the project. The first three years of manufacturing were plagued by double-digit inflation, punctuated by the 1979 oil crisis, eating into Lockheed's cost margins.

At the same time, the renewed defense buildup and a surge in the commercial airline business made both workers and materials hard to find. Boeing in particular was booming; in 1979 it was turning out twenty-eight large commercial airliners—including the jumbo 747—every month, which meant that on average a new plane rolled out of the Boeing

FIGURE 7.4

F-117 full-scale model on the RATSCAT radar range.

Source: Ben Rich papers, The Huntington Library.

plant almost daily.[50] For Lockheed it meant a shortage of experienced production workers, especially machinists and electricians. Contracting out the work was no help, in particular since many of Boeing's subcontractors were in Southern California (the 747 alone had almost a thousand subcontractors there), so that overbooked machine shops couldn't fill Lockheed's orders. It also meant a shortage of material: Boeing had cornered 30 percent of the aluminum destined for aerospace.[51]

Building Have Blue had required a few hundred people. Building the F-117 required a few thousand. Desperate for labor, the Skunk Works had to resort to hiring inexperienced workers. In addition, it could find few workers who already had a security clearance—and even fewer who could pass the security investigation. Over 40 percent of the Skunks Works' job applicants flunked the security screening because of drugs. Those who did pass the investigation had to wait several months for the clearance to come through, and during that time they couldn't start work on a classified project such as Stealth. So the Skunk Works

FIGURE 7.5
Hal Farley gets the traditional dousing from
Bill Fox after the first YF-117 flight.
Source: Lockheed Martin Skunk Works.

FIGURE 7.6

Skunk Works team party after the first YF-117 flight. Flight test was a man's world. Ben Rich is sixth from the right in the third row, to the left of the man in the dark T-shirt; Alan Brown is in the middle of the second row, to the right of the man in the checked shirt; Bob Loschke is fourth from left in the second row, in the hat.

Source: courtesy of Scratch Anderson.

had to hire them, apply for their clearance, and then send them to sit in the "ice box," an unclassified building where they were paid full-time to sort nuts and bolts or do other trivial make-work until their clearance arrived. Bob Murphy recalled his struggles to assemble a production workforce: "God dang, it was murder, just murder."[52]

The combination of double-digit inflation, labor and material shortages, clearance delays, and inexperienced shop workers more than doubled the F-117's planned cost, from $350 million to $773 million.[53] It also delayed the schedule. The YF-117 had its first flight in June 1981, eleven months behind schedule and thirty-one months after the contract signing. Test pilot Harold "Hal" Farley got the first flight, which was cut short due to overheating of the exhaust duct. The flight also confirmed suspicions that the tail fins were too small and flexible to control the plane, and engineers subsequently made them bigger. The test nevertheless proved that the plane flew, and Farley got the usual celebratory dousing by a bucket of water; that night the Skunk Works crew at Area 51 threw an all-night beer bash.[54]

The exhaust problem, however, was ominous. The exhaust ducts had been a constant problem in production. They were a flattened rectangular shape, lined with baffles and heat-absorbing tiles, which was great for reducing radar reflection and infrared emissions but not so great for delivering exhaust out of the plane. There's a reason pipes are usually round and open: the flattened shape was structurally weak, the baffles impeded the exhaust, and at high temperatures and pressures the whole duct tended to crack and split.[55] On a subsequent test flight the exhaust lining gave way and slipped, clogging up the exhaust duct. The exhaust had to go somewhere, and it blew a hole out of the exhaust duct, right out the side of the plane.

FIGURE 7.7

An F-117 in flight, viewed from above.
Source: Lockheed Martin Skunk Works.

That was not the last problem in the test program—a consequence in part of the rushed schedule, in part of the airplane's novelty, with the test engineers solving problems literally on the fly. The first production aircraft did not survive the test program. Workers on the production line had shifted a flight control and rewired it, and in the process unwittingly reversed the pitch and roll controls. Test pilot Bob Riedenauer was just getting airborne when the plane rolled on its side and skipped across the desert floor. Riedenauer survived but spent several months in the hospital.[56] Midway through a later flight one tail fin simply snapped off. The chase plane's pilot watched in horror as the fin fluttered down to the desert floor, though the test pilot calmly brought the airplane back.[57]

On another test flight, pilot Tom Morgenfeld had a nose wheel fall off at takeoff. Test engineers told Morgenfeld to eject; they feared the plane would pitchpole if he tried to land on the nose-gear stub. He landed it anyway, trying to pitch up the nose in a sort of wheelie, the metal nose stub trailing sparks as he careened down the runway. Kelly Johnson and Ben Rich later pranked Morgenfeld with a mock union grievance, for "grinding of a component by unauthorized personnel."[58]

The F-117 also demonstrated that the aircraft needed different types of managers at different times in their development. Since Alan Brown was oriented more toward research and design than manufacturing, Lockheed management and the Air Force agreed that they needed a new program manager for production and subsequent deployment, and in February 1982 they gave the job to Sherman Mullin. As a Princeton dropout, Mullin had wanted to write novels, but after enlisting in the US Army he discovered the Army had other plans for him. After teaching him electronics, the Army in 1955 put Mullin on the faculty of its Guided Missile School at Fort Bliss, Texas, at the ripe age of nineteen years old, teaching officers and enlisted men. He then learned the emerging art of digital computers at a couple of industry jobs, the last at a small company in New Jersey called Stavid, which was bought by Lockheed in 1959. After that Mullin learned systems engineering working on antisubmarine warfare projects, eventually including a five-year stint as program manager on the P-3 Orion aircraft. The P-3 taught him how to get along with operational commanders and maintenance crews during deployment of new aircraft, and its advanced avionics package also proved good training for the F-117.[59]

Mullin's career shows that there was more than one route to becoming an aerospace engineer. He had no college degree but was good at math and had extensive training in electronics courtesy of the US Army, a common experience for his generation. He also had a tremendous appetite for work. As F-117 manager Mullin developed a close rapport with colleagues and military managers, but as a former Army sergeant he could also express blunt if not pungent judgments on technical issues as well as people.

Mullin wrestled the flight-test and production problems to ground and made up some time in the schedule. One of the most critical remaining issues was the window for the infrared and laser targeting system, which inspired another piece of improvisation. The system sat inside a couple of small boxlike cavities in the fuselage, one at the front of the plane and one on the bottom. The infrared sensors would detect heat generated by potential targets, and the lasers would then guide the aircraft's bombs to the target. The trick was to screen off the aperture from radar waves, since a boxlike cavity would lead to a huge radar return, but still allow infrared waves and lasers to pass through. A regular glass window wouldn't work, since glass doesn't pass many infrared wavelengths. They tried more exotic solid-state crystals such as zinc selenide, but crystal panels a couple of feet across proved expensive (close to $1 million for the two windows on a single aircraft) and, perhaps worse, exceedingly fragile.

Alan Brown went home one weekend and had an idea: maybe the window didn't have to be airtight. If so, a grid of wire might screen out radar waves but pass the infrared. The wire would be under high tension, so Brown used piano wire. The shortest anticipated radar wavelengths were on the order of a half inch, much longer than infrared wavelengths, so a grid with spacing of about a tenth of an inch would suffice; it was wide enough to let infrared and laser radiation escape without interference, but fine enough to block radar waves and also avoid air turbulence. The Skunk Works shop floor ordered a bunch of

piano wire and made some prototypes. It was supposed to be a tempo-
rary fix until the engineering team came up with a better solution. They
never did, and the piano-wire grids were installed on all F-117s for the
lifetime of the aircraft.[60]

————

The F-117 was operational in October 1983—nine months later than
planned, but still less than five years from approval to deployment,
faster than the F-15 (six years) and F-16 and F-18 (seven years each).[61]
The Air Force deployed it in the 4450th Tactical Group, located on a
newly constructed, $200 million base at Tonopah Test Range, known
as Area 52.[62]

By this time it was well known that the US was pursuing Stealth aircraft, but the fact that it had built and deployed such airplanes was still
secret. That didn't stop speculation. In 1986 the Testor Corporation,
maker of toy model airplanes, came out with a model Stealth fighter.
It called the plane the F-19, logically assuming it would take the next
number in line after the F-18, the latest fighter. The model sparked controversy and front-page headlines. How could a toy company, which
had started out making glue during the Depression, have come up with
the top-secret Stealth design? Angry congressmen brandished models
on the floor of Congress and demanded to know why a toy company
knew a secret they didn't. In fact, the model's designer, John Andrews,
an aviation buff, had simply followed the stories about Stealth, made
some educated guesses, and come up with something that looked like
a scaled-down, tricked-out SR-71. Testor happily rode the publicity to half a million kits sold in the first year and a million lifetime
sales, making it the best-selling model plane of all time. The Soviet
Embassy supposedly dispatched staff to a Washington hobby shop to
buy models, only to find them sold out.[63]

With speculation building—and with plans under way to publicly unveil the B-2 Stealth bomber, whose existence was already well
known—the Pentagon announced the existence of the Stealth fighter on
November 10, 1988, five years after deploying it and seven years after
its first flight. (Having accused Carter of playing politics by announcing

Stealth just before the 1980 election, the Reagan administration delayed a planned press conference until just after the 1988 election.) The Pentagon's grainy, blurry photo yielded few details and only piqued public interest, although American taxpayers still did not know how much they had paid for the plane or why.[64]

The first combat use of Stealth was anticlimax, if not overkill. In December 1989 the US ran out of patience with Panama's Manuel Noriega, a onetime American ally turned drug-running strongman. After Noriega's regime declared war on the US and killed an American Marine, the Bush administration initiated Operation Just Cause to overthrow and capture Noriega. During the invasion two F-117s each dropped a one-ton bomb near a Panamanian army barracks, intending to hit close enough to stun the troops but not kill them. It was not an auspicious debut; thanks to a snafu with the targeting information, one of the bombs landed on a nearby hillside, and since Panama had few air defenses it didn't offer a serious test of Stealth. Some cynical observers thought the Air Force just wanted a chance to trot out its secret weapon.[65] A truer test for Stealth came a bit over a year later, in the skies over Baghdad.

CHAPTER EIGHT

SECRETS AND STRATEGIES

Up through deployment in 1983 the Stealth program was confined to a tight circle of engineers within the two firms, DARPA, and the Air Force. All of them worked under extreme secrecy, in what was known as the black world, a realm quite apart from the open, unclassified world. For seven years Stealth was one of the nation's most highly classified projects, a so-called Special Access Program; even the fact that the program existed was closely guarded. It had not always been so secret. Project Harvey was classified Confidential, the lowest level, and the classification increased through the XST program; only with Have Blue in 1976 did Stealth enter the special-access black world. Yet, as the anthropologist Mihir Pandya has shown, this invisible project to build an invisible plane was hidden in plain sight, in nondescript office buildings in Hawthorne and Burbank, and its secrecy represented profound implications of the Cold War for American society.[1]

There were good reasons for secrecy. Starting in the early 1970s the Soviets had a vigorous espionage program, under a KGB directorate known as Line X, to penetrate US defense and electronics firms. (*The Falcon and the Snowman*, the book and movie, was based on an engineer at TRW in Redondo Beach caught spying for the Soviets in the mid-1970s.) In 1981 a KGB source cultivated by French intelligence revealed the efforts of Line X, which the French shared with the US in what became known as the Farewell Dossier. The CIA turned the operation back on the Soviets, feeding them bogus designs and blueprints.[2]

Secrecy, however, came with costs. The investigation for a Secret clearance for a single employee could run $10,000, a more extensive Top Secret investigation two or three times that. These investigations could take weeks or months, and newly hired employees had to bide their time in the "ice box," playing cards or pursuing make-work projects, until their clearance came through and they could turn to their actual job. Then there were the daily hassles of security: storing and tracking classified documents, maintaining classified computers, storing typewriter ribbons used to type secret documents. An example of the measures taken: the US learned that the KGB (specifically Léon Theremin, inventor of the eponymous musical instrument) had developed a way to eavesdrop on conversations within a building by directing an infrared beam on the window, picking up the vibrations in the glass set off by human speech. Classified projects had to seal their windows or apply special coatings to cloak the vibrations.[3]

Other costs were incalculable. The scale of the black world in the Cold War boggles the mind. At any one time, several million people in the US had security clearances—perhaps one in sixty adult citizens. In regions like Southern California, the proportion of cleared individuals was far higher. Similarly, historians have estimated the volume of classified documents at several *billion* pages, perhaps greater than the entire contents of the Library of Congress.[4] So much of the historical record remains classified to this day that our picture of the Cold War is only a small corner of the canvas.[5]

This vast security regime shaped American society in ways that are still little understood. For Stealth, not only the design of the airplane but its budget and its very existence were kept secret from the public. The Pentagon briefed a few select congressmen—the chair and ranking minority members of key defense committees—but otherwise kept Congress in the dark; the briefed members had to persuade their congressional colleagues that the secret funding was for a worthwhile program.[6]

Such secrecy had benefits. On the Manhattan Project in World War II, for example, project leaders used secrecy to keep Congress or other executive agencies from meddling in and perhaps prolonging the work leading to the atomic bomb.[7] Similarly, secrecy on Stealth in the 1970s and 1980s fostered efficiency. Lockheed built Have Blue in twenty months from contract to first flight, and the F-117 in thirty-one months.

The Skunk Works could work so fast because, thanks to tight secrecy, it didn't have an army of auditors and procurement officers looking over its shoulder. But this administrative efficiency posed a fundamental dilemma to American democracy: How could citizens or their elected representatives cast informed votes if they didn't know about these programs?[8]

Perhaps most chilling were the personal or psychological costs of secrecy. The clearance process was not only expensive but also intrusive, asking probing, uncomfortable questions. Everything was fair game: an individual's relationships, mental health, drug and alcohol use, financial status, sexual orientation. And if you neglected to disclose an embarrassing detail—say, a failed relationship, or smoking some pot in college—and investigators found out, you were out of a clearance, and thus out of a job, with no right to appeal.[9]

Admission to the black world then brought the psychological costs of keeping secrets. Aerospace workers couldn't talk about work with their families; they couldn't explain to their spouses or kids where they were going or what they were doing when they disappeared for weeks at a time, to a place in a desert they still won't name. They developed a personal discipline about secrets, in effect internalizing the surveillance: always on guard about what one was saying or doing, and who was watching or listening. One retired aerospace engineer, trying to explain the difficulty he had talking about his job, said, "You have to understand, I spent forty years trying to be a gray face." Some participants still refuse to talk at all about their work, even in general terms and decades later, for fear of losing track of the boundary between the white and black worlds and letting slip a secret—and getting in trouble for it.[10]

The black world reflected an ultimate irony of the Cold War: to defend American liberties, aerospace engineers gave up civil liberties.

———

Despite this vast security regime, the Soviets learned about Stealth within a year of the first concept studies. They learned about it not through high-tech espionage or cloak-and-dagger tradecraft but rather simply by reading the American trade press, where magazines like *Aviation Week* (better known as "Aviation Leak") offered industry scuttlebutt. In June 1975 *Aviation Week* announced that ARPA had funded feasibility studies by Northrop, Lockheed, and McDonnell Douglas for a "fighter or attack aircraft that could escape enemy radar, infrared and visual tracking"—that is, for "high-stealth aircraft."[11] Subsequent articles in *Aviation Week* divulged the contest between Lockheed and Northrop, the contract award to Lockheed (for what became Have Blue), and then test flights of a Stealth demonstrator aircraft.[12]

The CIA was not entirely unhappy with the leaks. The articles often merged fact and fantasy; published estimates of the B-2 radar cross section ranged from 5.0 to 0.000001 square meters, from as big as a barn door to a pinprick. A later CIA report in 1988 noted that such speculation "keeps US Stealth programs shrouded in mystery, perpetuates false rumors about Stealth technology, and complicates the job faced by those Soviet analysts struggling to determine the capabilities of US Stealth systems."[13]

The Carter administration may not have minded the leaks either. After a flurry of news reports about the Stealth bomber in summer 1980, the Pentagon held a press conference at which Bill Perry and Secretary of Defense Harold Brown publicized the existence of Stealth. Given the timing, in the midst of a heated presidential campaign, some observers smelled a political motive behind the announcement—and perhaps behind the leaks that led up to it. The Carter administration had canceled the B-1 bomber in 1977, and in the 1980 campaign Ronald Reagan was using the issue to hammer Carter as being soft on defense. Carter asked Brown and Perry if the administration could reveal the Stealth program, and added that he would respect their judgment if they said no. But Brown and Perry decided it was safe to publicize the existence though not the details of Stealth. With the F-117 deployment about two years away, and the Stealth bomber about to start needing large budgets, they figured an announcement would occur in the next year or two anyway.[14]

Reporters weren't the only ones dubious about the timing of the announcement. Congress questioned the sudden shift, as a congressional investigation described it, "from a secrecy which prevented even the mention of its name, to a press conference in which it was unveiled to the whole world." The investigation, by a subcommittee of the House Committee on Armed Services, concluded that "the release of information about Stealth in the formal press conference was done to make the Defense Department and the administration look good in an election year." With the Stealth bomber still a decade from deployment, the report charged, the announcement had given the Soviets a ten-year head start not only to develop their own Stealth bomber but also to develop countermeasures.[15]

The committee's outrage was disingenuous, given that the trade press had been discussing Stealth for five years by that time. It was also curious, in that Democrats controlled Congress and were thus attacking a Democratic president in the middle of a crucial campaign. In fact, there were ample precedents for such friendly fire between Congress and a president on military issues (such as the Truman Committee in World War II and the Johnson Committee in the Korean War), which proved only that politicians often prized personal publicity over party loyalty—and that secret programs, ironically, made for great publicity. Stealth was already a political football, and it was still early in the game.[16]

The press conference also allowed Harold Brown to make a cryptic point, one that revealed an unintended consequence of Stealth. From eighteenth-century submarines to twentieth-century strategic bombers and atom bombs, the US had always been in pursuit of wonder weapons, some new technology that would deter adversaries and guarantee the nation's security. A subset of American fascination with the technological sublime, from intercontinental railroads to moon landings, this tendency often led to dazzling displays of engineering virtuosity, and Stealth was just the latest in this long line.[17]

Technological spectacles cannot dazzle, however, if they are kept under wraps. As the fictional Dr. Strangelove said of the Soviets' famous Doomsday Machine, "The whole point . . . is lost, if you keep it a secret!" In this sense the leaks about Stealth, and the press conference, served an important purpose, one Brown and Perry discussed at the time.[18] There is no evidence to suggest that the US revealed Stealth's existence as part of a campaign to frighten the Soviets (or that the technology itself was part of a sting operation, as some partisans would later claim about Reagan's Strategic Defense Initiative, also known as Star Wars). The US, after all, was still devoting vast resources to keeping Stealth secret—both with the security regime and by carefully coordinating test flights to avoid Soviet satellite overflights—because it was intended for combat use. But by proclaiming the existence of Stealth, the US achieved one of its most important though unintended consequences: its effect on Soviet thinking.

In this sense Stealth was like nuclear weapons, which served their purpose simply by existing. As Brown put it at the press conference, "The potential already has the effect."[19] The strategic function of these technologies was their mere existence, not their actual use. They acted on the adversary's imagination, not on his armed forces. And Stealth scared the daylights out of the Soviets.

———

The leaks fed a feverish yet fruitful bout of theorizing by Soviet strategists, leading to their conclusion that a "military-technical revolution" was at hand—and that the US was leading it.

In 1962 Marshal of the Soviet Union V. D. Sokolovsky described two military revolutions in the twentieth century, each one deploying new technologies to extend the reach and speed of warfare dramatically. The first linked tanks and airplanes with radio networks to enable quick, deep strikes, such as the Nazi blitzkrieg. The second revolution combined nuclear weapons with ballistic missiles to allow intercontinental attacks within a half hour.[20]

In the late 1970s the Soviet General Staff began writing about a third "military-technical revolution" (MTR), in which sensors, computers, precision-guided weapons, and Stealth technology would allow an adversary to identify and attack even heavily defended targets far behind the front lines. Although Stealth was just one of several components of this "reconnaissance-strike complex," as the Soviets called it, it was important in avoiding air defenses. The main proponent of this view,

Nikolai Ogarkov, was promoted to marshal and chief of the general staff in 1977. From that point forward, Soviet military journals were full of articles on the revolution's tactical and strategic implications, including the deep-strike capability opened up by Stealth aircraft.[21]

It was no surprise that the Soviets were first to perceive a revolution based on technology—they were, after all, trained in a revolutionary and materialist view of history, and they had experienced firsthand the devastating effects of the German Blitzkrieg. They also had a cultural as well as ideological fondness for systematic theories.[22] The MTR was a specific offshoot of a broader "scientific and technical revolution," in which computers and automation, combined with the limitless energy of nuclear power, would transform labor and production and realize the ultimate transition to communism.[23]

Soviet theorists recognized that the MTR presented a particular threat to the Soviet Union. First, it challenged the Soviet "deep battle" philosophy, since the leapfrog air strikes threatened the echelons at the rear of the Soviet front—the Soviet concept of the front as a box, not a line. Second, it offset their quantitative advantage in manpower and matériel with technology. Third, the role of computers and electronics had troubling implications for a military populated by poorly educated conscripts.[24] As Ogarkov put it to an American visitor in 1983, "Modern military power is based upon technology, and technology is based upon computers. In the US, small children—even before they begin school—play with computers. Computers are everywhere in America. Here, we don't even have computers in every office of the Defense Ministry."[25]

Finally, the MTR posed special challenges to the Soviet defense industry. After World War II, the Soviets decided that preparing for war meant stockpiling not only weapons but the factories to make them. Having this production capacity available, however, assumed that one knew what weapons the military would need; the Soviet system, after all, depended on planning. In the late 1970s, Soviet theorists realized that rapid changes in technology made it impossible to plan for productive capacity, since it took time to tool up manufacturing lines. The Soviets couldn't shift their production fast enough to keep up with American technology.[26]

This realization, summarized in a 1981 report for the general staff titled *The Economic Foundations of the Military Power of the Socialist State*, by Alexsandr Pozharov, persuaded Ogarkov—long before Gorbachev had entered office, let alone embraced perestroika—to urge the restructuring of the Soviet economy to a more flexible, responsive system. It also caused his downfall. The men who ran the Soviet defense industry had accumulated considerable power by the mass production of old-fashioned equipment, by churning out tanks, trucks, planes, and ships by the hundreds and thousands. These "metal eaters" had no interest in shifting from heavy industry to high-tech. In 1984 they helped engineer Ogarkov's ouster, abetted by Soviet leaders tired of his harping on American high-tech superiority.[27]

The MTR also had particular implications for the role of nuclear weapons. In a 1984 interview, Ogarkov noted that the new technologies—Stealth, precision-guided munitions, and cruise missiles—"made it possible to sharply increase (by at least an order of magnitude) the destructive potential of conventional weapons, bringing them closer, so to speak, to weapons of mass destruction in terms of effectiveness."[28] Stealth could help make a conventional attack as effective as nuclear weapons.

———

This line of thinking had already surfaced in the long-range R&D (LRRD) seminars cosponsored by DARPA and the Defense Nuclear Agency in the early 1970s—namely, that new conventional weapons could blunt a Soviet attack in Western Europe without nuclear weapons. In the 1980s, noting the alarm raised by Soviet theorists, some American strategists pushed for a fundamental reappraisal of America's Cold War strategy.

The push was led by Albert Wohlstetter, whom one scholar has called "the alpha male of strategic studies" in the Cold War. An influential architect of nuclear strategy at the RAND Corporation, Wohlstetter had then taught at the University of Chicago, from where his intellectual progeny propagated the neoconservative movement, and he now ran his own consulting firm, called Pan Heuristics.[29] Wohlstetter had chaired the LRRD seminars of the early 1970s, and now, a decade later, he developed the ideas they had introduced.

Wohlstetter believed that the strategic and political landscape had changed, along with the technology, since the development of nuclear doctrine.[30] For two decades the US had relied primarily on the strategy of mutual assured destruction, which assumed that the American threat to meet any Soviet assault with a thermonuclear apocalypse would deter the Soviets from attacking. But the vast growth of nuclear arsenals on both sides—the US and Soviet Union by 1980 had well over fifty thousand nuclear warheads between them—had rendered nuclear deterrence "increasingly incredible" in the literal sense. Neither side believed the other would really commit civilizational suicide to defend a swath of territory. A case in point: nuclear weapons had evidently failed to deter the Soviets from invading Afghanistan. The US was relying, Wohlstetter declared, on "empty threats." He also pointed out that the US and NATO's plan to rely on nuclear weapons to stop a Soviet invasion of Western Europe meant laying waste to NATO territory with its own nuclear weapons, not exactly an optimal strategy. As for politics, the US and NATO democracies would need to muster public support to fight a war, an impossible task if television broadcasts were showing the devastating effects of a nuclear exchange. If anything, Wohlstetter noted, the Freeze movement showed increasing public opposition to nuclear weapons.[31]

In short, Wohlstetter argued, basic strategic and political problems had emerged for nuclear weapons. New technologies, however, provided a solution. It now seemed possible to deliver conventional weapons with sufficient accuracy to destroy any target. That possibility, he added, undermined the need to rely on "suicidally indiscriminate responses" with nuclear weapons.[32]

Richard Brody, who worked for Wohlstetter at Pan Heuristics, summarized the shift. In general there were two ways to destroy a target: a small bomb close to the target, or a big bomb not so close to the target. Strategic bombing in World War II had used the big-bomb, brute-force approach, and American nuclear strategy took this philosophy to the extreme in the Cold War. The US planned to use nuclear weapons against the Soviets because bombs or missiles couldn't always get close to their targets; nuking a target was therefore the best way to make sure it was destroyed. Overkill, perhaps, but military planners did not like uncertainty. The ability to deliver conventional weapons with pinpoint accuracy changed the equation. Now you didn't need a big bomb—a small one would do. The new technologies, Brody concluded, made nuclear weapons "both wasteful and irrelevant."[33]

A group of American defense planners pursued these ideas in a series of "New Alternatives" workshops starting in 1982 under the Defense Nuclear Agency and then, starting in 1986, in an explicit sequel, called LRRD II, to the joint DNA-DARPA workshops of the early 1970s.[34] LRRD II planners included Stealth as one of the five high-priority technologies, alongside others such as precision-guided munitions and sensors, driving the revolution.[35]

These brainstorming sessions, and the basic concepts behind them, received little public notice. The ideas were ignored despite being featured in a prime-time televised speech by President Reagan on March 23, 1983. Without going into detail, Reagan asserted that "America does possess—now—the technologies to attain very significant improvements in the effectiveness of our conventional, nonnuclear forces."[36]

This message was ignored because Reagan used the same speech to reveal an extraordinary proposal to build a vast defense system against strategic missiles, what became known as the Strategic Defense Initiative, or Star Wars. The media and public focused overwhelmingly on the missile defense part of the speech and missed the point about conventional weapons.[37] It only later dawned on some administration officials, particularly George Keyworth, Reagan's science adviser, that the new conventional capabilities suggested another way to achieve the goal of Star Wars—namely, as Reagan had put it in his speech, to render nuclear weapons "obsolete."[38]

The neglect of the strategic implications of the new conventional weapons, however, was only in part due to Star Wars dominating the strategic conversation. There was also explicit resistance from the military services (Wohlstetter complained that both the Navy and Air Force were resisting new technologies), along with political opposition from both the left and right.[39] Some conservatives, Wohlstetter argued, saw nothing wrong with relying on nuclear weapons, since they believed nuclear war was survivable and winnable. Critics on the political left meanwhile saw little difference between the new conventional technologies and nuclear weapons and feared a new, nonnuclear arms race that would undermine deterrence, make war more likely, and further divert resources from social programs.[40]

Others bemoaned the trend of technological virtuosity, with ever more elaborate and costly weapons producing what one book title at the time described as "the baroque arsenal." The journalist James Fallows, in an influential 1981 *Atlantic* article on "America's high-tech weaponry," noted that the price of a single fighter aircraft, such as the F-14 or F-15, now ran in the tens of millions of dollars; "the search for more exacting technical triumphs has taken on a life of its own." The US, in this view, should build a greater number of simple weapons instead of a few costly high-tech ones; quantity, that is, instead of quality. In other words, the US should offset the Soviets' quantitative advantage by building more weapons itself, not trying to build better ones.[41] Similar sentiments inspired about two dozen members of Congress, mostly Republicans and conservative Democrats, to band together in 1981 as the Military Reform Caucus. Their platform included an effort to end what one defense analyst called an "infatuation with fancy weaponry whose design reflects pursuit of technology for its own sake"—a category that presumably could include Stealth.[42]

The strategic push for conventional weapons finally got broader attention in the Commission on Integrated Long-Term Strategy, a major study undertaken in 1986 for the Pentagon and Reagan's national security adviser, looking twenty years into the future for national security. The commission's prominent strategists included Zbigniew Brzezinski, Samuel Huntington, Andrew Goodpaster, and Henry Kissinger; its sympathy for the military-technical revolution was no surprise, since the cochairs both participated in the '80s strategic workshops: Fred Iklé . . . and Wohlstetter himself.[43]

The committee's report, entitled *Discriminate Deterrence*, urged that the US military make Stealth a top priority, touting its potential, in combination with precision-guided munitions, to replace nuclear weapons. "The precision associated with the new technologies will enable us to use conventional weapons for many of the missions once assigned to nuclear weapons. . . . Particularly important in this connection is the prospective use of 'low-observable' (Stealth) technology in combination with extremely accurate weapons and improved means of locating targets."[44]

––––––––

This argument, however, gained little traction, despite the prominence of its proponents. The fact that Stealth itself was by that time already enlisted in the strategic realm, with the B-2 as a delivery vehicle for nuclear weapons, demonstrates the sheer inertia—military, political, and intellectual—that nuclear strategy had acquired. The US had spent trillions of dollars on its nuclear capability and would not abandon it easily.[45] It would take more than a technological fix to solve the problem of nuclear weapons.

The US originally developed Stealth to meet a tactical problem: how to defeat Soviet air defenses in the event of a conventional invasion of Western Europe. This tactical, battlefield focus seemed far removed from the lofty intellectual realm of nuclear strategy. But Soviet theorists began to recognize that Stealth and other new technologies, especially precision-guided munitions, blurred the usual distinction between conventional and nuclear weapons. This outburst of theorizing helped provoke American strategists in the 1980s to a fundamental reconsideration of the role of nuclear weapons, including the possibility that they were, as Richard Brody declared, "both wasteful and irrelevant." If anyone wanted to make nuclear weapons "obsolete"—as Wohlstetter put it, echoing Reagan—here was a chance.[46] In the end, though, the military-technical revolution represented a missed opportunity for the US to wean itself from nuclear weapons even before the end of the Cold War.

CHAPTER NINE

THE WHALE

Although the F-117A and B-2 have become widely recognized aircraft, few have heard of one called Tacit Blue. This is perhaps understandable, since only one was ever built and it was never deployed. Yet the Tacit Blue project created another, totally different Stealth aircraft, one that provided a crucial stepping-stone between the two more famous planes.

Tacit Blue was another by-product of the LRRD seminars in the early 1970s and their vision of the high-tech battlefield—in this case, one battlefield in particular, among the most famous military sites of the Cold War despite the fact that it thankfully never saw a battle. The site was the Fulda Gap, a corridor along the Fulda River on the East German border with West Germany, and the presumed route of any Soviet invasion of Western Europe. The Fulda Gap offered a path from east to west through a series of mountain ranges. Once through the gap Soviet tanks would be on the doorstep of Frankfurt, the financial hub of West Germany as well as a major American military center, including an air base. Beyond Frankfurt lay open, gentle terrain leading to the Rhine.

The Soviet Red Army, as we know, embraced the concept of echelons, sending attacks in waves that made the battlefield not a line but a box. The response by the US and NATO was to leapfrog the initial attack and strike the follow-on echelons in the rear. (This leapfrog maneuver, known as "deep attack," would be codified in NATO's Follow-On Forces Attack [FOFA] doctrine, adopted in 1981, and the US AirLand Battle doctrine of 1982.)[1] The Soviet echelons would wait in the staging area behind the Fulda Gap, where Soviet tanks and troops collected at the end of East German rail lines. The staging area was shielded by the mountains around the gap, including the Vogelsberg and Rhön ranges, with peaks 2,000 to 3,000 feet high.

American defense planners intended to use an airborne radar to detect Soviet tanks far behind the front lines and then target the tanks with precision-guided munitions. The plan would eventually be known, starting in 1978, as Assault Breaker.[2] The catch: Assault Breaker required a way to see over the mountains to the Soviet staging area. To do that, the US needed a powerful radar that could loiter high in the air without getting shot down. The solution was a radar-bearing aircraft that incorporated Stealth, in order to evade Soviet air defenses. The radar antenna required a big boxlike shape. So the question was, How do you make a stealthy flying box—and one with its own powerful radar inside?

––––––

In April 1976 Northrop learned that it lost the XST shootout, but it soon got a consolation prize. In order to keep Northrop's Stealth team in the game, in December 1976 DARPA asked it to work on the stealthy flying box. Perhaps reflecting the airplane's awkward requirements, DARPA encumbered it with the name Battlefield Surveillance Aircraft—Experimental, or BSAX. The project required designers to make a stealthy airplane for the mission and then to put a radar in it that didn't compromise its stealthiness. The job fell initially to John Cashen, who started out as the project manager within Northrop.

BSAX required a big radar antenna inside the plane, adding another dimension to Stealth. The walls of the aircraft had to be transparent to the antenna's frequencies, so engineers needed to design the inside of the plane such that incoming radar waves, if they got through the walls, couldn't bounce around and then escape (again, the harmonica effect). Most people think of Stealth as referring just to the outside of the plane. BSAX had Stealth on the inside: essentially, the internal space for the radar was an anechoic chamber, with radar-absorbing cones lining the walls to diffuse inbound radar waves, something like the egg-crate-style absorbers in a music recording studio.

That took care of the cavity, but then Northrop's designers also had to make the radar itself stealthy. It did no good to make an invisible plane if the enemy could simply home in on its radar beam. Along with Stealth, Ken Perko's Tactical Technology Office at DARPA had under way a program called Pave Mover to develop a radar that, among other things, provided moving target indication, or MTI, in order to distinguish tanks from the background landscape. The MTI radar took advantage of the Doppler shift, the same effect that makes an ambulance siren or train horn change pitch as it moves: a radar wave that reflects off a moving target shifts in frequency. The system fed the received radar signal into a filter that compared it with the transmitted signal, and any stationary object that didn't display a Doppler shift—say, a boulder or a building—got filtered out.[3]

The BSAX airplane was intended to fly a long racetrack pattern on the friendly side of the battlefront, flying for many miles in one direction along the front, then making a U-turn and flying back in the opposite direction. The radar antenna looked out one side of the plane toward the enemy forces; on the other side the data-link antenna beamed a radio signal back to friendly troops on the ground, who would direct the antitank missiles to the targets. The radio signal carried the raw radar data, which required more computer power than an airplane at the time could carry, so computers on the ground would process the data to reveal the targets. Both antennas were mounted on a turntable, so that when the airplane made its U-turn at one end of the racetrack, the radar and the data link would switch sides.

BSAX was designed to test a classified version of the Pave Mover radar, built by Hughes, known as a low-probability-of-intercept radar. The radar had to be on all the time to track targets, but if the beam stood out like a searchlight, that would defeat the purpose of Stealth. To avoid detection, the beam couldn't stay in any one spot on the ground for too long—it couldn't "dwell"—and it also couldn't just sweep the ground in a regular, predictable pattern. It hence had to shift in a seemingly random pattern, darting from spot to spot on the ground. In addition, the radar transmitter tweaked the waveform and frequency-hopped across a wide bandwidth, so that it didn't produce a predictable sine wave at a single frequency.

For Pave Mover's frequency band Cashen, working with the Hughes engineers, chose the Ku band, between 12 and 18 GHz. The relatively short wavelength of the Ku band had the advantage of providing a smaller antenna, and it was also an uncommon band for tactical radars since it gets absorbed by heavy rainfall. Cashen argued that severe rain was usually localized in cells and was more common to the tropics than to Western Europe, and thus unlikely to affect performance. Furthermore, the wall of the airplane covering the radar was a "bandpass radome," featuring tiny slits that were tuned to allow only waves that matched the radar's frequency to pass through. So a bandpass radome for the Ku band would filter out radar waves in more prevalent frequency bands.[4]

Finally, BSAX added to the Pave Mover package a synthetic aperture radar, which combined radar data from many points along a flight path to simulate a large antenna and thus achieve higher-resolution radar images. It was a computation-heavy technique, requiring the integration of large amounts of radar data; BSAX was the first attempt at a real-time airborne synthetic aperture radar, using a data link to computers on the ground to do the real-time processing.[5]

All of this was new to the Stealth program, since the XST competition had not included a radar on the plane. For the outside of the plane, BSAX also presented different demands. Instead of an attack aircraft zooming in at low altitude and high speed, which needed to be invisible to radar from the front, BSAX was a high-flying reconnaissance airplane that had to be stealthy from all angles—what engineers call "all-aspect" stealth—and especially from the side, since the aircraft would mostly fly parallel to the battlefront and thus present its side to air-defense radars.

The first step was to lay out the planform, the outline of the airplane viewed from above. The planform largely determined the radar scattering in azimuth—that is, at any angle in the same geometric plane as the aircraft. As we know, Northrop, like Lockheed, believed in straight edges, accepting a single sharp spike, tall but narrow, in the radar signal—like a glint of light off a mirror—and then having the airplane's own motion sweep that glint across the ground faster than a radar could track it. An air-defense radar had to scan the sky, and if the glint was short enough—if the spike was narrow enough—the radar might be looking in another direction and miss it altogether, or it might catch only a glimpse, not long enough to start tracking it.[6]

A low-altitude strike aircraft needed highly swept wings to minimize reflections toward the front of the airplane. The challenge for BSAX was to minimize reflections to the side. As it happened, shortly after the XST decision DARPA had also asked Northrop to work on a stealthy cruise missile called Teal Dawn. Northrop eventually bowed out of that program, but before then it inspired some basic thinking. The cruise missile has a long, straight body, with stubby squarish wings and tail fins—what's called a wing-body-tail design, more like a conventional airplane than the blended wing-body, or delta wing, of the XST designs. Long straight edges provide large spikes, but very narrow ones. That helped persuade Cashen to embrace a wing-body-tail for BSAX, with a long, straight body.

Another design principle was the fewer edges the better, to reduce the number of glints. And, wherever possible, the edges should be parallel. Two parallel edges essentially provided a single radar spike in the same direction, the same as would reflect from a single edge. So the Northrop team embraced what they called parallel planforming. A simple, boxy airplane with parallel edges—in the fuselage, the wings, and the nose and tail—would produce just a handful of spikes. BSAX, in fact, was a six-spike airplane. The wings had minimal sweep, about 10 degrees, to keep radar from reflecting to the side, toward the enemy forces.[7]

Once the planform was set, the next step was to add volume to the aircraft. The ideal shape to minimize radar cross section is an infinitely thin flat plate. A real airplane, however, needs volume: it has to carry a pilot, engines, and fuel, and this one of course would carry a radar as well. So Cashen started with a flat plate and added the volume above it; the result was a fuselage rimmed with chines, the flat, flared-out surfaces that had helped give the SR-71 its distinctive shape. In this case, though, the chines were married to a boxy-looking aircraft, so

FIGURE 9.1

Tacit Blue in flight, viewed from above.
Source: courtesy of Northrop Grumman Corporation.

that rather than contributing to a sense of sleekness, the chines gave the plane the ungainly appearance of a butter dish. But the chines served a purpose: by putting all of the usual radar-cross-section vulnerabilities—the cockpit, engine inlet, engine exhaust—on top of the plane, above the chines, designers effectively screened them off from radars on the ground.[8]

The other main design challenge was to create space for the radar. Cashen envisioned something like the Huey helicopter, with a big rectangular hole running sideways through the central fuselage, from behind the cockpit to slightly ahead of the engine inlet and the engine itself. If you removed the radomes and the antennas behind them, you could look right through the airplane, through a big rectangular gap above the chines.[9] The walls of the box were inclined 15 degrees; that is, the base was bigger than the top, to deflect radar waves up and

FIGURE 9.2
Side view of Tacit Blue.
Source: U.S. Air Force.

away rather than back toward the ground. Finally, Cashen included one more unconventional element: instead of inward canted tails as on the XST, BSAX had an outward canted V-tail, inspired by the old Beechcraft Bonanza, a popular small plane for private pilots.

As the Beechcraft homage suggested, although BSAX introduced a passel of novelties, it was also a throwback in some ways. First of all, it was a traditional wing-body-tail design, a far cry from the sleeker blended wing-body of many recent aircraft. Second, its wings used the Clark Y airfoil, a profile introduced in the 1920s by Virginius Evans Clark, an American aircraft designer, and used on Lindbergh's *Spirit of St. Louis* as well as the Lockheed Electra that Amelia Earhart flew on her ill-fated around-the-world trip. Cashen wanted flat-bottomed wings to improve the radar cross section, and the plane only needed an airfoil that provided respectable performance at low speeds, not high-speed maneuverability. The old flat-bottomed Clark Y fit the bill.[10]

In a nod to an even older technique, the airplane used a form of wing warping—the same technique used by the Wright brothers seventy-five years earlier (and, far earlier, by birds) to control roll. Wing warping, as the name implies, flexes and bends the wing to make the airplane turn. It also causes much structural strain, and most airplanes had adopted ailerons, the familiar flaps on the trailing edge of wings. On BSAX, however, when conventional ailerons deflected to roll the plane, that hinged flap created an angle that lit up on a radar screen. Northrop designers thus pinned the aileron's inboard side and let the outer edge move, warping it along its length, which gave the needed control without lighting up on radar.[11]

———

By mid-1977 Northrop had laid out the wing-body-tail configuration for BSAX, a bulky, boxy shape with prominent chines around the base of the fuselage and a V-tail—in many respects, a complete departure from the sleek, sharply raked XST. But at that time BSAX still resembled the XST in one respect: toward the front of the plane, roughly where the cockpit met the chines, it included flat, faceted surfaces to mask the boxy structure from radar. Those facets, however, were dramatically increasing the aircraft's radar signature, adding additional spikes to the six-spike design. On every model they tried on the test range, the nose glowed on radar like Rudolph the Reindeer.

The facet problem had three consequences. First, Perko grew impatient with Northrop and quietly encouraged Lockheed to study the BSAX design. Second, Perko leaned on Northrop to shake up the project and get it unstuck. In July 1977 Northrop installed Irv Waaland as project manager, demoting Cashen to chief engineer on the project. Cashen, unsurprisingly, was not thrilled but took the move philosophically. "One of the rules of this game is when you're a good project manager you get fired." Or, as Waaland more pithily put it, "shit happens."[12]

Third, the facets sparked yet another intersection between Stealth and Disneyland—and, in the process, rekindled Northrop's embrace of curves. The inspiration came from Fred Oshiro, whom we met as one of the first members of Northrop's radar group in the early 1960s. He was of Japanese American background; during World War II Oshiro, then a young boy, and his family were sent to internment camps, an experience that apparently instilled a deep-seated discomfort with security regimes, including the Top Secret clearance his work at Northrop required.[13]

The occasion for Oshiro's inspiration was Northrop Night at Disneyland, an outing the company organized for employees and their families. As his kids rode the Matterhorn and Tea Cups (designed years earlier by his Lockheed colleague Dick Scherrer), Oshiro sat on a bench and mulled over the problem with the BSAX airplane's nose. He had the habit of carrying around a lump of modeling clay in his pocket, and as he sat he pulled out the clay and started playing with it. Perhaps the rides inspired him. The next morning he came to work, plopped the clay on the shop table, and said, "Build me a model of that." Oshiro had shaped the clay into a complex double curvature to replace the facets around the front of BSAX. When Northrop's team incorporated Oshiro's curves into a model and took it to the test range, lo and behold, the reflections were gone.[14]

Oshiro wasn't the only one who played with clay. A colleague in Northrop's radar-cross-section group, Kenneth Mitzner, an electrical engineer and the group's resident theorist, also modeled with clay (he liked to sculpt little clay animals that he would dispense as gifts.) Cashen, too, used clay to help design aircraft. They called it phenomenology, a way to visualize what the equations or codes were telling them, using a physicist's intuition for how radar waves would behave. Northrop's codes only worked for two dimensions; the clay allowed them to visualize in three. Cashen called it "seeing the waves," or better yet riding them in their imaginations, surfing them as the waves bounced off the aircraft.

This is not to say that Northrop's design team ignored computer codes, or that they relied solely on intuition and guesswork. Both Mitzner and Oshiro, who met at one of Ohio State's summer schools on radar-scattering theory, could go deep into the mathematics of diffraction. As Mitzner described it, "Look, I've agonized for weeks over whether an operator was compact or not. So don't get the idea this is low-tech."[15] But this intuitive approach did present a contrast with Lockheed's reliance on computer codes—and it helps explain the contrast between Northrop's embrace of curves and Lockheed's facets.

And there were more curves to come. Cashen had given BSAX a flat bottom, but when Waaland took over as project manager he quickly realized that wouldn't fly. Waaland, who was an aerodynamicist by training, pointed out that the flat bottom would play havoc with pitch—it would constantly make the nose want to pitch up. Cashen asked Mitzner to come up with a curve that wouldn't wreck the radar cross section. Mitzner worked through the equations and settled on what is known as Gaussian curvature, named after the German mathematician Carl Friedrich Gauss, of which the most familiar example is the bell curve. This became "Ken's Gaussian Bottom," otherwise known, with a Cold War smirk, as the KGB.[16]

With BSAX, Northrop's earlier flirtation with curves fully flowered. In addition to the KGB on the belly and Oshiro's curves around the

FIGURE 9.3

Head-on view of Tacit Blue. Note Oshiro's curves around
the cockpit and the flared tail fins.

Source: courtesy of Northrop Grumman Corporation.

nose, the exhaust duct was a tapered arc at the back of the plane, and the tail fins on either side of the exhaust flared out in graceful curves at the tips.

Northrop's weaknesses in the XST competition may have contributed to the curves. Northrop didn't allow radar experts to control the design, as they did at Lockheed, which gave aerodynamicists a stronger voice—and those aerodynamicists preferred curves. Also, Northrop hadn't turned to fly-by-wire as early as Lockheed, which reinforced the preference for aerodynamic stability. So Northrop's apparent shortcomings in the XST competition turned into a virtue on BSAX, encouraging the turn to curves. And in the end DARPA's stovepipe strategy on the XST worked: by not mingling the Lockheed and Northrop designs, it allowed the weaknesses as well as strengths of each side to play out in the long run.

———

After Northrop submitted its BSAX design in December 1977, DARPA decided to light a fire under its team by opening the follow-on contract to competition, with Lockheed the other competitor. Northrop managers made a remarkable gamble: they told DARPA they refused to enter a competition. They had been working on the assumption that they had the job, and they protested that the government was now threatening to give it to Lockheed. Northrop calculated that the government didn't want Lockheed to have a monopoly on Stealth, so the firm in effect said: if you don't give us the job, we walk. And that would mean Northrop was out of the Stealth business, leaving Lockheed with a monopoly and the government with no leverage on future projects. The gambit worked. DARPA backed down and in April 1978 gave Northrop a sole-source contract for Tacit Blue. The gamble was all the more remarkable given the stakes: this was Northrop's chance to get into Stealth, and indeed to revive its role with the Air Force in general.[17]

But before DARPA shut out Lockheed, the Burbank firm had made a key contribution. Upon returning to work after his stroke, Dick Scherrer had started work on a stealthy U-2, an upgrade of the old spy plane. Much earlier in his career he had toyed with a flying wing for a

Navy patrol plane, since flying wings could achieve long ranges. From Lockheed's work on Have Blue, he also knew about the importance for Stealth of parallel planforming—that is, having aligned edges in the planform—and of minimizing the number of parallel edges, each of which produced a radar spike. A flying wing, since it lacked fuselage or tail, minimized the number of spikes. The combination of the U-2 upgrade (another long-range mission) and Stealth made the flying wing a natural fit, and Scherrer sketched a flying wing with four spikes—two fewer than Northrop's BSAX design.[18]

After DARPA manager Perko grew frustrated with Northrop's struggles on BSAX and approached Lockheed, Scherrer showed him his flying-wing sketches. Perko promptly suggested applying the design to BSAX. Scherrer and a couple of others set about adapting his flying wing to the BSAX mission. Among other things, they chopped off the pointed nose, since for BSAX spikes to the side mattered more than spikes to the front. There was one catch, however. Given that Lockheed's ECHO code could only handle facets, and that Lockheed thus only knew the radar behavior of a faceted plane, Scherrer's flying wing was faceted. Scherrer recognized the aerodynamic disadvantage of facets and

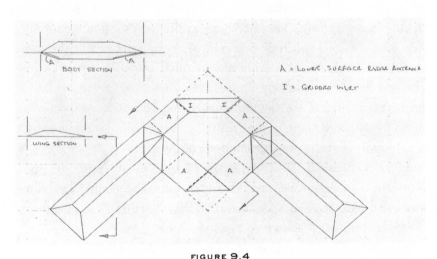

FIGURE 9.4

Reconstructed sketch of Lockheed's faceted
flying-wing design for BSAX.
Source: Richard Scherrer.

realized that curves might even help with radar, so he proposed radar and wind-tunnel tests of a curved airfoil for his flying wing. But Perko had only asked Lockheed to take a look; he hadn't provided any money for design work, merely the chance to compete for the follow-on contract. Lockheed management refused to fund the tests out of the firm's own pocket. So Lockheed's flying wing remained faceted and aerodynamically awkward, and since the BSAX mission required long times aloft, its degraded lift-to-drag performance doomed the design.[19]

The point was soon moot, since DARPA backed down in the face of Northrop's demands and shut down Lockheed's BSAX efforts. The seed of a stealthy flying wing nonetheless remained, ready for transplant into a new environment. DARPA manager Bruce James, Perko's boss, had been especially enthusiastic about the flying-wing concept. Sometime around New Year's Day 1978, James called Waaland back to Washington to discuss Northrop's design. James took Waaland into a classified vault, gave him a new target radar-cross-section number, lower than the current BSAX design had achieved, and gave Northrop three months to come up with a better design.

After Waaland returned to Hawthorne, it was immediately clear to him and Cashen that the only configuration that could meet the radar-cross-section target was a four-spike design. That is, a flying wing. Both men guessed that Lockheed had proposed a flying wing and that DARPA was now nudging Northrop in that direction. In the end they rejected the idea for simple reasons of geometry. BSAX had to carry a big radar, one that could look to the side. It was hard to fit a big radar in a flat flying wing, and harder still to have it look out the side of one—since on a flying wing, by definition there is no side; it's all wing. (Scherrer's design had the radar looking out at an angle from the front and back of the wing.) Northrop told DARPA that the flying wing would compromise the radar—and radar surveillance, after all, was the main point of the mission—and DARPA agreed to stick with the wing-body-tail design. Before Cashen and Waaland rejected the flying wing, however, they radar-tested a model and were surprised by how well it shed radar waves. Even as they went back to their original design, they filed away those test results in their memory.[20]

It is commonly thought that Northrop was the flying-wing company, thanks to Jack Northrop's fixation. In the end Northrop's BSAX design was wing-body-tail, even more conventional than the blended delta-wing of its XST proposal. In fact, it was *Lockheed* that first proposed a flying wing for Stealth, for BSAX. DARPA then pushed the idea on Northrop. By sharing Lockheed's idea, albeit indirectly, James and DARPA had violated the philosophy of stovepiping the two teams, rather than allowing ideas to flow between them. But DARPA's overall strategy to encourage competition between the two firms would once again bear fruit.

———

Just as XST was the design proposal phase leading to the Have Blue flight demonstration, the BSAX design led to a contract, in April 1978, for Tacit Blue, a flight demonstration prototype. Since Waaland was an advanced design engineer, and Tacit Blue required the actual manufacturing of an airplane, Northrop brought in a new program manager, Steven Smith. There may have been another reason to bring Smith on board: John Patierno, who oversaw all these projects as head of advanced design, was a gentle, pipe-smoking soul who had tired of refereeing the constant disputes between Cashen and Waaland and wanted someone to serve as a buffer between his squabbling charges and his own office.[21]

Smith had undergrad and master's degrees from Stanford in engineering and after landing at Northrop had worked his way into management. He became involved in foreign military sales, first for the T-38 (the Volkswagen Beetle of airplanes, which Smith was selling to West Germany—in other words, Germany sold extremely subsonic Beetles to Americans, and the US sold Germany a supersonic version) and then as program manager of the F-5. For three years in the 1970s Smith had lived in Iran, helping train the Iranian air force on flying and maintaining the F-5. Tacit Blue brought him back to the States in early 1978, which was fortuitous timing as the Iranian revolution soon made Americans unwelcome. (Lockheed also had a couple of hundred people in Iran, for the P-3 naval patrol aircraft, and they had a closer call than

Smith; their manager got them all out on a chartered flight just before the shah's regime fell.)[22]

Having won its first prototype production contract for Stealth, Northrop now faced the same problem Lockheed had: building an actual aircraft. Lockheed's facets had presented particular problems, and so too did Tacit Blue's curves entail a different set of manufacturing challenges. The sides of the airplane sported a complicated S-curve, where the flat of the chines blended through an arc to the flat of the fuselage sidewall, then blended through another arc to the flat roof. Oshiro's nose, meanwhile, involved double curvature—that is, curves both in plan view and elevation view on the blueprints. (A cylinder or cone represents single curvature, while a sphere or dome is double curvature; if you have a piece of paper, you can roll it into a cylinder, but you can't shape it into a dome or sphere without creasing it.)[23] Airplane builders had manufactured double curvature before, as anyone looking at the nose of an airliner could attest, but Northrop's shop floor now had to machine these curves to unprecedented tolerances.

Translating the designers' elegant curves from two-dimensional drawings to three-dimensional hardware involved the mysterious art of lofting, a crucial but oft-overlooked intermediate step between blueprints and bent metal. The term "lofting" itself came from shipbuilding and was also used in automobile manufacturing. The blueprints provided a plan for the aircraft from three directions: plan view (from above), profile (from the side), and form (head-on). From these three views, the lofter could provide a cross section of the fuselage or wing at particular intervals, or stations. For each station the lofter would lay out curves with flexible plastic strips or splines, held in place by small weights called ducks. Borrowing from boatbuilding, the horizontal slices in plan and head-on view were known as "waterlines," and the vertical slices in the head-on and profile view as "buttock lines." (Thus lofting was also sometimes known as "lines.") A shop-floor machinist working on a particular station of the airplane—say, Station 380, which would be 380 inches from the airplane's nose—could come over and get the template for the entire fuselage outline at that point. A mathematical formula then interpolated for the shape between these lines.[24]

As Waaland put it, good lofters "could see in three dimensions." It was crucial that lofters got the curves right when they transferred them to the shop floor. The problem was that Northrop's lofting department relied on a World War II–era manual, from a time of looser tolerances and simpler shapes. The lofters struggled in particular with Gaussians, which were unlike the conic sections—like ellipses or parabolas—they usually used. Waaland continued with a laugh, "So the RCS [radar-cross-section] guys would always say, 'We want Gaussian curves.' And our configurator, the guy who did all the layout of all the lines, said, 'Well, they think they're getting a Gaussian, but the shop can't make it, and they're getting conics.'" That, of course, did not satisfy the RCS guys. Mitzner fired off a memo insisting that Northrop's lofters get up to date, and Cashen assigned one of his mathematicians, Hugh Heath, as a sort of quality control for the loft. Heath's job was to make sure the lines in fact matched what the RCS people wanted—so that where the blueprints said "Gaussian," the loft and thus the airplane would have a Gaussian.[25]

Although Tacit Blue relied primarily on shaping to defeat radar, it also resorted to radar-absorbing material, or RAM, to solve a problem that the Pentagon had sprung on Northrop many months into the program, just before Tacit Blue entered production. In the 1970s cruise missiles had acquired a growing role in US strategy, for attacking the Soviet Union from standoff distances instead of with bombs delivered directly to targets. As the Air Force stepped up testing of cruise missiles against Soviet radars, it found that long-distance, early-warning Soviet radars at low frequencies, like the Tall Kings, easily spotted them. General Lew Allen, the Air Force chief of staff, insisted that Northrop address this low-frequency threat on Tacit Blue. Rather than change the shape of the airplane, the Tacit Blue team used RAM around the entire edge of the airplane, the chines, without changing the outer mold line. The edge RAM had to bear only air loads, not structural loads, to satisfy the structural engineers (that it, it only had to stand up to air pressure from the speed of flight, not support the weight of the aircraft). The change, however, introduced new problems for the shop floor and delayed production by perhaps a year.[26]

Like Lockheed's Skunk Works, Northrop benefited from an integration of design and manufacturing. For Tacit Blue, aircraft design and production were in the same place, in Building 360 in Northrop's Hawthorne plant. The design offices were on the second floor, right above the shop floor, so that design and production engineers only had to trot up or downstairs to talk with their counterparts.[27]

Before every new aircraft design flies it has a rollout ceremony, where it is rolled out of the hangar for the first time. Tacit Blue, being Top Secret, couldn't have a rollout, so it had a roll-in. The whole team was there, including the Air Force officer, Major Jack Twigg, in charge of the program. To avoid drawing attention to the Top Secret program, Twigg had always dressed in civilian clothes when he visited Northrop. Before the roll-in, however, he snuck into a restroom and changed into his dress uniform before walking out onto the stage. Steve Smith recalled, "It was the first time people had seen him in his uniform. Half of them didn't even know he was Air Force. It was electric. Everybody just went bonkers." The manufacturing team, meanwhile, gave Smith a baseball bat with an inscription: "S. R. Smith schedule control stick. Reminder: schedules must be met."[28]

Then they shipped the aircraft out to the desert to fly it.

———

When Northrop engineers rolled Tacit Blue out of the hangar at Area 51, some Lockheed engineers watching the exercise were bemused. One asked, "When are you going to take it out of the crate?"[29] Tacit Blue looked like an upside-down bathtub. Its ungainly appearance and bulbous nose, offset by the flaring V-tails that looked like flukes, earned it the nickname "the Whale." As a counterpart to the skunk logo of the Skunk Works, Northrop staff took to sporting a whale logo.

Tacit Blue didn't just look odd. It also flew funny. It was totally unstable in yaw, tending to swing around like a weather vane and end up flying tail first. It was also unstable in pitch: if it departed more than about 6 degrees from level flight it would flip over on its back. That earned it another nickname, "HUM," for Highly Unstable Mother.

To tame Tacit Blue, Northrop designers turned to flight controls, having learned from their mistake on XST, when they neglected to include fly-by-wire. Tacit Blue had a complete fly-by-wire system, developed by flight-control engineer Rudi Seamans, Northrop's counterpart to Bob Loschke at Lockheed. And, as Loschke had done with the Have Blue pilots, Seamans had Tacit Blue's test pilots log countless hours in the simulator, dialing in the flight controls, testing their response to various contingencies—say, a 10-foot-per-second gust of crosswind just as the pilot flared the plane for landing.[30]

Improvisation and jury-rigging continued on the flight line, as they had with Have Blue. Initial tests revealed a problem with the air intake of the topside engine inlet. If there was a crosswind, not enough air would reach the inlet, and the engine could stall. The inlet was made of fiberglass over an aluminum frame, so engineers on the flight line took out a coping saw and cut out the inlet lip, eyeballed a new mold line, and refiberglassed it. Not exactly high-tech. Also, to save money, instead of adding seals around the cockpit door, so that radar beams wouldn't reflect off the gap, Northrop engineers just used conducting tape—like aluminum duct tape. After the pilot climbed into place, the flight crew would tape him in.[31]

The test pilot for the first flight was Richard Thomas, whom Steve Smith brought into the project in 1978. A former Air Force pilot with an engineering degree, Thomas had gone through the Navy's test pilot school before joining Northrop in 1963. A dashing figure with swept-back hair and a pencil-thin mustache, an aviator analogue to Errol Flynn, Thomas had his share of close calls. In November 1965, flying out of Edwards, he had an aileron lock up on an F-5 and had to eject over the Sierras, knocking himself unconscious on the canopy. The airplane spiraled down and crashed in the Owens Valley, but Thomas landed in a boulder field high on the flanks of Mount Whitney, where, after coming to, he lit a fire to signal the rescue planes that were searching for him far below. A decade later he conducted over a hundred spin tests on the F-5, some versions of which had shown alarming instability. The tests called for Thomas to put the F-5 into an intentional spin at 35,000 feet and then try to recover. If he couldn't recover after drop-ping 10,000 feet, a parachute deployed from the aircraft at 25,000 feet to stop the spin. These were nonetheless long, unnerving rides.[32]

So Thomas was quite familiar with risky flights. Still, Tacit Blue gave him pause. The first flight was on February 5, 1982. The night before the flight, John Cashen walked into Sam's Place, the bar at the test site. As he recalled, Thomas was there nursing a beer. "Dick, it's getting a little late. You fly at dawn." Thomas replied, "I can't sleep." Thanks to his experience in the flight simulator, he knew as well as anyone just how unstable the aircraft was. Cashen proposed they shoot some hoops in the gym next door. The two men wore themselves out playing one-and-one, and Thomas went off and slept.[33]

That first flight did not inspire confidence in the plane's airworthi-ness. Upon takeoff a fuse blew and the data link to the ground cut out, so the flight engineers were getting no data. The controllers started yell-ing at Thomas to abort the flight, but he was already in the air and too far down the runway to put the plane back down. The airplane then began porpoising, dipping and rising and then dipping again in quick sequence, as Thomas and the flight computer each tried to stabilize the plane. Thomas finally synched his commands with the computer, and the airplane leveled out; he flew for another twenty minutes. He went on to fly more than half of Tacit Blue's 135 total test flights. One of the other pilots to fly Tacit Blue: Ken Dyson, who had recovered from his ejection on Have Blue. He was the only pilot to fly both of the first two Stealth aircraft.[34]

Despite the successful flight-test series, the Air Force canceled the program. Northrop built only one complete plane, and there was no follow-on production contract. Unlike Have Blue, which led to the F-117, Tacit Blue was a one-off. It's not known why the Air Force can-celed it: perhaps it was a case of "not invented here," since it started as a DARPA idea; perhaps the Air Force liked that the replacement, Joint STARS, which carried a similar radar on a simpler, nonstealthy platform, required an escort of fighter jets to protect it. Or maybe the Air Force simply never liked the look of the Whale. The one aircraft itself, still classified, went into storage for a decade and seemed to be a forgotten secret.

Tacit Blue's designers didn't have time to mourn its demise. Long before its cancellation—indeed, even before its first flight—Tacit Blue had left a more immediate and important legacy.

CHAPTER TEN

FACETS VERSUS CURVES

THE CONTEST FOR THE B-2

In the late 1970s, as Lockheed was pushing the F-117 into production and Northrop fine-tuning Tacit Blue—and long before either airplane flew—the Air Force began planning a third round of the Stealth competition, this time to develop a strategic bomber, a Stealth airplane to deliver nuclear weapons through Soviet defenses. As with the XST it was a winner-take-all contest, though one with even higher stakes, and Lockheed and Northrop once again geared up for a fight.

———

The strategic rationale for the Stealth bomber was a perceived window of vulnerability. America's deterrence strategy relied on the nuclear triad: bombers, land-based ICBMs, and submarine-based missiles. Military planners reasoned that while the Soviets might neutralize one or two of the three legs—say, bombers or ICBMs—they could not take out all three at once. The US would thus retain the ability to deliver a devastating counterstrike, the threat of which would deter the Soviets from launching a nuclear war.

The problem was that by the mid-1970s all three legs had emerging weaknesses, at least in the eyes of some strategists. Increasingly accurate and powerful Soviet missiles appeared capable of destroying Minuteman missiles in their hardened silos. In response, in the early 1970s the US began developing a new Missile X, or MX, to be bigger and more accurate than the Minuteman as well as more survivable. A contentious debate, however, arose about how best to deploy the MX, whether in ultrahardened silos or on mobile trucks or rail cars, among other schemes, which pushed back potential deployment of any system until well into the 1980s.[1]

Submarine-launched missiles similarly seemed to face a window of vulnerability. American scientists and engineers were developing new ways to peer deep into the ocean, such as by using blue-green lasers and synthetic aperture radars, and the techniques could potentially reveal either a submarine itself or the internal waves it left behind, something like a submerged wake. American military planners increasingly voiced fears that the Soviets would discover a breakthrough, a technique to, as Soviet admiral Sergei Gorshkov put it, make the oceans transparent, revealing the location of American submarines.[2]

The triad's third leg, bombers, had its own problems owing to the buildup of Soviet air defenses. Against the formidable Soviet radars, the aging B-52 bomber seemed to stand little chance: it was a twenty-five-year old design with a radar cross section of a hundred square meters, as big as a barn. The Air Force was reluctant to give up the bomber leg of the triad, and not just because airplanes, unlike missiles, needed pilots. Once you launch a missile, whether from an underground silo on the midwestern prairie or a submarine in the Atlantic, that missile won't stop until its nuclear warhead devastates its target. Missiles, as the saying went, were "fire and forget." A bomber, by contrast, could be recalled on the way to its target. That offered at least some assurance—not much, perhaps, but better than none—against an accidental nuclear strike. That factor alone helped keep bombers part of the triad.

The question was how to make the bombers more effective. One approach was to evade air defenses by flying them low and fast, literally under the radar. The proposed B-1 bomber pursued this route, using computer- and radar-guided ground-hugging navigation to skim a couple of hundred feet off the ground at close to the speed of sound. The other option was to skip trying to penetrate Soviet defenses and instead fire cruise missiles from a B-52 from a standoff distance, outside the range of Soviet air defenses. In this period, the mid-1970s, the Air Force began testing new air-launched cruise missiles, similarly using new electronic terrain-following navigation systems paired with much smaller jet engines. They could fly over a thousand miles as low as 30 feet off the ground.[3]

In June 1977 President Carter, after a contentious debate, canceled the B-1. The ostensible reason was that cruise missiles launched from B-52s could penetrate Soviet airspace easier and cheaper. Lurking in the background, however, was Stealth, which offered a new way to evade Soviet air defenses. Carter's new national security team, starting with Harold Brown and William Perry, had already embraced Stealth, and some observers later claimed that Stealth played a role in the decision. But Have Blue would not fly for another six months, and Stealth was still too uncertain a prospect to justify canceling a major program like the B-1. Thus Brown for good reason insisted, in the August 1980 press conference publicizing Stealth, that it was *not* a factor in Carter's decision. Stealth, however, may have played a secondary role in tamping down lingering resistance after the decision was made.[4]

Whatever the reason, it was no surprise that soon after the B-1's cancellation the Air Force thought to apply Stealth to a strategic bomber. A war-game study in the late 1970s concluded that by 1995 Soviet air defenses would shoot down most US aircraft before they released their weapons, whether the US deployed a fast-and-low penetrator like the B-1 or a standoff cruise-missile platform.[5] A Stealth bomber would solve the problem in a different way. It was not at all clear, though, that you could hide something as big as a bomber.

———

After Have Blue the Skunk Works had looked into two designs, one a scaled-up Have Blue as a small fighter/attack aircraft, the other a medium-sized bomber, around the size of an F-111, capable of carrying a 10,000-pound payload. The Air Force chose the first option and awarded Lockheed the F-117 contract in 1978, but the Skunk Works kept working on a Stealth bomber on the side.[6]

An old saying of Lockheed's Alan Brown—"Nothing fails like success"—became relevant again. Winning the F-117 meant Lockheed was soon preoccupied with building it, and the bomber study essentially got, as Brown put it, the "second team." Brown himself was one of those focused on the F-117, as its program manager. He was thus not involved in the design effort of the bomber, where his saying also applied.[7]

Whereas the Skunk Works had first resisted the idea of facets in 1975, by 1978 it had embraced them. Richard Scherrer, as we know, had sketched a faceted flying wing for a stealthy U-2 and then adapted that to BSAX, only to see the plan founder when Lockheed wouldn't fund tests of a curved airfoil. For the bomber design, Scherrer revived the idea of a stealthy flying wing; like BSAX, the bomber would have to fly high and long distances, which the flying wing's aerodynamic efficiency enabled. Scherrer again argued that facets would doom the plane aerodynamically, wrecking the lift-to-drag ratio. His managers, nevertheless, once again refused to fund wind-tunnel tests of a curved airfoil. Facets had won Lockheed the F-117, and the company was not going to mess with success. To Scherrer, it was "clear to me that the faceted ATB [bomber] was doomed because the Laws of Physics would not bend to fit Company policy."[8] Scherrer finally gave up and quit Lockheed in frustration in June 1979.

Lockheed's bomber design incorporated some elements of the flying wing—after all, they were the ones who had proposed it for Tacit Blue—but otherwise it was something like an expanded F-117. The big diamond-shaped body sprouted slender wings, which gave it some resemblance to a flying wing, but the effect was undermined by a tail boom with a V-tail, sticking straight off the back of the diamond like the spiky tail of a Stegosaurus. Scherrer and Denys Overholser had pushed for a pure flying wing, but Skunk Works aerodynamicists insisted on the tail for stability and control, and Scherrer and Overholser lost the argument. Most important, the design stuck with facets: flat plates, sharp edges, and obtuse angles. One of the Air Force managers described to Alan Brown the prevailing Air Force view of the design: "You just took an F-117 and you went *pffft*, like this, just pumped it up."[9]

———

One day during the Tacit Blue program some Air Force engineers were sitting around with a few Northrop counterparts, talking about the next step for Stealth. The Northrop group included John Cashen and Irv Waaland, as well as their boss John Patierno. Cashen recalled that one of the Air Force engineers said, How about a bomber? Patierno puffed on his pipe and replied to the effect of "Northrop is a fighter house. We don't do bombers." Cashen and Waaland were aghast. They had heard that Lockheed had a Stealth bomber study under way, and they surmised that the Air Force wasn't happy with Lockheed's progress and wanted Northrop in the game.[10]

Cashen and Waaland were right, and the Air Force didn't take no for an answer. It had agreed to Northrop's gambit on Tacit Blue to avoid precisely this situation, where one firm had a monopoly on Stealth. The Air Force brass called Tom Jones and made it clear that they had put Northrop in the Stealth business with Tacit Blue, and now they expected the company to play the game. Jones got the point and agreed.[11]

Around May 1979 Irv Waaland left Tacit Blue to lead the design team for the bomber, resuming his collaboration with Cashen. The designers first had to decide what kind of mission the bomber would fly: Subsonic or supersonic? Low altitude or high altitude? They ruled out supersonic; no one had yet built a Stealth plane that was also supersonic, and the challenges of combining aerodynamic with radar requirements were hard enough for subsonic—especially for features like engine inlets that would have to gulp vast quantities of thin air but not reflect radar. They next ruled out low altitude; that was what the B-52 and the now-canceled B-1 tried to do, and the thicker air at low altitude made it harder to fly long distances. That left subsonic and high altitude, around 60,000 feet, which would put more distance between the plane and Soviet radars and also allow longer-range flights.

As Waaland and Cashen toyed with potential bomber designs, they remembered the flying-wing model they had tested for Tacit Blue. The new bomber would be a long-range aircraft, and the flying wing's lift-to-drag performance gave it outstanding range. Moreover, the radar tests on Tacit Blue had shown that a flying wing could shed radar waves. Its simple shape minimized the number of parallel edges, which in turn minimized the number of spikes in the reflected radar—the sharp glints from a long, straight surface, like light reflecting off a mirror. By August 1979 Northrop's design team had in hand a flying-wing planform.

The flying-wing concept was necessary but not sufficient. The other key step was how to add volume. As facets had become the company

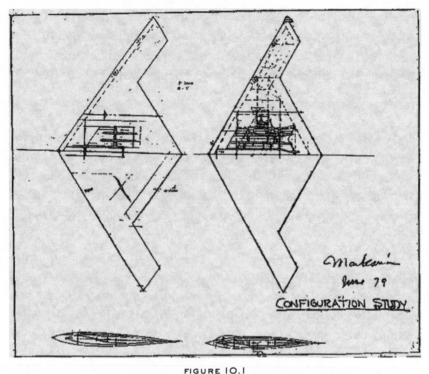

FIGURE 10.1

Sketch of Northrop's flying wing design by Hal Markerian, 1979.
Source: courtesy of Northrop Grumman Corporation.

line at Lockheed, Northrop's design embraced curves. The curves were clear in both profile and head-on views. The bottom and top of the aircraft were smoothly rounded. Although it was a flying wing, it had a rounded quasi-fuselage down the center to hold the cockpit and bomb bay, tapering to a flat tail; up front, where the cockpit blended into the wing, the design borrowed the curvature Fred Oshiro had conceived for Tacit Blue.[12] The engine inlets rose from the top of the wing in graceful arches, separated from the central quasi-fuselage by narrow gullies, lending a bug-eye effect; Cashen had added these gullies by running his thumb down a clay model of an early design, in order to create some distance between the propulsion path and the cockpit and bomb bay.

In short, Northrop combined the flying-wing idea with the curves from Tacit Blue. "We went a hundred percent to curvature," Cashen recalled. "Gaussian curvature had now become a religion among the lines and lofting folk."[13]

Northrop designers meanwhile heard that Scherrer had quit Lockheed and decided to hire him. After leaving Lockheed, Scherrer had lit out on a summer road trip up the Pacific Coast with his wife, driving a twin-engine, hot-rod bus that he had lowered by a foot and customized into a motor home. By Labor Day he had made it as far as the Olympic Peninsula when Northrop tracked him down and got him back in the game. When he arrived at Northrop he was overjoyed to see a flying wing already on their drawing board.[14]

Scherrer was proof that innovators could learn from the past even for cutting-edge technology. Stealth aircraft had already incorporated many old ideas, from wing warping and the Clark Y airfoil on Tacit Blue to the flying wing itself. Scherrer proved especially adept at ransacking, rummaging, and recycling past designs. He was put in charge of sizing the airplane's wings, which meant defining the aspect ratio— that is, the ratio of the wing length to its width (for nonrectangular wings, expressed as the square of the wingspan divided by the wing area). The flying wing featured an inner diamond shape for the cockpit and engines, with wings extending from the diamond's edges. Scherrer looked at a couple dozen older planes that had a similar design, with a short, narrow wing segment extending outboard of a much wider segment close to the fuselage. He found that most of their aspect ratios clustered around a particular figure, and he thought there must be a good reason, so he chose that number.[15]

Another bit of old made new was the wing's airfoil, or profile. The problem, as usual, was to balance aerodynamics and radar physics. Designers wanted a sharp leading edge to deflect radar, but for high-speed, long-range flights, they also needed a supercritical airfoil, one that would minimize the drag that occurs when flying near the speed of sound. Such an airfoil would have a flatter top surface, a cambered lower surface, and a rounded leading edge. Scherrer, working with an aerodynamicist named Leo Newman, came up with a supercritical airfoil from a decades-old Brooklyn Polytechnic report. (Recall that several Northrop engineers came out of Brooklyn Poly, including

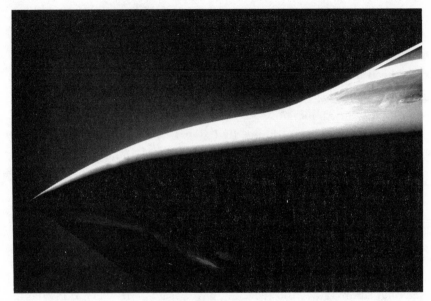

Close-up side view of B-2 hawkbill airfoil.
Source: courtesy of Northrop Grumman Corporation.

Waaland.) Scherrer and Newman made a couple of tweaks, then confirmed its performance with computer calculations and wind-tunnel tests. The result was a distinctive hawkbill profile, something like a downward pointed beak when viewed from the side, that combined the sharp leading edge with the supercritical curves.[16]

A final blast from the past influenced the control surfaces. The flying wing was relatively stable, at least compared to Have Blue and Tacit Blue. Like a falling leaf floating to the ground, it didn't tend to twirl or roll. The problem was in steering it, especially in yaw. Most planes use rudders on the tail to turn the plane left or right, and Northrop's first Stealth bomber design included small inward-canted tails for this purpose; designers also toyed with the idea of fins out on the wingtips.[17]

The prospect of tails or fins, however, drove Cashen and the radar physicists to distraction; anything sticking up from the wing surface ruined the radar signature. Someone—it's not clear who—remembered that the old YB-49, Jack Northrop's flying wing from 1947, flew fine without a tail rudder. It had used flaps on each wing, and opening the flap on one side or the other created differential drag. Waaland's team borrowed the idea for the Stealth bomber, using split flaps at each wing-tip that opened and closed like a clamshell, with the clamshell's mouth facing rearward. Opening the clamshell flaps on one wing created extra drag on that side and turned the aircraft in that direction. (Opening the flaps, of course, also affected the radar signature. When flying in Stealth mode, the bomber would use differential engine thrust for the same effect; the engines on one side pushing harder than the ones on the other turned the plane.)[18] The result: no tails and better radar performance.

In August 1979 Waaland's team briefed the design to the Air Force but assumed they were merely a stalking horse for Lockheed. The aerodynamic efficiency of the curved flying wing, however, got the attention of the Air Force, especially when compared to the aerodynamic inefficiency of Lockheed's facets. Northrop's plane had a projected range of up to 7,000 miles, and it also promised a stealthy radar cross section across a wide range of frequencies, from 0.1 GHz to 15 GHz (in wavelength, from about 300 cm to 2 cm). The Air Force offered Northrop a small study contract out of some leftover funding, and Northrop took another gamble, insisting on a bigger contract, not just for a study but for what was known as a demonstration/validation contract. Waaland's team laid out a detailed proposal for a substantial program, including wind-tunnel and radar testing of a large-scale model.[19]

Again, the gamble paid off. The Air Force agreed, and in January 1980 Northrop got a contract for a full-fledged design, to culminate in another radar pole-off against Lockheed. Lockheed still had a year's head start, and the Air Force made clear to Northrop that it was just an "insurance policy" in case Lockheed slipped up. But Northrop was now in the contest, and the battle was once again joined.[20]

———

Both firms realized that for this contest they would need help. The bomber was going to entail a huge program, involving the production of well over a hundred planes, each one a huge and vastly complicated machine, requiring both a workforce and facilities beyond what each firm on its own could muster. Around the summer of 1980 the two firms went looking for partners, with the obvious candidates being the big airframe firms: Rockwell, McDonnell Douglas, and Boeing. Lockheed started first and snapped up Rockwell, which was adrift at the time after the B-1 cancellation and had lots of empty factory space to fill.[21] Northrop was already working as a subcontractor with McDonnell Douglas on the F-18, but the relationship had devolved into a legal fight: after McDonnell Douglas had tried to cut Northrop out of a percentage of foreign sales, Northrop sued, in October 1979, and McDonnell Douglas quickly countersued. The lawsuits would take six years to resolve, and meanwhile soured Northrop on the idea of teaming with McDonnell Douglas again.[22]

That left Boeing. Patierno had been right about one thing: Northrop was not a bomber house, not having built one since the original flying wing thirty years earlier. Boeing, on the other hand, had built lots of big aircraft in general and bombers in particular, including the workhorse B-52. Northrop invited Boeing's CEO, Thornton Wilson, and several of its top engineers to Hawthorne for a briefing on the Stealth bomber. Wilson, known simply as "T," had been project engineer on the B-52 and head of Boeing's winning bid on the Minuteman ICBM, and he was a formidable, hard-nosed manager.

Waaland and Cashen gave the briefing, and at the end of it, as they both recalled, Tom Jones, with ever-present cigar in his left hand, extended his right hand across the table toward Wilson and said, "Well, you've heard it, T. Now, what do you think? Are you with me?" Wilson hesitated, then finally replied, "I'm with you, Tom. This time." He shook Jones's hand, then turned to his engineering staff behind him and growled, "Don't ever let this happen to me again." Boeing was not accustomed to playing second fiddle on big bombers. Wilson and his firm had been caught entirely flat-footed on Stealth.[23]

Lockheed and Northrop also split between them the two major engine builders, Lockheed going with Pratt & Whitney, Northrop with General Electric. In addition, Northrop brought on as a smaller partner Vought Aircraft, part of the LTV conglomerate. Vought, based in Texas, had manufacturing capability and also expertise in composites.[24]

In September 1980 the Air Force issued a formal call for proposals for what it now called the Advanced Technology Bomber, or ATB, with the proposals due in December. The request went only to Lockheed and Northrop, whose responses followed the pattern for Stealth program names with a "Senior" designation: the F-117 contract had been called Senior Trend, and Lockheed had a Stealth cruise missile program called Senior Prom. Northrop's ATB proposal was thus called Senior Ice and Lockheed's was Senior Peg; Ben Rich, ever the canny salesman, supposedly got Lockheed's entry named after Peggy Ellis, the wife of Air Force General Richard Ellis, head of Strategic Air Command.[25]

As Northrop ramped up its efforts for the formal proposal, it brought in a new program manager named Jim Kinnu. Until Kinnu's arrival Waaland had been managing the proposal, but his specialty was advanced design. The ATB proposal, with its several corporate partners and subcontractors, had become more than a design job; Northrop had 250 people working on it in a separate, dedicated building in Hawthorne, and Kinnu came on board to run it. The program soon outgrew that building and moved over to several floors of a nondescript office building on Century Boulevard, nestled unobtrusively among the hotels and parking garages around LAX. Northrop blocked off the windows to foil potential spies, and the countless commuters heading down Century to catch a flight had no idea they were driving past a military revolution in the making.[26]

Kinnu's father was an Assyrian immigrant from northern Iran who had worked on radar for Western Electric during World War II, and Kinnu inherited his father's technical aptitude. He was yet another aerospace engineer who built and flew model airplanes as a kid. After earning a degree in physics at Notre Dame and another degree in business management at UCLA, he spent the first seventeen years of his career at Lockheed, most of it in the unclassified side of the company, the last few years in the Skunk Works. He then bounced around several firms in the 1970s before landing, in January 1979, at Northrop, just before the Stealth bomber program got under way there.

At the time Kinnu was approaching fifty, with almost twenty-five years of experience in the aviation business. John Patierno, as head of advanced design, soon tapped that experience and in the process introduced Kinnu to Stealth—not on the bomber but on Tacit Blue. Northrop's Tacit Blue team had given a sloppy briefing to the Air Force managers, and the Air Force was thinking of canceling the program. Patierno assigned Kinnu as a short-term fixer, a fresh outside perspective to identify the risks in the design and then figure out how to eliminate them. When the Air Force showed up for another briefing several weeks later, Kinnu had laid out a detailed plan for cost, schedule, and risk for each design group, and the first-rate briefing persuaded the Air Force to keep Tacit Blue alive.[27]

As the episode demonstrated, Kinnu had abundant engineering acumen, but his real specialty was program management, an ambiguous term that essentially meant figuring out what needed to be done and then getting it done. Many aerospace institutions, including NASA, had learned the hard way that management was a distinct skill in its own right, and one not usually taught in engineering schools.[28] Knowing science and engineering was necessary but not sufficient; a good manager was always a good engineer, but a good engineer did not always make a good manager. Kinnu knew how to identify the obstacles within a program and then lay out a plan to deal with them. As important, he knew how to manage *people*: when to grant engineers freedom and when to direct them; how to align the various interests of many individuals toward the collective project goals; how to hire and promote good engineers, and how to fire poor ones. The B-2 program would test these skills to the limit.

Kinnu had one other outstanding characteristic: his work ethic. He was not just a workaholic himself, at it every day from seven in the morning until ten at night, including weekends during the proposal period. He was also, as more than one of his colleagues noted, a "driver," inspiring—or at least expecting—that same dedication from those working with him. And he apparently had little trouble getting it. Once again, the willingness of Stealth engineers to devote almost all of their waking hours to the job came from a mix of motivations, including patriotism—the sense, as Waaland put it, that "the big bear is out there," and the Stealth bomber was vital to defend against it. And of course there was the engineering challenge.[29]

As before, this remarkable dedication came with a cost, to the individuals themselves and perhaps even more so to spouses and families. When Patierno first approached Kinnu about coming on the project full-time, Kinnu hesitated. He knew it meant he would rarely see his wife and their two daughters, just entering their teens. Kinnu went home and talked it over with his wife. He couldn't describe the program, but he told her it was important for the country. She said, "It's up to you," before adding, pointedly, "But we do have a family." He took the job.

Kinnu recalled, decades later, "It turned out to be 24/7 for six years." For his wife, he realized, this period was "pure hell," and she eventually made it clear that something had to change. They went to Palm Springs one weekend and bought a condo on a golf course, and he made a commitment: the family would go to Palm Springs every Friday night and return Sunday night, with no work, no phone calls allowed. It saved his marriage.[30]

In the fall of 1980, however, Kinnu focused on the bomber, whipping Northrop's team into the home stretch. The flying wing's aerodynamic efficiency gave it outstanding range-payload capability—the ability to fly farther, with more weight—and it seemed to carry no penalty in the radar cross section. Northrop's team had reason for confidence.

At the end of 1980 engineers from the two firms once again trooped out to RATSCAT for a pole-off. It had been almost five years since the last contest. This time the facility seemed to live up to its name. In some of the radar tests engineers were getting mysteriously large radar returns. A family of burrowing owls was using the aircraft models, high up on the mounting pole, as a hunting perch; the mouse carcasses and owl turds they left behind were playing havoc with the radar return. (Some brave engineers tested the scat and found that owl turds are in fact conductive and reflective.)[31]

Once the owls were shooed away, the shootout proceeded. Once again the two teams tested models made out of plywood coated with silver paint to mimic the conductivity of a metal airplane surface. The contest's outcome almost turned on that silver paint. Northrop got lousy radar data, with a cross section far greater than expected, and the engineers couldn't figure out why. It looked like Lockheed was going to win this second shootout—and with it the bomber contract.

Lockheed, however, unaware of Northrop's problems, meanwhile filed a protest, arguing that Northrop's model had violated the terms of the test by not including simulated doors and other features an actual airplane would have. Northrop happily agreed to go back and retest, having finally figured out the problem. The tests used four-tenths scale models, but those models were still big: four-tenths of the Northrop design's wingspan was still almost 70 feet. The sheer weight of Northrop's model on the pole was causing it to flex, creating tiny cracks in the paint. The web of cracked paint was reflecting the radar and thus blowing up the signature. The Northrop team fixed the paint, fiberglassed the wood to prevent flexing, went back to the range, and indeed got a far better radar cross section. Lockheed's protest had bailed out Northrop.[32]

———

The teams submitted their final designs in summer 1981. The Air Force went through them in close detail, but the question at that point was perhaps not *who* would build the Stealth bomber but whether *anyone* would build it. Reagan's inauguration had revived the B-1 bomber, now called the B-1B, and some elements within the Air Force sought to stifle the Stealth bomber in order to save the B-1. They argued that a Stealth bomber was years away, and that while you could hide an F-117, hiding something as big as a bomber was a far harder proposition.

A pitched political battle ensued. Democrats had long opposed the B-1, and they backed the Stealth bomber as a way to justify that opposition without being seen as "soft on defense." Republicans continued to support the B-1 as the safest bet, leading Washington wags to joke that the B-1 was a Republican plane and the Stealth bomber a Democratic one. There were other fault lines, both legislative—the House backed the B-1B, the Senate backed the Stealth bomber—and corporate. Rockwell, the B-1B contractor, launched a lobbying campaign; Northrop, Lockheed, and Boeing did the same for the B-2. (Boeing was also teamed with Rockwell on the B-1B but placed its bets on the ATB because of the access it would provide to Stealth, including lightweight composite technology.) It probably didn't hurt that Northrop chief executive Tom Jones was a friend of Reagan.[33]

In the end Reagan decided not to decide: the US would build *both* bombers. The Air Force would build 100 B-1Bs, followed by 132 Stealth bombers, a plan soon approved by the House and Senate. Letting the B-1B go first gave an edge in the Stealth contest to Northrop, which would have more time to work out the risks in its design. On October 3, 1981, the Air Force announced that Northrop had won the bomber contest, and with it a contract for $36 billion.

Or, rather, the Air Force did *not* announce it, in keeping with the strict classification policy. The only public notice of the Stealth bomber contract came not out of any interest in informing the public but from Wall Street. The Reuters news service heard that Northrop had gotten a contract for a major program, and ran a short item about it that provided no details. Jones knew this meant trouble: if the New York Stock Exchange believed that Northrop was withholding material information from stockholders and the market, it would delist the company. He alerted the Defense Department, which sent a lawyer to talk to the leaders of the stock exchange, explaining that national security meant there could be no public comment. The stock exchange replied, in effect, "Fine, Northrop can choose not to reveal the information, and we will just delist the firm."

Jones persuaded Pentagon officials to craft a press release that addressed the stock exchange's basic question—did Northrop have a contract or not?—without revealing what the contract was for. The twelve-line statement, released two weeks after the decision, revealed that Northrop had a contract to study the development of a manned penetrating bomber, and it named the main subcontractors: Boeing, Vought, and General Electric (plus Hughes for the radar). Terse as it was, it provided enough information to appease the stock exchange. It was also enough to allow savvy observers to connect the dots. In its next issue, *Aviation Week* identified it as a contract for the Stealth bomber—and Northrop shares climbed $2.25, to $42.50, on the stock market.[34]

Lockheed's reaction was not unlike Northrop's five years earlier, when Northrop had believed that the XST contest rules had been rigged against them. Ben Rich protested that the Air Force had told the Skunk Works at the outset that it should take an incremental approach to a Stealth bomber. Rather than try immediately for a big bomber, to compete with the B-52 or B-1, the Stealth bomber would be medium-sized, on the order of the F-111, with a correspondingly smaller range and payload. Given the evolving state of knowledge on Stealth, the Air Force had suggested that going for broke with a big bomber was too risky. According to Rich, Lockheed had therefore stuck with a smaller design, only to see the Air Force reward Northrop for proposing a bigger bomber, with greater range and payload and more risk.[35]

The military's referees, however, said the contest wasn't even close. As Paul Kaminski, who now ran the Air Force low-observables office, put it, "Lockheed got cleaned in the competition."[36] The two firms had similar radar performance, and Lockheed's smaller aircraft would cost less, but Northrop won handily in aerodynamics, which translated into range and payload. Lockheed's design range of 3,600 miles required refueling to reach anything beyond the northern fringes of the Soviet Union; Northrop's design range of 6,000 miles could reach any Soviet target without refueling.[37] Lockheed's facets imposed a high aerody-namic penalty, while Northrop's design provided the aerodynamics of a conventional airplane in a Stealth platform. This time, curves won.

Northrop held a jubilant celebration in the atrium of the Century Boulevard building. Tom Jones, Patierno, Cashen, Waaland, Kinnu, and the rest of the team toasted the win, beneath a big banner on the stage stating simply, "We Won It!"[38]

At Lockheed, meanwhile, the loss was particularly painful because Rich had sold the company's leadership on the original Stealth project with the promise of an eventual bomber. This included getting them to put in $10 million in cost-sharing for Have Blue, in addition to accepting a risky contract to deliver the F-117 on a greatly accelerated schedule. When Rich had first asked Lockheed chair Roy Anderson and president Lawrence Kitchen for the $10 million, they had understandably balked, since Lockheed had just lost billions on the L-1011 commercial airliner. But Rich had persuaded Kitchen, and Kitchen had persuaded Lockheed's board to put up the money as an investment on future payoffs. The

FIGURE 10.3

Northrop celebrates winning the contract for the Stealth bomber.
Irv Waaland is at the podium. Behind him, left to right, are
John Cashen (with mustache), John Patierno, and Welko Gasich.
Source: courtesy of Northrop Grumman Corporation.

F-117 had proved it a good bet, but the bomber would have provided a
far greater windfall. At $36 billion, the B-2 contract was a hundred times
bigger than the $350 million in the early F-117 contract.[39]

Lockheed was a victim of success. Buoyed by its XST victory, the
Skunk Works stuck to a similar formula based on facets. Northrop
struck out in a new direction. In particular, Tacit Blue gave Northrop
three crucial advantages in the B-2 contest. First, it was on Tacit Blue
that Northrop designers first considered a flying wing, then undertook
the radar tests that persuaded them that a flying wing worked both for
aerodynamics and avoiding radar. Second, Tacit Blue had immersed
Northrop's designers in the use of curves to defeat radar. Curves not
only helped the plane fly better; they also improved its stealthiness

across a broader range of radar frequencies. Third, the B-2 had to have a radar in it for navigation and targeting, and Northrop had learned from Tacit Blue how to incorporate a radar in a Stealth plane.

Tacit Blue was the crucial stepping-stone to the B-2. In addition to teaching Northrop how to use curves and incorporate a radar inside a Stealth plane, it exposed it to the idea of the flying wing and taught it to embrace fly-by-wire flight controls to boot. Losing the F-117, in other words, was crucial to winning the B-2. The consolation prize for the first round, Tacit Blue, held the key to the last round.

The B-2 contract restored Northrop's luster. It also seemed a vindication of its founder's fixation on the flying wing. It is sometimes believed that the B-2 was a flying wing because that's what founder Jack Northrop had always wanted to build. The real story is more interesting. Northrop's original Stealth proposal for the XST contest, like Lockheed's, was a blended wing-body design. Then Northrop had gone in the other direction, away from the flying wing and toward a standard wing-body-tail for Tacit Blue. It was *Lockheed* that had proposed a flying wing for Tacit Blue, and Air Force program managers then nudged Northrop in that direction. The flying-wing idea for the B-2 first came from outside Northrop—indeed, from its main competitor.

Nonetheless, the mythical, almost mystical connection to Jack Northrop was cemented when Northrop designers laid out the dimensions for the Stealth bomber. After sizing the wings to the engines for the right aspect ratio, they found that the wingspan, by sheer coincidence, was 172 feet—exactly that of Jack Northrop's YB-49 flying wing from the 1940s.[40]

Jack Northrop was still alive. In April 1980 Northrop company brass got a special clearance to brief him on the Stealth flying-wing design. The old engineer, aged eighty-five, was suffering from Parkinson's disease, and he apologized for his poor health as he shuffled into the room. When the briefing began, however, any signs of decline disappeared: he locked in and began firing sharp technical questions. As he left the briefing, he turned to his escort and said, "Now I can die in peace."[41] His dream of an all-wing airplane was coming true. He died ten months later.

CHAPTER ELEVEN

BUILDING THE B-2

Some Northrop engineers recognized that winning the contract was just the start. At the victory party in fall 1981, Jim Kinnu tempered the celebration with a sobering message. "Today you're going to start running," he told those assembled, "and you're never going to stop running for the next eight or nine years, because endurance is going to be most important." Kinnu had seen the F-104, P-3, and L-1011 projects firsthand at Lockheed and understood what it took to build a big, complex airplane.[1]

For starters, there was the usual feedback among propulsion, aerodynamics, flight controls, and so on, so that changes in any one component sent ripples through the entire design. Aerospace engineers had developed the discipline of systems engineering to control the interfaces and the trade-offs among different components, but the Stealth bomber had the added complications of radar cross section. And the Stealth bomber presented other major challenges: making composite materials and then forming structures out of them, which aircraft companies had done but never on the scale now contemplated; achieving the close tolerances required to achieve Stealth; and incorporating all-digital, fly-by-wire flight controls. Kinnu had also decided that for the first time Northrop would use a computer-aided design and manufacturing system, or CAD/CAM, with all blueprints and drawings laid out on computer screens instead of paper. Above all, building a Stealth aircraft out of complex curvature imposed a daunting task on Northrop's engineering and manufacturing organizations. "I knew what we were up against," Kinnu would later say. "I knew what we were going to have to go through as a company. I don't think a lot of the people in the company recognized it."[2]

————

The Air Force added two major complications. One was an engineering challenge; the other, administrative or even philosophical.

The first complication came from an exercise organized by Paul Kaminski in 1981. Kaminski, previously Bill Perry's assistant in defense research and engineering, was now head of the low-observables office for the Air Force, which ran all Stealth programs. Operating with a handful of staff out of a small, unmarked office in the bowels of the Pentagon, he would soon be overseeing billions of dollars in Stealth contracts, around 10 percent of the total Air Force budget. Kaminski wanted to make sure the Air Force knew what capabilities it was up against. What exactly did the Soviets have in the way of air defenses; what new defenses might they field in the next decade or so; and how stealthy did US planes have to be to get through?

Kaminski's exercise had two purposes. First, since the existence of Stealth was now public knowledge, the exercise aimed to look at how the Soviets might adapt to defend against it. Second was to think about what defenses the US might have to develop should the Soviets pursue their own version of Stealth. The first looked like the more immediate problem, so Kaminski set up two Red Teams, who would play the part of Soviet air-defense planners. The first Red Team assumed that Soviet intelligence was very good (or American security very poor) and that the Soviets had all information about the program, including the actual capabilities of Stealth aircraft, and were designing defenses against it. The second Red Team operated only with the information that the US knew the Soviets had. Both Red Teams consisted of engineers from the aircraft contractors as well as the radar firms and were overseen by Lincoln Lab, the MIT spin-off that was a center of radar expertise.

The Red Teams discovered a couple of things. One was that most of the models underestimated the effects of clutter. An air-defense radar wouldn't pick out aircraft against a completely clean background. In the real world there would be background noise: the radar antenna would send out a bunch of radar waves, and some of them would re-flect from the ground, rocks, and mountains, in addition to an airplane. If there was more clutter than expected, an airplane flying close to the ground could take advantage of it, hiding in the noise. The second discovery by the Red Team, less encouraging, was that at high alti-tudes certain new Soviet radars might in fact be able to detect a Stealth aircraft.

These two discoveries led the Air Force to issue a change in the re-quirements. The Stealth bomber could no longer fly only at high alti-tudes, up around 60,000 feet. At particular points in its route it would need to fly at altitudes as low as 200 feet off the deck, down in the clut-ter. And it would have to do it at speeds as high as Mach 0.8—subsonic, but still very fast.[3]

That change presented a basic problem. The Northrop ATB was lightly wing-loaded, which is defined as the weight of the aircraft di-vided by the wing area. Hang gliders have light wing loading, since they have a lot of wing area and don't weigh much. Airliners have high wing loading, with skinny wings in order to minimize the effects of tur-bulence. Fighter aircraft also have high wing loading, because at high speeds they don't need as much wing area to create lift.

Northrop's flying-wing design had a huge wing area, which made it aerodynamically efficient with a high lift-to-drag ratio. The wing load-ing of the original design was 32 lb/ft^2. The B-52, by contrast, had wing loading of 122 lb/ft^2, and most big airliners were also in the 100–150 lb/ft^2 range. That meant the flying wing was vulnerable to getting tossed around or bent by wind gusts the same way a hang glider would be.[4]

The Air Force had issued this new requirement in early 1981, and Northrop's engineers first believed their design could meet it. The more they studied it, though, the worse it looked, and they eventually deter-mined that an ATB flying at high speed near the ground and subjected to a worst-case gust could either break apart or veer out of control and crash. Kinnu called Cashen, Waaland, and the rest of the team to a meeting one evening in early 1983 to go over the problem. At the end of it Kinnu announced grimly, "Okay, guys, we have no airplane." Back to the drawing board.[5]

The gust-load problem presented the biggest single challenge during the airplane's development. The Northrop team didn't panic, nor did the Air Force program manager when Kinnu phoned and told him Northrop didn't have an airplane. It was nonetheless a tense time. They were scheduled to lock in the external configuration of the aircraft in just a few months, so once again engineers faced some long hours. Some Northrop engineers suspected Boeing of a whisper campaign, suggesting to the Air Force that Northrop was botching the job and didn't know how to design a big airplane. Kinnu also brought in some outside experts, including a few NASA engineers who had worked on similar aeroelastic problems for the Space Shuttle.[6]

Northrop actually faced two problems rolled into one. One was structural, to limit the bending. Kinnu hadn't liked the structural design in this respect anyway, as it carried too much of the structural load through a single spar in the back of the plane. He wanted the load distributed more evenly between the plane's front and back, which meant a basic redesign of the middle, moving the cockpit forward and the engine inlets aft, creating room for a strong box through the center of the wing. The redesign added a lot of weight, several thousand pounds, but it resulted in a much stronger airplane, one with nearly double the original wing loading.[7]

The other problem was in the control surfaces, which could be used to moderate the bending of the wing by changing its position. The control surfaces were concentrated on the outboard tip of the wing. Engineers had always struggled to have sufficient aerodynamic control for the flying wing, finally scuttling plans for tails or fins (which ruined the radar signature) in favor of the clamshell controls. At low altitudes, though, a gust could bend the airplane enough to steal the airflow from those outer surfaces, rendering them useless. The airplane needed control surfaces closer to the centerline, but the current planform didn't have a place to put them. The solution involved adding notches to the inboard diamond, under the engine exhaust path, which gave an inboard trailing edge to add elevons for pitch and roll. The result was the striking double-W planform, the bat-wing shape, when viewed from above, that characterizes the Stealth bomber.

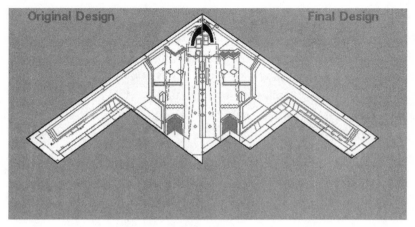

FIGURE II.I

Northrop's original planform and revised
W planform for the Stealth bomber.
Source: courtesy of Northrop Grumman Corporation.

Engineers changed not just the location but also the motion of control surfaces. The flight-control group, led by Al Myers, cranked up their speed so that they could rotate at 100 degrees per second (that is, going from horizontal to vertical in less than a second). Such a rate was unheard of for a plane that size, faster than those on a fighter plane; the F-16's much smaller control surfaces, for comparison, moved at 80 degrees per second.[8] Later, during checkout before a test flight, a mechanic was sitting in the hangar watching the pilot test the elevons. The mechanic leaned back in his chair just as the elevons whipped up at their max rate, and the wind they produced blew him over.[9]

The combination of the new structural design, the revised planform, and the new control surfaces solved the problem of low-altitude flight, but one more design problem soon emerged. The Air Force required the bomber to operate from any large airfield in the world with a full payload. Northrop conducted a study and found that if its airplane took off from a high-altitude airport on a hot day, it would stall and crash. The problem stemmed from the sharp leading edge of the wing, which Cashen's radar team needed in order to reduce the radar cross section. The edge made the airflow over the wing tend to turn sideways, along the wing, instead of going straight back over the top of the wing. The sideways flow caused the wing to lose lift, and the aircraft could stall on takeoff—especially in the thin air of higher altitudes. To keep the airflow going front-to-back Waaland began looking at various tricks used by the aerodynamicists, such as spoilers or pop-up vanes. But, again, such features would ruin the radar signature and thus frustrated Cashen and the radar engineers. The other option, a rounded leading edge for airflow, also ruined the radar signature.[10]

Ken Mitzner, the specialist in electromagnetic theory, whose work exemplified the connection between seemingly esoteric physical theory and the nuts-and-bolts of building an airplane, came up with a solution. Years earlier Mitzner had written a paper on what he called the incremental length diffraction coefficient. Elaborating on Pyotr Ufimtsev's theory, the paper provided a way to calculate the contribution to radar scattering from edge currents—that is, the electric currents a radar wave generated along the edge of a surface. One result was what Cashen called "the experiment of one hand clapping." In effect, the theory predicted that most of the radar scattering came from the end of an edge and not from the middle. In the case of an airplane, most of the radar scattering came from the wingtips.[11]

Northrop's solution, then, was to keep the leading edge thin and sharp out at the wingtips and have it thick and rounded in the middle. The rounded edge would keep most of the airflow going where it needed to, from front to back, and the sharp edge at the tips would keep the radar signature low. Viewed from head-on, the resulting profile was thicker and rounded in the middle, thin at the ends. Thus the name: the toothpick.[12]

The toothpick required careful tapering of the radius of the rounded leading edge as it went from the nose to the wingtip, which in turn required several iterations on the radar range—thus combining Mitzner's mathematical theory with the empirical, cut-and-try approach.[13] In the end the toothpick accommodated both the aerodynamic and radar demands and thus solved the last major design problem on the bomber.

There were a few other design issues, and they involved fields besides aerodynamics and radar. Stealth technology helped make an airplane

FIGURE 11.2
The "toothpick": head-on view of the B-2.
Note the clamshell control surfaces at the wingtips.
Source: courtesy of Northrop Grumman Corporation.

hard to see with radar waves, but that did no good if you could detect it by sight, or sound, or heat. Radar was by far the top priority, with detection by heat (or infrared) a distant second. For heat, engine exhaust was the main culprit. Northrop's design put the engines and exhaust outlets on top of the wing, to block them from view from the ground, and it mixed the exhaust with cold air from bypass inlets. After heat was visual detection. Since contrails were a dead giveaway at high altitudes, like a giant arrow pointing to the plane, the bomber injected chemicals into the jet exhaust. It also had dark paint to blend into the sky at high altitudes. Northrop retained a special consultant for the paint job, and it turned out the consultant was an avid birdwatcher. Ken Mitzner, a birdwatcher himself, noted, "If you're going to become an expert on visual camouflage, birds are an excellent place to start."[14]

The designers worried least about sound. The Red Team studied acoustic detection and concluded that at high altitudes there was usually too much background noise to detect aircraft, as anyone might guess from watching passenger jets pass silently overhead at their cruising altitude (and the Stealth bomber would fly twice as high). At low altitudes, the bomber would be flying near the speed of sound, so by the time you heard the plane it was already over you.[15]

———

The redesigns added several months and an estimated $2 billion to the schedule and budget of the ATB, which the Air Force officially renamed as the B-2 in September 1984. Those costs were exacerbated by another Air Force requirement: classification. Like the other Stealth planes, the B-2 was highly classified. The Air Force Program Management Directive listed the project's priorities, in order, as (1) security, (2) performance, (3), schedule, and (4) cost.[16]

Northrop again faced the same complexities presented by the other highly classified Stealth programs: the difficulty in building up the workforce, since new hires had to sit in unproductive limbo waiting for their security clearance; the loss of other workers, who found the security regime too oppressive and simply quit; storing and tracking classified documents; the need for special equipment, such as classified computers, and secure facilities, with blocked-off windows, restricted access, and a force of security guards. Less visible was the personal toll for private lives under public surveillance, families left ignorant of one's work or whereabouts.

The B-2, however, brought a whole new set of security challenges. Lockheed's Skunk Works had been building Top Secret planes for decades and therefore had facilities and processes in place not only to design but also to manufacture them in quantity. Northrop had designed and built the Tacit Blue, but that program was nowhere near the numbers or scale needed on the B-2. Northrop now had to create a Top Secret world essentially from scratch.

Furthermore, the Pentagon imposed a more intrusive security regime on the B-2. On the F-117 the Skunk Works enjoyed its usual isolation.

Northrop had enjoyed the same on Tacit Blue, with the program contained in one building. One might call it the Mark Twain theory of security: put all your eggs in one basket, and *watch that basket*.[17] The B-2, however, was too big a project to put in one building. For starters, Boeing and Vought were building large parts of the plane as subcontractors, and they were in other states. On top of that, the Pentagon imposed more oversight than before. It wasn't enough for Northrop to have a classified building and then control all the information within that building. Even within a classified building, the new procedure required workers to track every piece of paper and hardware through the security office.

Secrecy came with costs. It added perhaps 10 to 15 percent to the B-2's cost, and much more in inefficiency. For example, Northrop, like the Skunk Works, tried to integrate design and manufacturing, allowing free communication between them, but secrecy imposed a barrier. The radar group worked in a top-secret vault, and the shop floor couldn't talk to them. Waaland recalled, "We were dying with the things they were demanding, and the guys on the floor were saying, 'I can't build that.'" The shop floor, however, couldn't work directly with the radar group to resolve such problems. Eventually they took a structural engineer who worked closely with the shop floor and got him the special clearance to go into the radar vault; he became the translator between the radar designers and the shop floor.[18]

Again, there was a reason for secrecy. In 1981 the FBI discovered that a Hughes engineer for several years had been sending microfilm of classified reports on Stealth radar, including the B-2 system, to the Soviet bloc in exchange for $110,000. And in 1984 the FBI arrested a Northrop engineer for seeking to sell B-2 secrets to the Soviets. A Northrop worker snuck up to the factory roof and painted a giant vulgar insult in Russian, giving the figurative finger to the Soviet spy satellites that regularly orbited overhead.[19]

The B-2's tight classification, however, fueled suspicion that the Air Force imposed secrecy not so much for national security as to deflect political criticism. An executive from Rockwell, maker of the B-1B, complained, "I can't make a comparison with the [Stealth bomber] because I'm not allowed to know anything about it." Another civilian Air Force adviser declared that only a few military programs deserved high classification, "and Stealth isn't one of them."[20]

Some within the Pentagon, aware of the mounting costs, concurred. Paul Kaminski's Red Team exercise had a secondary purpose, which was to figure out what exactly the US needed to keep classified and what could be released.[21] Richard DeLauer, successor to William Perry as undersecretary of defense for research and engineering in the Reagan administration, pushed to reveal some information about the B-2, as did Reagan's science adviser, George Keyworth, who noted, "There's no deterrence in a black program." Defense Secretary Caspar Weinberger, however, insisted on keeping the B-2 deep black.[22]

As public and political criticism of baroque military projects zeroed in on the secrecy around Stealth, *Defense News*, a normally sympathetic trade journal, issued a warning in 1985: "In the coming months, the taxpayers gradually will realize that too many weapons projects and too many billions of dollars are hidden from public view in the rats' maze of highly classified 'black' programs. . . . It is only a matter of time before the public gets a peek inside the rats' maze and is repelled by what is there." Indeed, in January 1986 Democratic congressman John Dingell angrily wrote Weinberger to note "the rapidly increasing size of the Air Force's so-called 'black' programs" and complain that "the Air Force has been hiding virtually all relevant data on 'black' programs from the Congress." [23]

Weinberger ignored Dingell's demand for information on black projects, but a few months later, in April 1986, he got another letter from the House Armed Services Committee that was harder to disregard. Both the Republicans and Democrats on the committee expressed concern about the "growing volume of defense programs that now fall under the . . . 'black' umbrella" and noted in particular that much of the special-access funding went to the B-2. The letter concluded, "We are not convinced that there is a legitimate requirement to keep the wraps any longer on the most basic numbers involved," such as funding for the fiscal year and the total program costs. One of the committee staff quipped, "The best example of stealth technology is where the Air Force hid the money."[24]

———

In response to the congressional prodding, the Defense Department in June 1986 finally released a "fact sheet" on the B-2 revealing a total program cost of $37 billion (in 1981 dollars), or $277 million per plane.[25] The program costs would continue to mount because, as Kinnu had warned, Northrop was learning how hard it was to turn the elegant curves on conceptual drawings into an actual airplane.

For starters, there was the basic problem of translating drawings into hardware, which again involved the mysterious art of lofting. The catch: the drawings for the B-2 resided not on paper but on computer screens. Northrop for years had been using in-house R&D funds to develop a computer-aided design system, and the CAD group had been pushing to turn it into a full-fledged three-dimensional system covering all three phases: design, lofting, and production. Instead of requiring the shop floor to interpolate between stations on a blueprint, translated by the lofters into curves etched in metal, the CAD system had the advantage of defining every point on the airplane by coordinates on the computer. Kinnu decided to go for it: the B-2 would be the first aircraft designed entirely on CAD.[26]

Northrop's CAD team, whose engineers had both computing and manufacturing backgrounds, was given three years to perfect it. In the first three years, as Northrop ironed out the risks in the design, they would support just the designers, but in the fourth year the B-2 program would kick into high gear, and into production. At that point the system would have to incorporate lofting and production drawings of all the plane's 400,000 parts—and also extend to contractors Boeing and Vought, along with other suppliers, in a classified network.[27]

To build the B-2, in April 1982 Northrop acquired a vast plant at Pico Rivera in LA, site of a former Ford auto factory. Workers who had previously built Ford Thunderbirds were rehired to build a Stealth bomber.[28] As with the F-117, Stealth made stiff demands on the shop floor. The B-2's innards included the structural box, made out of titanium, a metal notoriously difficult to machine. Most of the airplane's skin consisted of carbon-fiber–graphite–epoxy composites, which were lighter than aluminum. Northrop had previously undertaken research on these materials, but the B-2 required manufacturing and machining them on a huge scale, due to the airplane's 172-foot wingspan.[29]

Northrop had to learn how to make the new materials, then how to form them and connect them, all of which required R&D beyond that needed just to design a radar-dodging plane. They produced the material by curing it at high temperature and pressure in massive heat chambers called autoclaves; for the mammoth wing sections, Boeing—which was, along with Vought, one of the major subcontractors—built the world's biggest autoclave, 90 feet long. Then they had to figure out how to detect bubbles, voids, or other defects inside the composite without tearing it apart (for instance, by using ultrasound), develop techniques to cut the material using water jets, and invent new fasteners to take the place of metal rivets. Without the usual racket of rivet guns, the B-2 production line was eerily quiet.[30]

In addition to new composite materials, Stealth required extraordinarily tight tolerances to ensure the curves would indeed shed radar. Most airplanes are built from the inside out, starting with the internal framework as a sort of skeleton and then putting the skin on at the end. Building from inside out, however, means that errors in tolerance multiply. In order to maintain the rigid specifications for the B-2's skin, Northrop built it from the outside in, which required production tooling that allowed the shop floor to put the surfaces together, then assemble the interior framework to match the skin.[31]

From 1980 to 1985 Northrop added 17,000 jobs, a 56 percent increase. In addition to the Pico Rivera plant with its 12,000 workers, Northrop built an 800,000-square foot factory on a 250-acre site outside Palmdale, California. The Northrop factory was part of what the Air Force called, with high-security blandness, Plant 42. It consisted of a complex of factories, hangars, and runways carved out of the Mojave Desert: a high-tech island amid the desert scrub. The Palmdale factory, bigger than sixteen football fields, would eventually house another

FIGURE 11.3
B-2 production line in Palmdale.
Source: courtesy of Northrop Grumman Corporation.

2,400 workers for the B-2's final assembly. In early 1987 it was estimated the B-2 program as a whole had more than 40,000 workers
throughout the country.[32]

Since the B-2 was built, literally, all over the map, Palmdale was where
the various parts came together. The Pico Rivera plant built the forward
fuselage and all leading and trailing edges; Boeing in Seattle built the
aft fuselage and outboard wings; Vought, near Dallas, built the inboard
wing sections. General Electric, near Cincinnati, supplied the engines,
and Hughes in El Segundo the radar system. The parts from Vought
and Boeing arrived at Palmdale in C-5 transports, and the huge airplane
wings were stuffed (gently) into even bigger airplanes. The Palmdale

plant had positions to assemble fifteen airplanes at a time, to fit the original plan of eventually turning out twenty-four planes per year.[33]

Stealth was a reminder that Southern California's economy—along with its middle-class culture and its leisure lifestyle—was built on defense dollars. Good times returned to the Golden State in the 1980s, thanks in part to the B-2 jobs at Northrop, plus the many thousands more jobs in the aerospace substrate, the workers at all the machine shops and suppliers scattered around Southern California that made the fasteners, gauges, switches, wiring, and so on that went into the bomber. Stealth also provided a reminder that the sunny days of the Reagan era had dawned before his presidency. The investment in Stealth started quietly under Nixon and Ford and redoubled under Carter.

The economic rebound was not just due to Stealth. The southland had several major defense contracts under way in the early 1980s, including the B-1B at Rockwell, the Trident missile at Lockheed, and the MX missile at Northrop and Rockwell—plus, of course, the F-117A at Lockheed. And the knock-on effects propagated through other economic sectors, such as real estate and construction. Aerospace employment around Los Angeles rose over 40 percent between 1979 and 1986, a surge that appeared more remarkable when compared to the contemporary decline of manufacturing sectors in the eastern and midwestern US.[34]

By 1987, Northrop's burgeoning programs, crowned by the B-2, led the *Los Angeles Times* to declare that the previously small firm had "the potential to run away with the leadership of the US aerospace industry by the turn of the century."[35]

———

Even as the *Times* lauded Northrop's bright future, storm clouds were gathering. Because of the B-1B program, the B-2 had a cushion built into the schedule: the Air Force had planned to build the B-1B first and get it into service quickly as a stopgap, then follow with the Stealth bomber a few years later. The B-1B went first because its contractor, Rockwell International (which had subsumed North American Aviation, the longtime Southern California aircraft firm), had already built preproduction versions of the B-1A before President Carter canceled it in 1977. When Carter canceled the program, he hadn't said anything about destroying the production tooling. (When the Pentagon canceled the SR-71, by contrast, it ordered Lockheed to destroy all the tooling.) So Rockwell stashed away the tooling, planning to wait out the Carter administration and see if the next president revived the program. Sure enough, when Reagan came into office and revived what was now called the B-1B, Rockwell pulled the tooling out of mothballs and had it ready to go.[36]

The Pentagon's plan was that from 1982 to 1984 the B-1B program would go all-out and Northrop's ATB funding would be constrained while it focused on identifying and dealing with the uncertainties in Stealth. Then as the B-1B neared completion in 1985, the B-2 would shift gears and go all-out. The original contract called for first flight in 1987, six years from contract signing.[37] That was a year slower than Lockheed built the F-117, but it was the same amount of time it took to build the F-15 and a year faster than the F-16 and F-18. And it was a far from leisurely pace for an airplane as big and complex as the B-2.

In defense-industry terms, the B-2 was a "concurrent program," meaning its development, production, and testing overlapped in the schedule. When problems appeared, concurrency magnified them. The design changes had already cost substantial time and money by 1985, and production brought more challenges, not just technical ones but managerial as well. For example, Northrop had to ensure quality control in all those 400,000 parts. Defective fasteners from a supplier in the San Fernando Valley made it into Boeing's parts of the plane, and thence into Northrop's final assembly, without being inspected. Since most of Northrop's managers were technical engineers, not business administrators, Northrop brought in a deputy to Patierno with a background in purchasing, pricing, and contracts to help prevent such problems.[38]

As problems mounted, the first flight slipped by several months, and then another several months, and then again into 1989. Northrop planned first to build six complete aircraft for flight test, then immediately proceed to full production at a rate of thirty per year. The delay of the first flight meant a delay in getting flight-test data—and some of those data revealed problems that needed correcting, such as unexpectedly hot temperatures from the engine exhaust on the aft deck (similar to the problem that Lockheed engineers encountered on Have Blue).[39]

The Pentagon's fact sheet released in mid-1986 had revealed that the B-2 cost $277 million per plane. That price tag worried Pentagon managers, who thought in terms of cost-to-kill ratios, and who wondered what Soviet targets were worth risking a $300 million plane. A former undersecretary of defense for acquisition, Robert Costello, joked, "If I want to hit the men's room in the Kremlin, I've got a lot of cheaper ways of doing it."[40] The rising costs also did not please the Congress. In 1987 the House Armed Services Committee startled Northrop by proposing to reopen the competition on the B-2, either by holding a new open contest for the final assembly job or by adding a second main contractor alongside Northrop. The Defense Department, at the request of Congress, asked RAND to study possible alternatives to Northrop's sole-source contract; the results were briefed to Defense Secretary Weinberger and to Congress by a RAND vice president named Michael Rich—the son of Lockheed's Ben Rich.[41]

The congressional threats to the program, together with the problems, alarmed investors, since half of Northrop's revenue depended on the B-2. The B-2 was a cost-plus contract, which meant that the government guaranteed it would cover all the costs of building the aircraft plus a negotiated profit. Such a contract protected the company against losses, but it also included performance incentives and fees for hitting certain dates. As Northrop missed these milestones, it had to write off $214 million against profits in 1986 and 1987. In the second half of 1987 its stock price dropped almost 50 percent, making it a candidate for a hostile takeover.[42]

Not all of Northrop's financial problems stemmed from the B-2. Delays and overruns also plagued Northrop's contract for the MX missile guidance system, eventually leading to federal charges of fraud. Northrop also suffered from Tom Jones's huge bet on the F-20 fighter, a lightweight, inexpensive competitor to the F-16. As he had with the F-5, Jones built the F-20 without a contract in hand from the Defense

Department, banking on foreign sales; but when the DOD refused to buy any of the planes itself, foreign governments backed away, leaving Northrop with a billion dollars in losses. The F-20 also competed for scarce engineering staff with the B-2, which was already struggling to find sufficient workers. To top it all off, Northrop's attempts to sell the F-20 abroad again landed it in hot water, with allegations of bribes paid to South Korean officials. Northrop denied the charges, but the episode revived unpleasant memories of the 1970s-era payola scandal.[43]

In April 1989, with Northrop beleaguered, Tom Jones announced his resignation as Northrop's chief executive—not, he insisted, because of the controversies but because at age sixty-eight he was ready to retire. That year the Air Force announced that the B-2's cost had risen to $44 billion in 1981 dollars; including inflation, that made it $70 billion for 132 bombers, or $530 million per plane.[44] The cost-conscious Jones, known for inexpensive aircraft, had now overseen the world's most expensive airplane. Some of this was due to the Air Force stiffening the requirements during development, some to Northrop (and the Air Force) underestimating the difficulty of building a Stealth bomber. Whatever the reason, the resignation of Jones after nearly thirty years at Northrop's helm seemed like the end of an era. And indeed it was— for reasons that reached far beyond the corporate suite at Northrop.

———

Jones remained at Northrop for several more months, long enough to preside over the B-2's first flight. The airplane had its public unveiling in November 1988 at Plant 42 in Palmdale, to great fanfare (literally: a military band played a tune, "Stealth Fanfare," composed for the occasion). A crowd of two thousand, including no fewer than forty-one Air Force generals, gathered for the occasion, watched over by two hundred armed guards and attack dogs. A tractor towed the plane out of the hangar, the crowd went wild, the press snapped photos, and then the tractor pushed it back out of sight.[45] The Air Force carefully controlled media access, allowing the crowd to see the plane only from the front—but ironically had failed to secure the airspace above the plant. An intrepid *Aviation Week* editor named Mike Dornheim, himself an amateur pilot, hired a plane and took photos of the B-2 from above, while his competitors on the ground shook their fists at him in vain.[46]

To some, the rollout celebration seemed a bit forced. By 1988 Mikhail Gorbachev's glasnost policy in the Soviet Union had thawed the Cold War, undermining the B-2's primary justification. A few months before the unveiling, Reagan had visited Moscow and strolled amiably through Red Square with Gorbachev. Inside the Kremlin, a reporter asked Reagan about his famous reference, just five years earlier, to the Soviet Union as an "evil empire"; Reagan replied, "I was talking about another time, another era."[47]

Meanwhile the B-2 headed toward flight testing, which meant that the test pilots again spent thousands of hours in the simulators, working with the flight-control engineers to iron out the bugs in the fly-by-wire software. The B-2, as we know, incorporated several links to the past, starting with the flying wing itself. Another throwback emerged in the flight-test program. When working on the flight controls engineers had worried about what is known as ground effect: when it approached the runway, the B-2, with its exceptional lift, might tend to float and not want to land. Northrop old-timers recalled that the YB-49 flying wing in the 1940s had the same problem, so they brought in Max Stanley, the original YB-49 test pilot, now in his seventies. They got Stanley a security clearance and put him in the flight simulator, and after a few test landings the old pilot assured them that the B-2 would land fine.[48]

The plane unveiled in November 1988 was not a finished aircraft. Among other things, it lacked engines. The B-2's actual first flight occurred in July 1989, a year and a half behind the original schedule. Another large crowd gathered in Palmdale on Saturday, July 15— Cashen and Waaland, long since moved on to other jobs, made the trip up—only to be disappointed. The flight aborted at the last second because of clogged fuel filters. Test engineers quickly traced the clogs to lint from the jumpsuits worn by production workers when they sealed the inside of the fuel tanks.[49]

Two days later, after workers cleaned out the lint and with a much smaller group on hand, the B-2 finally flew. Northrop's chief test pilot, Bruce Hinds, and Air Force test pilot Colonel Richard Crouch took off

FIGURE 11.4

B-2 first flight, July 17, 1989, over the Mojave Desert.
Source: US Air Force.

from a runway at Plant 42, circled at 10,000 feet above the Mojave Desert for an hour and a half with wheels down, and landed 25 miles north at Edwards Air Force Base. An anticlimax to some, to others the flight was the culmination of years of labor. It brought tears to Kinnu's eyes. The managers and engineers threw a party afterward at the Edwards officers club; when anyone who worked on the B-2 walked in the door, they got thrown in the pool.[50]

The B-2 entered full production, and Northrop delivered the first Stealth B-2 bomber to the Air Force at Whiteman Air Force Base in Missouri at the end of 1993. The Pico Rivera built its last B-2 components in 1997, and the following year the last B-2 rolled off the Palmdale assembly line. In 2001 the Pico Rivera plant was demolished and a shopping mall was built on the site. The evolution of the place—from Ford cars to Stealth planes to shopping mall—revealed an arc of American history.

CHAPTER TWELVE

FROM THE SHADOWS
TO THE SPOTLIGHT

The Gulf War was Stealth's first true test. Iraq had spent billions in the 1980s on a Soviet-style integrated air-defense system; downtown Baghdad bristled with seven times the density of defenses that had been deployed at Hanoi during the Vietnam War, which had decimated American aircraft. Baghdad was the second-most-defended city in the world, after Moscow.[1]

Those defenses could not see the F-117s. A total of forty-two Stealth fighters destroyed almost a third of the Iraqi sites targeted on January 17, 1991, the first night of the war. Over the entire air campaign, F-117A flights flew 2 percent of sorties but attacked 40 percent of Iraqi targets. Eighty percent of those sorties hit their target within 10 feet of their aim point. Military planners began redefining their targets not as a particular building or aircraft shelter but as a particular part of it: a window, say, or a door. American news viewers were mesmerized by the strike video of one F-117 in the first wave, which dropped a smart bomb down the ventilation shaft of Iraq's air force headquarters.[2]

Stealth gave the US overwhelming air superiority. Fifty years earlier, during World War II, the American 8th Air Force lost one out of every twenty planes it sent into the skies over Germany, and only a third of the survivors dropped bombs within 1,000 feet of targets. In Iraq, Stealth aircraft were delivering bombs down airshafts, and not one was shot down.[3] A single F-117 with two smart bombs was as effective as 108 B-17 bombers in World War II carrying 648 bombs. Even in the Gulf War itself, it took a wave of eight nonstealthy attack aircraft, escorted by thirty fighters and ECM (electronic countermeasure) aircraft, to attack one target—a ratio of almost forty airplanes per target.

Meanwhile, twenty-one F-117s without escorts struck thirty-seven targets. Stealth essentially flipped the script; instead of dozens or hundreds of aircraft being needed to take out a single defended target, a single aircraft could take out multiple targets.[4]

As Iraq collapsed with far fewer American and allied casualties than many observers expected, the money spent on the F-117 seemed well worth it. Testimonials to Stealth poured in from generals and military officials, as well as from the public.[5] *Vanity Fair*, in a gallery of Gulf War heroes photographed by Annie Leibovitz, included the F-117A in its annual Hall of Fame. (The magazine called it the "Stealth bomber"— no harm, and not inaccurate since that was in fact the plane's mission.) "It takes a smart plane to drop a smart bomb," the article gushed. "To the Iraqi radar it was no larger than a butterfly, but it stung like a B-52. Stealth was the air force's cool tool, the Pentagon's own Batplane." The F-117A, in short, was a technological celebrity. The editors concluded, "There's no such thing as a lovely war, but at least Desert Storm wasn't Vietnam."[6]

As the Vietnam analogy made clear, Stealth helped restore confidence in the American military. Surrounding events at the time reinforced the message of American dominance: the Berlin Wall had fallen, a wave of democracy was sweeping through Eastern Europe, and the Soviet Union itself was tottering and would eventually collapse, with remarkably little bloodshed, at the end of the year. Stealth merged the one-sided American victory in the Gulf War with Cold War triumphalism: as the American public saw it, here was a vivid demonstration of the value of the national investment in Cold War technology, which not only deterred and defeated the Soviet empire but also trounced Iraq.

Kelly Johnson, the founder and guiding spirit of the Skunk Works, died on December 21, 1990, at the age of eighty, a month before the opening attack of the Gulf War. He did not get to see the Stealth fighter, an airplane he never thought would fly, play its decisive role.

———

The B-2 hadn't yet entered service by the time of the Gulf War and the Soviet collapse, and it did not enjoy the same éclat. The Cold War ended just as Northrop was ramping up for mass production, removing the bomber's original strategic justification. At several points Congress and Presidents George H. W. Bush and Bill Clinton considered canceling the whole program. After years of extreme secrecy, Northrop now began inviting reporters to tour the B-2 production line, part of a public relations push to counter congressional critics. In the end Congress backed down, unwilling to pull the plug on the program with tens of billions of dollars already invested. The Defense Department, however, scaled back from 132 planes to 75 planes, then eventually cut the order to 20 planes, plus one of the test-flight aircraft—a fraction of the original plan. Spreading the final development cost of $45 billion over only 21 planes sent the price per plane skyrocketing, and the B-2 became known as "the $2 billion airplane."[7]

The demise of the Soviet Union meanwhile made the B-2 an airplane looking for a mission. The Air Force proposed using it for conventional strikes on rogue nations in the developing world, such as Libya, but at $2 billion per plane such missions were harder to justify. What targets were worth risking $2 billion to hit?[8] (The F-117, by comparison, cost about $110 million per plane, including the prototypes.) Maintenance issues also plagued the B-2. Test flights revealed that rain and snow, humidity, and extreme temperatures damaged the radar-absorbing material and undermined the plane's stealthiness. That meant that B-2s in service needed climate-controlled aircraft shelters and long and costly maintenance after each flight. During flight test the B-2 required 80 man-hours of maintenance for every hour in the air; during deployment at Whiteman Air Force Base, that figure soared to 124 maintenance hours per hour of flight in 1996. As a result, only one-fourth of the deployed B-2s were actually mission-capable on average.[9]

The B-2 saw action in 1999 during the Balkan conflict, destroying a third of all Serbian targets in the first eight weeks, flying nonstop from Missouri to the Balkans and back with refueling. Over the course of the war the B-2 accounted for 50 out of 34,000 total NATO sorties, yet it struck 11 percent of the targets, including a crucial bridge over the Danube in Serbia that had stymied other aircraft for two weeks. (An F-117 was shot down over Serbia, not because Stealth failed to avoid radars but, in part, because the Air Force had gotten tactically lazy: the F-117s flew the same routes over and over, and the predictability allowed Serb defenses to zero in on them.) After 9/11 B-2s flew missions to Afghanistan and then participated in the Iraq War.[10]

———

Long before Stealth's major combat debut in the Gulf War in 1991, the military sought to apply its technology to other platforms. Both Lockheed and Northrop had pursued Stealth cruise missiles, Lockheed with the Senior Prom project in the 1970s, based on the Have Blue design, and Northrop with the Tri-Service Standoff Attack Missile (TSSAM) in the 1980s, which was basically the Tacit Blue design turned upside down. The Air Force eventually canceled both projects.[11]

The Navy also pursued Stealth, with similarly mixed results. Lockheed built a Stealth ship, the *Sea Shadow*, which it tested in the Santa Barbara Channel, off Southern California. In the end both the ship and the concept were scrapped. One problem was that the ocean surface scattered radar waves, while the Stealth ship did not—so it showed up on radar displays as a hole in the ocean.[12] The Navy also pursued a carrier-based Stealth bomber, designated the A-12 (not to be confused with Lockheed's earlier A-12 spy plane). A team from McDonnell Douglas and General Dynamics won the contract in 1988, with a design for a flying wing about half the size of the B-2 and with a triangular planform. Cost overruns and schedule delays, combined with the end of the Cold War, led the Defense Department to cancel the project in 1991, a multi-billion-dollar debacle.[13]

The Air Force meanwhile looked to incorporate Stealth in an actual fighter. Despite its "F" designation the F-117 was an attack aircraft, not an air-to-air fighter. The Air Force called the new project the Advanced Technical Fighter (ATF), and seven aircraft firms entered the initial competition. In 1986 the Air Force narrowed the field down to two: Lockheed and Northrop. Once again these two squared off in a Stealth contest, with Lockheed teamed now with Boeing and General Dynamics, Northrop with McDonnell Douglas. The ATF presented a tough challenge: supersonic cruise, without afterburners; long range, without external fuel tanks; maneuverable enough for dogfights; and, of course, a minuscule radar cross section.[14]

Lockheed had learned its lesson about facets versus curves. Its design incorporated the familiar large flat panels—for instance, around the engine inlets—and twin tails canted outward, but it also featured distinct curves, around the forward fuselage, cockpit, and aft deck. Lockheed's team drew heavily on the F-117 experience, starting with its program manager, Sherman Mullin, who had previously overseen F-117 production.[15] After testing of the two prototypes in late 1990, Lockheed's YF-22 versus Northrop's YF-23, Lockheed came out on top. The F-22 first flew in 1997 and entered service in 2005. Lockheed and Northrop finally teamed up in the contest to build the stealthy Joint Strike Fighter, now known as the F-35, beating out Boeing. The F-35 was deployed starting in 2015 by the Air Force, Navy, and Marines.

In 2011 the Air Force announced a new contest for a second-generation Stealth bomber. Once again it was Northrop (now called Northrop Grumman) versus Lockheed (now Lockheed Martin, and teamed with Boeing). This time Northrop won, with a bat-shaped flying wing clearly descended from the B-2. The trend held: Lockheed won the smaller Stealth fighters; Northrop won the Stealth bombers. And, also once again, Northrop embarked on a hiring spree at its Palmdale plant, ramping up the workforce to build the B-21 under extreme secrecy—although, owing to automation, it planned not to hire as many workers as for the B-2.[16]

Lockheed and Northrop also competed on Stealth drones, or UAVs, intended to fly not just in largely uncontested airspace, such as Afghanistan, but also in defended airspace, such as Iran. The Skunk Works built the RQ-170 and Northrop Grumman the larger, longer-range RQ-180. Both designs were a modified version of the flying wing, providing an even more harmonious marriage of aerodynamics and Stealth than the B-2, and both were highly classified. The RQ-170 was first spotted in grainy photos from Kandahar Air Base in Afghanistan in 2007 and publicly outed by *Aviation Week* in 2009, and the RQ-180 was similarly revealed by *Aviation Week* in December 2013.[17]

Stealth had one other impact. The Black Hawk helicopters used in the raid that killed Osama bin Laden in 2011 apparently incorporated

Stealth—and the stealthy RQ-170 drone provided the crucial surveil-lance of bin Laden's compound.[18]

The US no longer has a monopoly on Stealth. In 2010 Russia first flew the stealthy Sukhoi T-50 (also known as the Su-57), and the fol-lowing year China's stealthy J-20 fighter made its first flight. Both Russia and China have also developed so-called counterstealth: new air-defense radars designed to detect Stealth planes.[19]

————

To many aerospace engineers, the end of the Cold War was a cause for national celebration but personal distress. Southern California's aero-space economy entered another nosedive, with hundreds of thousands of workers sacked and the survivors looking over their shoulder for the next round of pink slips. Southern California had come full circle: from the dark days of the early 1970s to the boom times of the 1980s to another recession in the early 1990s.

By 1994 California's aerospace industry had cut one-third of its jobs from the mid-'80s peak; in LA County alone, aerospace employ-ment was cut in half—returning, more or less, to the levels of the early 1970s.[20] The movie *Falling Down*, in which Michael Douglas plays an aerospace engineer who snaps after being laid off, came out in 1993. The Rodney King riots had occurred a year before—sparked by a racist attack but aggravated by economic dislocation. Southern Californians confronted images of burning buildings, billowing black smoke, and armed troops patrolling the streets—the outcome not of war with the Soviets but of strife at home.

As defense funding dwindled, a wave of mergers swept through the aerospace industry, washing out still more employees in the process. In late 1993 Defense Secretary Les Aspin asked his deputy Bill Perry—the same Perry who, fifteen years earlier, had championed Stealth—to arrange a dinner with a dozen leading defense executives. Perry told them that there was no longer enough funding to go around. There were twice as many defense contractors as the Pentagon could support, and they either had to merge or perish. Norman Augustine, Martin Marietta's puckish president, dubbed it "the Last Supper."[21]

Augustine got the message. In 1995 Martin Marietta merged with Lockheed, which had already acquired the General Dynamics aircraft division, to form Lockheed Martin. Northrop had bought out Grumman in 1994 to form Northrop Grumman. Several firms got swallowed up by larger competitors in the aerospace shakeout, and it is no coincidence that of the few survivors, two were the Stealth developers.[22]

As fewer defense contractors chased fewer defense funds, they began scrambling to find nonmilitary markets for their products. It was easier to turn swords into plowshares, however, than to find commercial uses for Stealth aircraft and laser-guided munitions, and these conversion efforts were, Augustine joked, "unblemished by success." Augustine continued, "Why is it rocket scientists can't sell toothpaste? Because we don't know the market, or how to research, or how to market the product. Other than that, we're in good shape."[23]

———

For the time being, though, Stealth eased the pain of the aerospace cutbacks, and with the Cold War's end the military further lifted the veil of secrecy around Stealth. The Skunk Works came out of the black world, blinking, into the bright light of celebrity. Its management style became a trend in management circles, and Ben Rich wrote a bestselling book about his outfit's innovative history. American companies rushed to form their own in-house "skunk works," a buzzword for advanced, blue-sky projects unencumbered by bureaucratic red tape.

Although Lockheed had the first and most public association with Stealth, Northrop may have benefited even more. Stealth had changed Northrop. Before the B-2 it was one of the smaller aerospace firms, occupying specialized niches. It hadn't built a big bomber since Jack Northrop's YB-49 half a century earlier, and the fighters it built were small, cheap, and designed for foreign markets. The B-2 brought Northrop into the big leagues, capable of the biggest projects, both physically and managerially, and thus a leading contender for the latest generation of aircraft, the F-22, F-35, and B-21.[24]

Stealth may have saved Northrop. In the 1980s Northrop had a few other good-sized contracts, but had it lost the B-2 on top of the F-20 debacle, the cupboard would have been bare. When the Cold War ended, Northrop would have been one of the little fish getting swallowed up by a bigger one. Instead, Northrop was the one buying Grumman.

Then, in July 1997, the Stealth giants made an announcement: Lockheed Martin and Northrop Grumman planned to merge. The Justice and Defense Departments subsequently blocked the merger, although apparently more for antitrust concerns in electronics than in Stealth. Blocking the merger, however, helped preserve the competition between the two Stealth stalwarts.[25]

———

By that time, though, the original Stealth teams at Lockheed and Northrop had largely scattered. Some moved on to other projects, but most simply went into retirement. Denys Overholser had long since left Lockheed for his own consulting business; Ben Rich stepped down from the Skunk Works in December 1990, and Alan Brown retired the following year. At Northrop, Kinnu retired in 1992, Cashen and Waaland in 1993, and Ken Mitzner in 1995; Cashen moved to Australia. Epic arguments between Cashen and Waaland no longer resounded in Northrop's offices, and Rich's laughter no longer echoed down Lockheed's hallways. In fact, the hallways themselves sat empty. Lockheed moved the Skunk Works out to Palmdale, in the Antelope Valley near Edwards Air Force Base, and shuttered its historic Burbank plant.

Some observers feared that the nation had just lost a priceless piece of hard-won expertise. Perhaps there was no pressing need for Stealth technology, with the Soviet Union defunct, but if the nation ever needed it, reassembling that knowledge base might not be easy. The *Los Angeles Times* warned of a Stealth "brain drain." Stealth knowledge, the article declared, was more an "arcane art form" than established science, and while young engineers might have learned the basics, "none have the experience and know-how of a Cashen or Rich."[26] Whether or not one agreed, there was a clear sense of a generational shift in the Stealth world.

Meanwhile, the public fanfare around Stealth demonstrated the old saying that success has many fathers, while failure is an orphan.

Determining who got credit for inventing Stealth was complicated by the fact that outsized personalities were involved. It couldn't have been otherwise. To accomplish something as audacious as Stealth took ambition, and not a small amount of ego.

In 1979 Lockheed had filed a patent for a Stealth aircraft, which was granted in 1993. The names on the patent were Scherrer, Overholser, and Watson. The patent described "A vehicle in free space or air, with external surfaces primarily fashioned from planar facets. The planar facets or panels are angularly positioned to reduce scattered energy in the direction of the receiver." For prior art, the patent noted that attempts to reduce the radar cross section of aircraft had mostly relied on materials, not shaping, and had been largely unsuccessful. It also identified the key distinction of Lockheed's approach: "With the possible exception of minor regions, few rounded external surfaces exist on the vehicle."[27]

Northrop filed a patent for the B-2 in April 1989, shortly before its first flight; it was granted in 1991. The patent was only for the "ornamental design for an aircraft," that is, the B-2's shape; the patent included no text, just drawings of the B-2 from various perspectives. The names on the patent were Waaland, Cashen, and Kinnu, in that order (after one more squabble between Cashen and Waaland; Kinnu threw his hands up and walked away from it). There was talk of adding more names, including Scherrer and Hans Grellman, another aerodynamicist, but they recognized the list would get long quickly. Some at Northrop, including Waaland, thought Oshiro deserved more credit. One of Kinnu's staff at one point tried to get Oshiro an award, perhaps as compensation for being left off the patent.[28] Even if Oshiro himself thought he had been slighted, he was not one to make a fuss about it. He refused interviews in later years and receded into the background. Like the planes he helped design, Oshiro became invisible.

The assignee for each patent was the firm, Lockheed and Northrop. None of the engineers, patent holders or otherwise, got rich off Stealth. Although a few of them worked their way into upper management, most were happy to earn a comfortable living, and they retired to Southern California beach towns, the Northern California coast, or the Pacific Northwest. It was striking how modestly most of them lived in retirement. The companies made the money, not the scientists and engineers.

One other man, however, almost entirely escaped attention. In 1989, amid Gorbachev's glasnost, Pyotr Ufimtsev was allowed to attend a conference in Stockholm. At the conference was Nick Alexopoulos, UCLA's engineering dean. Alexopoulos called John Cashen, himself a UCLA graduate, and said, "You won't believe it. Ufimtsev's here!" Cashen immediately urged him to invite Ufimtsev to the US. Cashen raised some money from Northrop and other aerospace firms, and the following year Ufimtsev came to UCLA on sabbatical to teach electromagnetism. He attended a talk on Stealth by Cashen and Alan Brown and was stunned to see his theory realized in airplanes. His first apparent reaction, according to Brown: "The enemy is using my stuff!" His second reaction: "Well, at least somebody is."[29]

American scientists expected Ufimtsev to be a cold Soviet ideologue; they found instead a charming Old World gentleman whose enthusiasm for science quickly won them over. For his part, Ufimtsev warmed to Southern California, after arriving with his wife and two children. He had first disliked Los Angeles. "I thought, what is this city? It is just a village. It is not a city. A city is Moscow, and maybe Odessa. Los Angeles is just a big village." But after a few years, he changed his mind. "I found, yes, it is a village, but it is a *good* village!" His family liked it, too. The Soviet Union's death spiral had ruined the research opportunities back home, and Ufimtsev decided to stay in LA. After the *New York Times* ran an article highlighting his contribution to Stealth, security agents showed up at his old institute and asked its managers why they allowed him to leave.[30]

In a final irony, Ufimtsev wound up working in the B-2 group at Northrop.

CONCLUSION

THE SECRET OF STEALTH

Five years after DARPA managers first started hunting invisible rabbits in Project Harvey, the United States had three Stealth airplane designs, each starkly different: the angular F-117; the ungainly Tacit Blue; the minimalist B-2.

Why did Stealth aircraft emerge when they did, and why did Lockheed and Northrop arrive at such different solutions to the problem of Stealth? One standard explanation is that digital computers in the 1970s became powerful enough to do the calculations needed for these designs. Lockheed's computers could calculate radar diffraction patterns but could only handle flat panels, which explains the faceted Have Blue and F-117. Then, this story goes, with the benefit of more powerful computers, Northrop added curves to the B-2. As Ben Rich put it in 1991, "The three-dimensional calculations you need to design stealthy curves, the kind you see on Northrop's B-2 . . . , were beyond us at the time."[1]

This argument assumes that Northrop had such computers and that it relied on them. It hadn't and didn't. Northrop's XST design, produced at the same time as Lockheed's faceted approach, already had curves, and within a couple of years Tacit Blue incorporated many more curves. Northrop's curves did not stem from the fact that it had better computers than Lockheed. It is rather that Northrop had relied *less* on computers.

Moreover, to say that one firm relied on computers more than the other just removes the explanation one step. So why did one firm rely more on computers? The answer lies in the people involved, and the relation between different engineering disciplines. And it also explains why Lockheed won the first round of the Stealth competition, for the F-117, and why Northrop won the next, for the B-2.

Lockheed won the first round for the F-117 not because of its legendary Skunk Works but in spite of it. Against the protests of Skunk Works stalwarts steeped in traditional aerodynamics, Lockheed put radar experts in charge, leaned on computer codes to design the plane, and turned to fly-by-wire flight controls to tame the unwieldy craft that resulted. Northrop gave aerodynamic traditionalists a greater voice, relied on intuition and modeling clay more than computers, and shunned fly-by-wire—and lost that initial round. Those same characteristics encouraged Northrop to pursue curves in its Stealth designs, and thus set up its victory in the B-2 contest. In short, the same factors that allowed Lockheed to win the first round with flat facets enabled Northrop to win the second round with curves.

Between those two rounds was Tacit Blue, which has been largely lost to history and seemed a dead end. In fact, Tacit Blue provided the stepping-stone from the faceted F-117 to the B-2 flying wing. The story that the B-2 was a flying wing because that's what Jack Northrop had always wanted to build is mainly myth. The real story is more interesting. Northrop's original Stealth proposal, like Lockheed's, was a blended wing-body design. Then for Tacit Blue Northrop went the other direction, *away* from the flying wing, to a standard wing-body-tail. It was *Lockheed* that proposed a flying wing for Tacit Blue, and Air Force program managers then nudged Northrop in that direction. The flying-wing idea for Stealth aircraft first came from Northrop's main competitor.

Although the two firms differed in several ways in their approach to Stealth, they shared one trait: the incendiary arguments that echoed through their design offices. One lesson of Stealth is that different viewpoints can spur innovation—and that engineers are not all cold and dispassionate. Whether it was Richard Scherrer taking on the Skunk Works traditionalists at Lockheed or, along different lines, John Cashen going head to head with Irv Waaland at Northrop, Stealth drew on the creative tensions between individuals and disciplines.[2]

The two firms shared another characteristic: the essential importance of the shop floor, and with it the need to integrate design and production engineering. Both firms learned the hard way that it was one thing to design a Stealth airplane on blueprints or computer screens. It was another thing altogether to turn those designs into flying hardware, made of exotic materials, machined to unprecedented tolerances, and manufactured in volume. That helps explain why both the F-117A and the B-2 encountered problems in manufacturing, and why aerospace firms in other countries, even decades after it debuted, have struggled to replicate Stealth.

Finally, the firms shared one more, seemingly simple characteristic, namely, their location. They were based 20 miles apart in Southern California, suggesting that another key to the story of Stealth is not only why it emerged *when* it did but also *where* it did. Southern California was already home to much of the nation's aerospace industry, but several major builders of military fighters or bombers—Boeing, Fairchild, Grumman, General Dynamics, McDonnell Douglas—were located outside Southern California, and none of them came up with Stealth. Stealth provides another example of what can happen in a creative, boundary-pushing culture, and perhaps only happen there.

So was the Cold War indeed won in El Segundo? Did scientists and engineers in the aerospace firms of Burbank, Hawthorne, and other blue-sky Southern California suburbs finally persuade the Soviets that they couldn't keep up with the US, technologically or economically, and that their system had fatal flaws? The poster child for this argument is the Strategic Defense Initiative, President Reagan's proposed missile-defense system in the 1980s, which some commentators have credited with introducing a new generation of space-based directed-energy weapons such as lasers and particle beams, forcing the Soviets into a high-tech arms race they could not afford, let alone win.[3]

Stealth may have presented an even bigger threat than Star Wars. First of all, the American investment in the F-117 and B-2 was roughly twice that of the $25 billion devoted to SDI. Stealth was also at hand, with the F-117 operational by 1983, whereas SDI was at best decades away from deployment.[4] Stealth also presented a particular peril to the Soviets, who had a historic fear of sneak attacks and had spent decades and billions of rubles creating a sophisticated air-defense network.

We have an indicator of Stealth's effect on the Soviets. After the initial vast buildup of their air-defense system in the 1950s and 1960s, Soviet investment in air defense leveled off in the 1970s. After the F-117 deployed, however, the Soviets undertook a redoubling of their air defenses, increasing the budget 8 percent per year to field new radars, antiaircraft missiles, and interceptors.[5]

Why the Cold War ended, however, defies simple explanation. Many factors caused it: the Afghanistan war, Poland's Solidarity movement, falling oil prices, ethnic nationalism, and general Soviet economic decline. Although Stealth probably did not play a direct role, it did unsettle the Soviets as part of a broader "military-technical revolution," what would later be called, in the US, the Revolution in Military Affairs. Soviet military theorists perceived that Stealth, in combination with precision-guided weapons, presented a fundamental threat. It posed a deepstrike capability against the Soviet echelon strategy, and it represented a rapidly evolving, high-tech approach, in stark opposition to the low-tech, mass-production mode of the Soviet defense industry. Marshal Ogarkov, chief of the Soviet General Staff, led a vocal campaign to persuade Soviet leaders of the peril, at the eventual cost of his job.

One can, of course, question whether Stealth was revolutionary. It may appear as just another shift in the long seesaw between offense and defense in the air, where first the attacking aircraft and then the antiaircraft batteries claim the advantage. The development of Stealth, like many purported revolutions, was also far from quick. Although Stealth may seem to have been a product of the Reagan military buildup in the 1980s, the program started in 1974, reinforced by subsequent actions in the Ford and Carter administrations.

The 1970s are sometimes viewed as a time of stagnation and malaise, as the Vietnam War and Watergate sapped public faith in the government and American industry was overtaken by competitors in Western Europe and Japan.[6] But the decade also saw the emergence of the personal computer, consumer electronics, and biotech, new high-tech industries that would revitalize the American economy. So too were the 1970s a crucial time of technological innovation for the US military, with Stealth as an exemplar. The Vietnam War in particular spurred the invention of Stealth, both in the specific realization that Soviet air-defense systems had the upper hand on American aircraft, and in the general intellectual ferment in strategic circles, seeking technological solutions to the problems plaguing the American military.

Furthermore, the concepts behind Stealth traced back at least three decades before deployment, to work in the 1950s on radar-absorbing materials and on the theory of radar diffraction. Compare the lead time for ballistic missiles, with early experiments in the 1920s and realization in the 1950s. And the Stealth aircraft themselves were throwbacks in several respects, with engineers hard-wiring components on circuit boards, digging up airfoils from old aerodynamics catalogs, wing-warping control surfaces, and reviving the flying wing.

There is a counterargument to the view that the Cold War was won in El Segundo. Far from winning the Cold War, one might say that scientists and engineers in fact *prolonged* it, leading the world to the brink of Armageddon by driving the arms race. In this telling, technological enthusiasm funneled trillions of dollars and bottomless brainpower into inventing better ways of killing people: the hydrogen bomb, the neutron bomb, the nuclear-driven x-ray laser, and so on. From this perspective, Stealth appears as just another ratchet of the Cold War arms race. The US devoted vast resources to develop Stealth, all to meet a Soviet invasion of Western Europe that was never going to happen.

This misallocation of resources, the argument continues, not only vastly inflated the federal deficit but also left the economy at a tremendous disadvantage against countries like Japan and West Germany, which then began to dominate high-tech industry. Although one may point to a few spin-offs from Stealth—say, the graphite-composite wings on Boeing's new airliners—it otherwise had few civilian applications. The $50 billion or so spent on Stealth aircraft, in this view, would have been far better invested in, say, electronics or molecular biology, not to mention social programs such as education or health care. A more cynical view sees Stealth, and especially the B-2, as just a billion-dollar boondoggle, a pork-barrel project pushed through in secret, serving no pressing military need but generating giant profits for the companies involved.[7]

Stealth, however, did offer one revolutionary implication: as an *alternative* to nuclear weapons and a way out of the looking-glass labyrinth of nuclear strategy. Both Soviet and American strategists viewed Stealth, together with precision-guided munitions, as a way to deliver conventional weapons with sufficient accuracy and confidence to make a conventional attack as effective as nuclear weapons. This enabled a small bomb to destroy a target, thus obviating the need for a huge bomb to do the job. In short, as one American strategist declared, Stealth and the other new technologies could render nuclear weapons "both wasteful and irrelevant."

This reconsideration of strategic fundamentals failed to gain traction. Instead of weaning American strategy from its reliance on nuclear weapons, the US embraced the new conventional technologies, including Stealth, as a complement to, not a replacement of, nuclear weapons. The B-2 itself, a Stealth nuclear bomber, demonstrated the inertia of nuclear strategy.

This is not to say that the invention of Stealth went for naught. Stealth had fundamental strategic import in demonstrating US technological preeminence. It presented a remarkable advance in military technology, with its performance in the Gulf War providing an exclamation point. With Stealth, and with personal computers, the internet, and cell phones in commercial technology, the US threw down a gauntlet to potential economic and military competitors. They would have to match America's seemingly boundless ability to generate new technologies or get left behind.

Although the American commitment to the Cold War aimed to demonstrate the superiority of free enterprise against a command economy, Stealth itself was a product not of an unfettered free market but rather of a vast integration of the state and private industry.[8] President Eisenhower had perceived this integration decades before. In his farewell address, in January 1961, he issued a dire warning about the emergence of "a permanent armaments industry of vast proportions," which the old Army general viewed as a dangerous incursion both by the state into private enterprise and by private interests into public policy.

Eisenhower gave it a name: the "military-industrial complex," thereafter usually invoked in the pejorative sense Ike intended.[9]

More recent scholars have taken a more positive view of the military-industrial complex, framing the public-private partnership as a remarkable engine driving technological innovation. What has been called the "hidden developmental state," "entrepreneurial state," or "innovation hybrids" was every bit the match of Japan's vaunted Ministry of International Trade and Industry, or MITI, which was heralded in the early 1980s, just when Stealth was emerging, as the reason for Japan's high-tech lead over the US.[10] Japan's MITI, of course, promoted commercial consumer technologies, whereas Stealth projected military strength but did little for economic competitiveness. But both the personal computer and the internet, later linchpins of the high-tech economy, similarly derived from computing research funded by the US military and conducted in nongovernmental institutions.[11]

Stealth represents a prime example of the civil-military, public-private partnership and the American commitment to technological preeminence. That commitment included a willingness to invest in R&D with uncertain and long-term payoffs. The military, for example, funded the work on radar scattering and cross sections at Michigan's Willow Run Labs and the Ohio State's Antenna Lab in the 1950s, which provided the theoretical foundation for later work on Stealth; it then funded Northrop's radar cross section group in the 1960s.

Northrop's radar theory group was also supported initially by Northrop itself, through in-house, discretionary R&D funds, thus demonstrating that technological innovation derived both from federal investment and from a long-term outlook by the private sector. In Northrop's case, company managers in the early 1960s suspected that knowledge of radar diffraction would be important, though they didn't know just how it would manifest itself—or that would it produce as dramatic an advance as Stealth. Similarly, Lockheed used internal discretionary funds for its initial efforts on Stealth. For decades the Hughes Corporation, the source of Stealth radar for Tacit Blue and the B-2, funded the Hughes fellowships, an extensive program supporting students pursuing advanced degrees in science and engineering at local universities—and it did not even require that the fellows then go to work at Hughes. The Hughes fellows included two of the key developers of Stealth at Northrop, John Cashen and Ken Mitzner.

In this civil-military, public-private partnership, particular individuals served as crucial mediators. The initiative for Stealth did not come from presidents or generals operating from a grand strategic vision. Nor did it come from the bottom up, from the soldiers—or, in this case, pilots—who would be the ones to wield the new technology. It came rather from the middle, from engineers and program managers who translated technology into strategy and policy, and vice versa. People who worked in the Stealth program, whether in DARPA, DDR&E, and the Air Force on the one side, or Lockheed and Northrop on the other, have universally praised the sense of teamwork between the public and private sector, and between the military and the civilian contractors.[12]

History from the middle is a longer-term tale of technological creativity and personal sacrifice by many unsung actors, from engineers and physicists to test pilots to shop-floor machinists. This book has tried to account for many of them, even if it cannot do justice to all of them. Although these engineers succeeded in the quest for Stealth, they knew better than anyone else the price they and their loved ones paid, in the long hours committed to the job, the effects on their health and their relationships, and the civil liberties sacrificed to secrecy.

A corollary: although there were certainly dramatic moments in the development of Stealth, from the raging arguments in design offices to death-defying deeds in test flights, much of the history was not romantic or heroic. It consisted rather of countless mundane meetings, memos, and briefings, interspersed with trips to the remote, ramshackle outposts of RATSCAT and Area 51.[13] No Eureka moment made Stealth aircraft possible. Indeed, the fact that Lockheed and Northrop took two different paths to Stealth shows there was no magic formula. The concept's strategic importance and technological challenge inspired a large number of smart people to work exceptionally hard for a long time to realize it. That was the true secret of Stealth.

ACKNOWLEDGMENTS

I first thank Bill Deverell and Dan Lewis, my co-conspirators on the Aerospace History Project at the Huntington-USC Institute on California and the West. Bill helped me find a professional home at USC, while Dan helped me navigate the archival landscape at the Huntington Library. Both have provided boundless good humor over the years as we worked to preserve the history of Southern California aerospace. Our archival efforts from the outset have benefited from the generous advice and friendship of Sherman Mullin, who along the way taught me much about what life and work was like in the aerospace business. The archives project has enjoyed grant support from several institutions, including the National Science Foundation and the Northrop Grumman and Lockheed Martin foundations. It is important to note that the research and writing of this book was not supported by these funds, and the two companies had no editorial control.

I thank also the people who contributed interviews, some in informal conversations, many in formal oral histories, several for multiple sessions: Andrew Baker, Alan Brown, John Cashen, Malcolm Currie, Ken Dyson, Welko Gasich, Tom Jones, Les Jonkey, Paul Kaminski, Larry Kibble, James Kinnu, Kent Kresa, Robert Loschke, Hal Maninger, Ken Mitzner, Tom Morgenfeld, Sherman Mullin, Robert Murphy, Denys Overholser, William Perry, Maggy Rivas, Kevin Rumble, Steven Smith, Pyotr Ufimtsev, and Irv Waaland. The formal oral histories are being archived with the Aerospace History Project at the Huntington Library. Richard Scherrer generously shared documents and answered questions by email. Alan Brown and Irv Waaland also shared documents. Alan Brown, John Cashen, and Sherm Mullin read parts or all of the manuscript and corrected important details, though they may not agree with my interpretations; Bob Loschke also enlightened me on technical points. I also thank the Pioneers of Stealth organization for preserving the stories of participants and sharing their work.

Fellow historians provided advice and encouragement, including Glenn Bugos, Ruth Schwartz Cowan, John Heilbron, Dan Kevles, Bill Leslie, Patrick McCray, Peter Neushul, and Nick Rasmussen. Volker Janssen conducted several of the interviews. Tony Chong, Layne Karafantis, and Mihir Pandya read the manuscript and provided valuable feedback. I owe special thanks to Mihir for many collegial conversations and for sharing his insights into Southern California aerospace in general and Stealth in particular.

I thank archivists at the Hoover Institution, Smithsonian Institution/ National Air and Space Museum, and Ronald Reagan Presidential Library; at the Huntington Library, I must single out Brook Engebretson, Mario Einaudi, and Brooke Black for their help. For help with photos, I thank Tony Chong at Northrop Grumman, Melissa Dalton and Kevin Robertson at Lockheed Martin, and Scratch Thompson and Jessica Conway.

Many thanks as well to Andrew Stuart, my agent, for understanding what I wanted to do with this book and providing wise guidance on how to do it. At Oxford University Press, Timothy Bent went above and beyond the usual editor's role in helping me tell this story, India Cooper's keen-eyed copyedits sharpened the prose, and Joellyn Ausanka shepherded the manuscript to publication.

Finally, I once again thank my wife, Medeighnia, and our children, Dane and Caden, for their support and patience.

GLOSSARY OF
TECHNICAL TERMS

ailerons. Flaps on an aircraft's horizontal surface, such as a wing, used primarily to change an aircraft's roll.

airfoil. The cross section of an aircraft wing, whose shape determines the flow of air over the wing and hence the lift.

aspect ratio. The ratio of the wing length to its width; for nonrectangular wings, expressed as the square of the wingspan divided by the wing area.

chine. A horizontal surface extending from the fuselage of an aircraft, in addition to but shorter than the wings.

clutter. Background noise in a radar pattern caused by radar waves reflected from the ground, rocks, trees, or buildings; the background obscures the signal returned from a target.

control surfaces. Flaps on an aircraft wing or tail, such as ailerons or elevators, that change pitch, roll, or yaw.

ECM. Electronic countermeasures to prevent radar waves from detecting an aircraft, in which the aircraft sends out electromagnetic waves to jam or interfere with a radar.

elevators. Flaps on an aircraft's horizontal surface, such as the tail, used to control pitch.

elevons. Control surfaces on delta-wing or flying-wing aircraft that combine the functions of elevators and ailerons.

MTI. Moving target indicator; a radar system that uses the Doppler shift in reflected radar waves to distinguish moving targets from stationary objects.

PIO. Pilot-induced oscillation, which occurs when feedback loops in flight-control computers amplify a pilot's response, sending the aircraft out of control.

pitch. The degree of rotation around a lateral axis of an aircraft, moving the nose up or down.

planform. Outline of an aircraft viewed from above.

RAM. Radar-absorbing material, applied to the surface of an aircraft and consisting of a base material such as rubber or fiberglass impregnated with graphite or other materials to absorb radar waves instead of reflecting them.

RCS. Radar cross section, or the size an aircraft appears to a radar. Usually represented as the cross-sectional area of a sphere that provides a radar return equivalent to that of the aircraft, given in square feet or meters. The radar cross section varies depending on the frequency, polarization, and direction and angle of the incident radar waves.

roll. The degree of rotation around the longitudinal axis of an aircraft, tipping the wings up or down.

rudder. Control surface to control yaw, usually mounted on a vertical surface such as a tail.

supercritical airfoil. An airfoil that minimizes the drag that occurs when flying near the speed of sound.

wing loading. The weight of the aircraft divided by the wing area.

yaw. The degree of rotation about a vertical axis of an aircraft, moving the nose left or right in a horizontal plane.

NOTES

INTRODUCTION

1   Richard P. Hallion, *Storm over Iraq: Air Power and the Gulf War* (Washington, DC: Smithsonian Books, 1992), 166–76.

2   Paul Kennedy, "History from the Middle," *Journal of Military History* 74:1 (Jan 2010), 35–51; Kennedy, *Engineers of Victory: The Problem Solvers Who Turned the Tide in the Second World War* (New York: Penguin Random House, 2013); see also Max Boot, *War Made New: Technology, Warfare, and the Course of History, 1500 to Today* (New York: New York Times Books, 2006).

3   Quoted in David Bloor, *The Enigma of the Aerofoil* (Chicago: University of Chicago Press, 2011), 9.

4   Orville Schell, "Jerry Brown: Economics in an Era of Limits," *Los Angeles Times*, August 5, 1979; Jimmy Carter, "Energy and National Goals: Address to the Nation," July 15, 1979 (available at https://www.jimmycarterlibrary.gov/assets/documents/speeches/energy-crisis.phtml).

5   Edward Berkowitz, *Something Happened: A Political and Cultural Overview of the Seventies* (New York: Columbia University Press, 2007); Dominic Sandbrook, *Mad as Hell: The Crisis of the 1970s and the Rise of the Populist Right* (New York: Penguin Random House, 2011); Daniel T. Rodgers, *Age of Fracture* (Cambridge, MA: Harvard University Press, 2011); David Kaiser and W. Patrick McCray, eds., *Groovy Science: Knowledge, Innovation, and American Counterculture* (Chicago: University of Chicago Press, 2016).

6   E.g., Boot, *War Made New*.

CHAPTER ONE: ROOTS OF THE REVOLUTION

1   Guy Hartcup, *Camouflage: The History of Concealment and Deception in War* (Barnsley, England: Pen and Sword Military, 2008), 7–13; Hannah Rose Shell, *Hide and Seek: Camouflage, Photography, and the Media of Reconnaissance* (Cambridge, MA: MIT Press, 2012), 15; Tim Newark, Quentin Newark, and J. F. Borsarello, *Brassey's Book of Camouflage* (London: Brassey's, 1996),

8–19. On modern military organizations: William H. McNeill, *The Pursuit of Power: Technology, Armed Force, and Society since* AD *1000* (Chicago: University of Chicago Press, 1982).

2 Hartcup, *Camouflage*, 14–15.

3 NRC Division of Physical Sciences, annual report for 1918, January 26, 1919 (Robert A. Millikan papers, 5/11, Caltech archives); M. Luckiesh, "The Visibility of Airplanes," *Journal of the Franklin Institute* 187 (March 1919), 289–12 and (April 1919), 409–57.

4 Michael S. Sherry, *The Rise of American Air Power* (New Haven, CT: Yale University Press, 1987), 22–46; Sven Lindqvist, *A History of Bombing*, trans. Linda Haverty Rugg (New York: The New Press, 2001).

5 Stanley Baldwin, "The Bomber Will Always Get Through," in *The Impact of Air Power: National Security and World Politics*, ed. Eugene M. Emme (Princeton, NJ: Van Nostrand, 1959), 51–52; Ronald W. Clark, *The Rise of the Boffins* (London: Phoenix House, 1962), 24–27. David Zimmerman, *Britain's Shield: Radar and the Defeat of the Luftwaffe* (Gloucestershire, UK: Amberley Publishing, 2001), chap. 2, gives an average detection range of 18 miles with the largest (200-foot) mirror but adds that "first detection frequently took place at less than 10 miles range."

6 W. Bernard Carlson, *Tesla: Inventor of the Electrical Age* (Princeton, NJ: Princeton University Press, 2013), 381–89; Marc Raboy, *Marconi: The Man Who Networked the World* (Oxford: Oxford University Press, 2016), 582; R. V. Jones, *The Wizard War: British Scientific Intelligence, 1939–1945* (New York: Coward, McCann & Geoghegan, 1978), 15–16; Louis Brown, *A Radar History of World War II: Technical and Military Imperatives* (Bristol, UK: Institute of Physics Publishing, 1999), 40–52; Clark, *Boffins*, 41.

7 Cat anecdote in Lt. Col. Daniel T. Kuehl, "The Radar Eye Blinded: The USAF and Electronic Warfare, 1945-1955" (PhD diss., Duke University, 1992, available at www.dtic.mil/dtic/tr/fulltext/u2/a265494.pdf), 16n2.

8 Brown, *A Radar History*, 73–83; Robert Buderi, *The Invention That Changed the World* (New York: Simon & Schuster, 1996), 202–5.

9 Daniel J. Kevles, *The Physicists: The History of a Scientific Community in Modern America* (Cambridge, MA: Harvard University Press, 1995), 302–8, 315–23; Brown, *A Radar History*. See also Henry E. Guerlac, *Radar in World War II*, 2 vols. (New York: American Institute of Physics, 1987); Guy Hartcup, *The Effect of Science on the Second World War* (New York: Palgrave Macmillan, 2000), 18–59; Jack Nissen and A. W. Cockerill, *Winning the Radar War* (New York: St. Martin's Press, 1987).

10 Otto Halpern, "Method and Means for Minimizing Reflection of High-Frequency Radio Waves," US Patent 2,923,934, issued February 2, 1960; Winfield W. Salisbury, "Absorbent Body for Electromagnetic Waves," US Patent 2,599,944,

issued June 10, 1952; William H. Emerson, "Electromagnetic Wave Absorbers and Anechoic Chambers through the Years," IEEE *Transactions on Antennas and Propagation* AP-21:4 (July 1973), 484–90. HARP and other approaches using conductive particles worked by absorbing radar and dissipating the energy as heat. The Salisbury Screen worked by reflecting radar waves; spacing the reflective surfaces a quarter wavelength apart caused the reflected waves to interfere destructively with incident waves and cancel them out.

11 "Nazis Were Close to Building Stealth Bomber That Could Have Changed Course of History," *Daily Telegraph*, July 8, 2009; Thomas L. Dobrenz, Aldo Spadoni, and Michael Jorgensen, "Aviation Archeology of the Horten 229 V3 aircraft," 10th AIAA Aviation Technology, Integration, and Operations (ATIO) Conference, *Proceedings*, AIAA report 2010–14 (September 2010), 1–9. See the analysis by the Smithsonian's National Air and Space Museum, "Is It Stealth?" (available at airandspace.si.edu/collections/horten-ho-229-v3/about/is-it-stealth.cfm).

12 Von Hardesty and Ilya Grinberg, *Red Phoenix Rising: The Soviet Air Force in World War II* (Lawrence: University Press of Kansas, 2012), 8; Andrew Krepinevich and Barry Watts, *The Last Warrior: Andrew Marshall and the Shaping of the Modern American Defense Strategy* (New York: Hachette Book Group, 2015), 130–31; Steven J. Zaloga, *The Kremlin's Nuclear Sword: The Rise and Fall of Russia's Strategic Nuclear Forces, 1945–2000* (Washington, DC: Smithsonian Books, 2002), 166–67.

13 Col. Gen. Yuriy Votintsev, "Unknown Troops of an Extinct Superpower," *Voyenno-Istoricheskiy Zhurnal* 9 (1993), 26–38, and 11 (1993), 12–27; Steven J. Zaloga, "Defending the Capitals: The First Generation of Soviet Strategic Air Defense Systems, 1950–1960," *Journal of Slavic Military Studies* 10:4 (1997), 30–43; James D. Crabtree, *On Air Defense* (Westport, CT: Praeger, 1994), 106–13.

14 L. A. DuBridge, E. M. Purcell, G. E. Valley, and G. A. Morton, *Radar and Communications,* vol. 11 of Army Air Forces Scientific Advisory Group, *Toward New Horizons* (Dayton, OH: AAF Scientific Advisory Group, 1946), 166, emphasis in original.

15 William F. Bahret interview by Squire L. Brown, August 22, 2006, Cold War Aerospace Technology History Project, Wright State University Archives.

16 William F. Bahret interview by Squire L. Brown, May 27, 2009, Cold War Aerospace Technology History Project, Wright State University Archives.

17 Bahret interview, August 22, 2006.

18 On another aspect of Ohio State's Cold War research, geodesy, see John Cloud, "Crossing the Olentangy River: The Figure of the Earth and the Military-Industrial-Academic-Complex, 1947–1972," *Studies in History and Philosophy of Modern Physics* 31:3 (2000), 371–404.

19 John Walsh, "Willow Run Laboratories: Separating from the University of Michigan," *Science* 177 (August 18, 1972), 594–96; see also Thomas B.A. Senior, "Radlab History" May 2011 (available at eecs.umich.edu/radlab/images/history.pdf).

20 K. M. Siegel and H. A. Alperin, "Studies in Radar Cross Sections III—Scattering by a Cone," Willow Run Research Center, University of Michigan, report UMM-87 (January 1952); K. M. Siegel et al., "Studies in Radar Cross Sections, XII: Summary of Radar Cross-Section Studies under Project Miro," Willow Run Research Center, University of Michigan, UMM-127 (December 1953); J. W. Crispin, Jr., R. F. Goodrich, and K. M. Siegel, "A Theoretical Method for the Calculation of the Radar Cross Sections of Aircraft and Missiles," July 1959 (available at www.dtic.mil/dtic/tr/fulltext/u2/227695.pdf).

21 Leon Peters Jr., "A Brief History of the ElectroScience Laboratory" (available at https://electroscience.osu.edu/sites/electroscience.osu.edu/files/uploads/about/history.pdf).

22 Kuehl, "The Radar Eye Blinded," 252. On the Quail, see Glenn A. Kent, *Thinking about America's Defense: An Analytical Memoir* (Santa Monica, CA: Rand Corporation, 2008), 149–53.

23 Bernard C. Nalty, *Tactics and Techniques of Electronic Warfare: Electronic Countermeasures in the Air War against North Vietnam, 1965–1973* (Newtown, CT: Defense Lion Publications, 2013); Richard P. Hallion, *Storm over Iraq: Air Power and the Gulf War* (Washington, DC: Smithsonian Books, 1992), 57–61. On the Christmas Bombings: Marshall Michel, *The Eleven Days of Christmas: America's Last Vietnam Battle* (New York: Encounter Books, 2002). On the Arab-Israeli war: Dima Adamsky, *The Culture of Military Innovation* (Stanford, CA: Stanford University Press, 2010), 94, and David C. Aronstein and Albert C. Piccirillo, *Have Blue and the F-117A: Evolution of the "Stealth Fighter"* (Reston, VA: American Institute of Aeronautics and Astonautics, 1997), 11.

24 On American estimates of Soviet capabilities: Phillip A. Karber and Jerald A. Combs, "The United States, NATO, and the Soviet Threat to Western Europe: Military Estimates and Policy Options, 1945–1963," *Diplomatic History* 22:3 (1998), 399–29; on NATO forces and the second Soviet echelon: Michael J. Sterling, "Soviet Reactions to NATO's Emerging Technologies for Deep Attack," RAND report N-2294-AF (August 1985), 3.

25 William E. Odom, *The Collapse of the Soviet Military* (New Haven, CT: Yale University Press, 1998), 722–75; Adamsky, *Culture of Military Innovation*, chap. 2; Mikkel Nadby Rasmussen, *The Risk Society at War: Terror, Technology, and Strategy in the Twenty-First Century* (Cambridge, UK: Cambridge University Press, 2006), 46.

26 The story of the CIA's efforts on Palladium in these paragraphs is taken from Gene Poteat, "Stealth, Countermeasures, and ELINT, 1960–1975" (2008), available at https://www.cia.gov/library/readingroom/docs/stealth_%20count.pdf.

27 Alan Brown interview, November 15, 2010.
28 On the Fighter Mafia: Robert Coram, *Boyd: The Fighter Pilot Who Changed the Art of War* (New York: Hachette Book Group, 2002); Grant Hammond, *The Mind of War: John Boyd and American Security* (Washington, DC: Smithsonian Books, 2004). For a dimmer view of Boyd, see Kent, *Thinking about America's Defense*, 172–79.
29 Brown interview.

CHAPTER TWO: TOMORROWLAND

1 Ann Markusen, Peter Hall, Scott Campbell, and Sabina Dietrick, *Rise of the Gunbelt: The Military Remapping of Industrial America* (New York: Oxford University Press, 1991), 93; on the aerospace industry in Southern California, see also Allen J. Scott, *Technopolis: High-Technology Industry and Regional Development in Southern California* (Berkeley: University of California Press, 1993); Roger Lotchin, *Fortress California, 1910–1961: From Warfare to Welfare* (New York: Oxford University Press, 1992); and Peter J. Westwick, ed., *Blue Sky Metropolis: The Aerospace Century in Southern California* (Berkeley: University of California Press, 2012).
2 Greg Hise, *Magnetic Los Angeles: Planning the Twentieth-Century Metropolis* (Baltimore: Johns Hopkins University Press, 1997), 117; Peter J. Westwick, introduction to Westwick, *Blue Sky Metropolis*, 4; on Chandler and Douglas: David Halberstam, *The Powers That Be* (New York: Knopf, 1975), 114.
3 Richard P. Hallion, "The Impact of the California Institute of Technology on American Air Transport and Aeronautical Development, 1926–1941," appendix 1 in *Legacy of Flight: The Guggenheim Contribution to American Aviation* (Seattle, 1977).
4 Anita Seth, "Los Angeles Aircraft Workers and the Consolidation of Cold War Politics," in Westwick, *Blue Sky Metropolis*, 79–104.
5 Scott, *Technopolis*.
6 George Paulikas interview with Volker Janssen, September 4, 2009.
7 Richard Neutra, *Life and Shape* (New York: Appleton-Century-Crofts, 1962), 207.
8 Carey McWilliams, *Southern California: An Island on the Land* (Salt Lake City: Gibbs Smith. 1946), 369.
9 Kevin Starr, *Golden Dreams: California in an Age of Abundance* (New York: Oxford University Press, 2009), xi, 219.
10 Stuart W. Leslie, "Spaces for the Space Age: William Pereira's Aerospace Modernism," in Westwick, *Blue Sky Metropolis*, 127–58, and Leslie, "Aerospaces: Southern California Architecture in a Cold War World," *History and Technology* 29:4 (2013), 331–68.

11 Starr, *Golden Dreams*, 414; Matt Warshaw, *The History of Surfing* (San Francisco: Chronicle Books, 2010), 48; Jesse Birnbaum and Tim Tyler, "California: A State of Excitement," *Time*, November 7, 1969, 60–66; Wallace Stegner, "California: The Experimental Society," *Saturday Review*, September 23, 1967, 28. Stegner's actual quote: "Like the rest of America, California is unformed, innovative, ahistorical, hedonistic, acquisitive, and energetic—only more so."

12 Norman Mailer, *Of a Fire on the Moon* (New York: Little, Brown, 1970), 430.

13 On intersections of the counterculture with science and technology in the late 1960s and 1970s, see David Kaiser and W. Patrick McCray, *Groovy Science: Knowledge, Innovation, and American Counterculture* (Chicago: University of Chicago Press, 2016).

14 Tom Morgenfeld interview, July 26, 2011.

15 Leslie, "Aerospaces" and "Spaces for the Space Age."

16 Stephanie Young, "'Would Your Questions Spoil My Answers?' Art and Technology at the RAND Corporation," in *Where Minds and Matters Meet: Technology in California and the West*, ed. Volker Janssen (Berkeley: University of California Press, 2012), 293–320; Lawrence Weschler, *Seeing Is Forgetting the Name of the Thing One Sees: A Life of Contemporary Artist Robert Irwin* (Berkeley: University of California Press, 1982), 125–31.

17 Ted Johnson, "A Tour de Force," *Los Angeles Times*, April 20, 1995.

18 On aerospace and surfing, see Peter Westwick and Peter Neushul, *The World in the Curl: An Unconventional History of Surfing* (New York: Crown Publishers (Random House), 2013), 98–103, 106–8, 222–24; on the windsurfer, see James R. Drake, "Wind Surfing: A New Concept in Sailing," RAND report P-4076 (Santa Monica, CA, 1969). Drake obtained the patent on the windsurfer together with his friend Hoyle Schweitzer, though others, most notably S. Newman Darby, claimed to have earlier invented a similar craft. Drake's design, however, became the popular standard.

19 David Livingstone, *Putting Science in Its Place* (Chicago: University of Chicago Press, 2003); on Soviet aircraft: Scott W. Palmer, *Dictatorship of the Air: Aviation Culture and the Fate of Modern Russia* (Cambridge, UK: Cambridge University Press, 2006), and Leon Trilling, "Styles of Military Technical Development: Soviet and U.S. Jet Fighters, 1945–1960," in *Science, Technology, and the Military*, ed. Everett Mendelsohn, Merritt Roe Smith, and Peter Weingart (Dordrecht: Springer, 1988), 155–85.

20 Eric Avila, *Popular Culture in an Age of White Flight: Fear and Fantasy in Suburban Los Angeles* (Berkeley: University of California Press, 2004), 106–44, quote on 115.

21 Neal Gabler, *Walt Disney: The Triumph of the American Imagination* (New York: Knopf, 2006), 580; James D. Skee, "By the Numbers: Confidence, Consultants, and the Construction of Mass Leisure, 1953–1975" (PhD diss., UC

Berkeley, 2016). See also "Disneyland's Enchanted Tiki Room and the Invention of Audio-Animatronics," *Entertainment Designer*, December 3, 2011.

22 Ray Bradbury, "The Machine-Tooled Happyland," *Holiday*, October 1965, 100–104.

23 Richard Scherrer email to Westwick, November 24, 2015.

24 Robert C. Post, *High Performance: The Culture and Performance of Drag Racing, 1950–2000* (Baltimore: Johns Hopkins University Press, 2001), 81–82, 172.

25 On the history of Arrow and Disneyland: Robert Reynolds, *Roller Coasters, Flumes and Flying Saucers* (Minneapolis: Northern Lights, 1999).

26 Scherrer email.

27 Carey McWilliams, *Southern California: An Island on the Land* (Salt Lake City: Gibbs Smith, 1946); Starr, *Golden Dreams*, and other books in Starr's *Americans and the California Dream* series; Mike Davis, *City of Quartz: Excavating the Future in Los Angeles* (New York: Verso, 1992); Avila, *Popular Culture in an Age of White Flight*, 106–44.

28 *Aviation Week* quoted in David Beers, *Blue Sky Dream: A Memoir of America's Fall from Grace* (New York: Doubleday, 1996), 135; job statistics from fig. 1 in Gavin Wright, "World War II, the Cold War, and the Knowledge Economies of the Pacific Coast," paper for conference "World War II and the West It Wrought," Stanford University, April 4–5, 2017. I thank Prof. Wright for permission to cite his paper.

29 Lisa McGirr, *Suburban Warriors: The Origins of the New American Right* (Princeton, NJ: Princeton University Press, 2001), on 240.

30 Michael Davie, *California: The Vanishing Dream* (New York: Dodd, Mead, 1972), xi.

31 David De Voss, "Whatever Happened to California?" *Time*, July 18, 1977.

32 On California as the epitome of "a world of make-believe," see Daniel Bell, *The Cultural Contradictions of Capitalism*, 20th anniversary ed. (New York: Basic Books, 1996), 72.

CHAPTER THREE: BREEDING INVISIBLE RABBITS

1 Sharon Weinberger, *The Imagineers of War: The Untold Story of DARPA, the Pentagon Agency That Changed the World* (New York: Knopf, 2017); Roger Geiger, *Research and Relevant Knowledge: American Research Universities since World War II* (New York: Oxford University Press, 1993), 190–91.

2 William D. O'Neil, "What to Buy? The Role of Director of Defense Research and Engineering (DDR&E): Lessons from the 1970s," Institute for Defense Analyses, IDA paper P-4675 (Alexandria, VA, January 2011), v, 20–22, 49–54.

3 J. J. Martin, memo on DNA New Alternatives Workshop, June 17, 1985 (Albert J. and Roberta Wohlstetter papers, box 88, folder 22, Hoover Institution archives);

Joseph Braddock to Albert Wohlstetter and George Blanchard, February 25, 1985 (Wohlstetter papers, box 89, folder 6); Henry Rowen interview, January 12, 2010; Richard H. Van Atta and Michael J. Lippitz, *Transformation and Transition: DARPA's Role in Fostering an Emerging Revolution in Military Affairs*, vol. 1, *Overall Assessment*, Institute for Defense Analyses, IDA paper P-3698, April 2003 (available at www.fas.org/irp/agency/dod/idarma.pdf), S-2, 6–8; Stephen J. Lukasik, "Towards Discriminate Deterrence," in *Nuclear Heuristics: Selected Writings of Albert and Roberta Wohlstetter*, ed. Robert Zarate and Henry Skolnik (Carlisle, PA: Strategic Studies Institute, 2009), 512–15.

4   For Stealth engineers and model airplanes: Alan Brown interview, November 15, 2010; John Cashen interview, December 15, 2010; James Kinnu interview by Volker Janssen, December 8, 2010; Steven R. Smith interview by Janssen, February 21, 2011. See also John (Jack) C. Duffendack interview by Bill Deverell, Sherman Mullin, and Peter Westwick, June 12, 2008.

5   Philip J. Klass, "Mini-RPVs Tested for Battlefield Use," *Aviation Week and Space Technology*, January 22, 1973, 76–78; Kent Kresa and Col. William F. Kirlin, "The Mini-RPV Program: Big Potential, Small Cost," *Astronautics and Aeronautics*, September 1974, 48–62; Thomas P. Ehrhard, *Air Force UAVs: The Secret History*, Mitchell Institute report, July 2010 (DTIC report ADA526045), 20.

6   Mini-RPV RCS values from Kresa and Kirlin, "The Mini-RPV Program." F-15 RCS value from "Radar Cross Section," www.globalsecurity.org/military/world/stealth-aircraft-rcs.htm.

7   "Stealth" is used in Kresa and Kirlin, "The Mini-RPV Program." For the story about the ZSU-23 test: Cashen interview.

8   Dennis Jarvi, "William Elsner," in *Pioneers of Stealth*, ed. John Griffin (Morrisville, NC: Lulu.com, 2017), 151–52; Irv Waaland interview by Volker Janssen, November 15, 2010; Cashen interview.

9   Waaland interview; Cashen interview; "Ken Perko," in Griffin, *Pioneers of Stealth*, 264–66.

10 Malcolm Currie interview, May 9, 2013; Weinberger, *Imagineers of War*, 246; Van Atta and Lippitz, *Transformation*, 8.

11 David C. Aronstein and Albert C. Piccirillo, *Have Blue and the F-117A: Evolution of the "Stealth Fighter"* (Reston, VA: American Institute of Aeronautics & Astronautics, 1997), 13–14; Weinberger, *Imagineers of War*, 243–44.

12 James P. Stevenson, *The $5 Billion Misunderstanding: The Collapse of the Navy's A-12 Stealth Bomber Program* (Annapolis, MD: Naval Institute Press, 2001), 11–19; Weinberger, *Imagineers of War*, 241–44; O'Neil, "What to Buy," 61–65. Aronstein and Piccirillo say that there was no actual Project Harvey at DARPA, but Stevenson cites memos that refer to it.

13 Aronstein and Piccirillo, *Have Blue and the F-117A*, 13–15.

14 Cashen interview.

15 Currie interview; Aronstein and Piccirillo, *Have Blue and the F-117A*, 28; Jones quoted in O'Neil, "What to Buy," 64–65; Stevenson, *The $5 Billion Misunderstanding*, 19–23.

16 Aronstein and Piccirillo, *Have Blue and the F-117A*, 15; Alan Brown interview, November 15, 2010; Ben R. Rich and Leo Janos, *Skunk Works: A Personal Memoir of My Years at Lockheed* (New York, 1994), 23–25. The sources conflict on which Lockheed engineer got wind of the Stealth contest: some say it was Warren Gilmour (Alan Brown; Rich and Janos); others (Overholser; Aronstein and Piccirillo) say Ed Martin; others (Weinberger and O'Neil, both apparently following Chuck Myers interviews) say Rus Daniell. Weinberger, *Imagineers of War*, 248–49; O'Neil, "What to Buy," 64.

17 McDonnell Douglas had designed a low-radar-cross-section aircraft with a curving planform and curved leading and trailing edges. When the design looked like it would fail, Perko encouraged them to team with Teledyne Ryan, which like McDonnell Douglas had earlier built some of the stealthy RPVs. Aronstein and Piccirillo, *Have Blue and the F-117A*, 26.

18 "Ken Perko," in Griffin, *Pioneers of Stealth*, 264–66; Aronstein and Piccirillo, *Have Blue and the F-117A*, 28–29.

CHAPTER FOUR: LOCKHEED:
TIN SHED IN A HURRICANE

1 For the history of Lockheed, see Walter J. Boyne, *Beyond the Horizons: The Lockheed Story* (New York: St. Martin's Press, 1998); Sherman N. Mullin, "Robert E. Gross and the Rise of Lockheed: The Creative Tension between Engineering and Finance," in *Blue Sky Metropolis: The Aerospace Century in Southern California*, ed. Peter J. Westwick (Berkeley: University of California Press, 2012), 57–78; Wayne Biddle, *Barons of the Sky: From Early Flight to Strategic Warfare: The Story of the American Aerospace Industry* (New York: Simon & Schuster, 1991).

2 Mullin, "Robert E. Gross."

3 Boyne, *Beyond the Horizons*, 358–68, 428.

4 "Performance Problem," assignment for Aeronautics 1, January 1931 (Clarence L. Johnson papers, box 12, folder 1, Huntington Library); Clarence L. Johnson, *Kelly: More than My Share of It All* (Washington, DC: Smithsonian Institution Press, 1985).

5 Johnson, *Kelly*; Ben R. Rich and Leo Janos, *Skunk Works: A Personal Memoir of My Years at Lockheed* (New York: Little, Brown, 1994), 113–14.

6 Johnson, *Kelly*, 139, 161.

7 Ben Rich notebook on aerothermodynamics, c. late 1950s (Ben Rich papers, box 9, folder 1, Huntington Library).

8 Rich and Janos, *Skunk Works*, 62–63, 291.

9 Rich and Janos, *Skunk Works*, 281–89.

10 Paul A. Suhler, *From Rainbow to Gusto: Stealth and the Design of the Lockheed Blackbird* (Reston, VA: American Institute of Aeronautics & Astronautics, 2009), 13–30; Peter W. Merlin, *Images of Aviation: Area 51* (Charleston, SC: Arcadia Publishing, 2011), 26–27.

11 Edward Baldwin, Archangel notebook, 1957–58, and blueprints of B-2 and other models up to the A-11A (Edward P. Baldwin papers, box 1, National Air and Space Museum archives, Udvar-Hazy Center); Suhler, *From Rainbow to Gusto*, 55–86; Edward Lovick Jr., *Radar Man: A Personal History of Stealth* (New York: iUniverse, 2010), 118–19.

12 Frank Rodgers quoted in Suhler, *From Rainbow to Gusto*, 85–86, also on 90; Norm Taylor seconded Rodgers's account. See also Lovick, *Radar Man*, 116–17.

13 Suhler, *From Rainbow to Gusto*, 137, 159, 163.

14 Suhler, *From Rainbow to Gusto*, 11–13, 123, 142.

15 Suhler, *From Rainbow to Gusto*, 172–75.

16 Lovick, *Radar Man*, 125–26; Suhler, *From Rainbow to Gusto*, 197, 203; Merlin, *Images of Aviation*, 63–66.

17 Suhler, *From Rainbow to Gusto*, 180. The B-47, though only a few feet longer than the A-12, had twice the wingspan.

18 Pyotr Ufimtsev interview, October 23, 2016. Unless otherwise indicated, material in these paragraphs is from this interview.

19 P. Ya. Ufimtsev, "The 50-Year Anniversary of the PTD: Comments on the PTD's Origin and Development," IEEE *Antennas and Propagation Magazine* 55:3 (June 2013), 18–28.

20 A. Sommerfeld, "Theorie der Beugung," in *Die Differential- und Integralgleichungen der Mechanik und der Physik*, vol. 2, ed. P. Frank (Physics) (Braunschweig, 1927).

21 J. B. Keller, "Geometrical Theory of Diffraction," *Journal of the Optical Society of America* 52:2 (1962), 116–30.

22 P. Ya. Ufimtsev, *Metod krayevykh Voln v Fizicheskoy Teorii Difraktsii* (Izd-Vo Sovetskoye Radio, 1962), translated as *Method of Edge Waves in the Physical Theory of Diffraction* (report FTD-HC-23-259-71, USAF Foreign Technology Division, September 1971). For a general introduction to Ufimtsev's theory, see Pyotr Y. Ufimtsev, "Comments on Diffraction Principles and Limitations of RCS Reduction Techniques," *Proceedings of the IEEE* 84:12 (1996), 1830–51; also Kenneth Mitzner, foreword to *Theory of Edge Diffraction in Electromagnetics*, ed. Pyotr Ufimtsev (Raleigh, NC: Tech Science Press, 2009), v–x.

23 Ufimtsev interview; Ufimtsev, "50-Year Anniversary of the PTD," 20.

24 Ufimtsev interview.

25 Michael Gordin, *Scientific Babel: How Science Was Done before and after Global English* (Chicago: University of Chicago Press, 2015), 213–66.

26 Kenneth Mitzner interview, January 25, 2016; John Cashen interview, December 16, 2010; Ufimtsev's report is cited as a machine translation in Richard D. Moore, "Translator's Note," in Ufimtsev, *Theory of Edge Diffraction in Electromagnetics*, xiii–xiv.

27 Mitzner, foreword to Ufimtsev, *Theory of Edge Diffraction in Electromagnetics*, v–x, on v. On Soviet contributions to US military technology in the Cold War, such as Stealth and the x-ray laser for SDI, see Peter Westwick, "The International History of the Strategic Defense Initiative: Economic Competition in the Late Cold War," *Centaurus*, 52 (2010), 338–351, and Mihir Pandya, "Security, Information, Infrastructure," talk at American Anthropological Association annual meeting, 2016.

28 Moore, "Translator's Note."

29 Richard Scherrer to Westwick, November 24, 2015; David C. Aronstein and Albert C. Piccirillo, *Have Blue and the F-117A: Evolution of the "Stealth Fighter"* (Reston, VA: Institute of Aeronautics & Astronautics, 1997), 16–17.

30 Lovick, *Radar Man*, 186.

31 Capi Lynn, "Secret Weapon for Stealth Tech Is from Dallas," *Salem Statesman-Journal*, April 16, 2016; Denys Overholser telephone interview, March 9, 2018.

32 Rich in Rich and Janos, *Skunk Works*, 29; Overholser interview.

33 Overholser interview.

34 Overholser interview.

35 Aronstein and Piccirillo, *Have Blue and the F-117A*, 16–18.

36 Aronstein and Piccirillo, *Have Blue and the F-117A*, 18–20.

37 Lovick, *Radar Man*, 187.

38 Rich and Janos, *Skunk Works*, 26.

39 Aronstein and Piccirillo, *Have Blue and the F-117A*, 20–21.

40 Richard Scherrer to John Griffin, August 9, 1996 (courtesy of Scherrer).

41 Andrew Baker interview with Volker Janssen, May 5, 2010; Lovick, *Radar Man*, 188; Scherrer to Westwick; Scherrer to Louis Dachs, June 1, 1994 (courtesy of Scherrer).

42 Brown interview; Aronstein and Piccirillo, *Have Blue and the F-117A*, 21, 30.

43 Brown interview; Scherrer to Griffin.

44 Scherrer to Dachs.

45 Scherrer to Westwick, emphasis added; Rich and Janos, *Skunk Works*, 119.

46 Scherrer to Westwick.

47 Scherrer to Westwick.

48 "F-117A Cost Performance and Contracts History," n.d. (Ben Rich papers, box 2, folder 10); Aronstein and Piccirillo, *Have Blue and the F-117A*, 27–29; James P. Stevenson, *The $5 Billion Misunderstanding: The Collapse of the Navy's A-12 Stealth Bomber Program* (Annapolis, MD: US Naval Institute Press, 2001), 19–23.

49 Ben Rich, handwritten notes on Have Blue, n.d. (Rich papers, box 2, folder 10); on Baldwin's work on the aft fuselage: Sherman Mullin email to Westwick, October 21, 2017.

50 Brown interview.

51 Bill Sweetman, *Inside the Stealth Bomber* (Osceola, WI: Zenith Press, 1999), 50.

52 "Shouting matches" in Aronstein and Piccirillo, *Have Blue and the F-117A*, 30; "tin shed" in Ken Dyson and Robert Loschke interview, January 9, 2012.

CHAPTER FIVE: NORTHROP: SEEING THE WAVES

1 Wayne Biddle, *Barons of the Sky: From Early Flight to Strategic Warfare: The Story of the American Aerospace Industry* (New York: Simon & Schuster, 1991), 68–70, 150–51.

2 Fred Anderson, *Northrop: An Aeronautical History* (Century City, CA: Northrop Corporation, 1976), 1–7; Biddle, *Barons*, 268–69.

3 Tony Chong, *Flying Wings and Radical Things* (Forest Lake, MN: Specialty Press, 2016), 22–25; Anderson, *Northrop*, 44.

4 Chong, *Flying Wings*, 12–13; Biddle, *Barons*, 268.

5 Anderson, *Northrop*, 90–113; Chong, *Flying Wings*, 25, 39–42.

6 Bud Baker, "Clipped Wings: The Death of Jack Northrop's Flying Wing Bombers," *Acquisition Review Quarterly* 8:3 (2001), 197–219; Biddle, *Barons*, 314–15. Northrop dated the meeting to 1949, but it most likely occurred in July 1948.

7 Baker, "Clipped Wings."

8 Douglas A. Lawson, "Pterosaur from the Latest Cretaceous of West Texas: Discovery of the Largest Flying Creature," *Science* 187 (March 14, 1975), 947–48, and "Could Pterosaurs Fly?" *Science* 188 (May 15, 1975), 676–77; Malcolm W. Browne, "2 Rival Designers Led the Way to Stealthy Warplanes," *New York Times*, May 14, 1991.

9 "Technology: A Place in Space," *Time* (October 27, 1961), 89–94. For Jones's biography, see Thomas V. Jones interviews with William Deverell and Dan Lewis, October 10, 2005, with William Deverell, March 3, 2006, and with Peter Westwick, February 16, 2010; "Thomas V. Jones," *Aviation Week & Space Technology* 176:1 (January 13, 2014), 11; Ralph Vartabedian, "Thomas V. Jones," *Los Angeles Times*, January 9, 2014.

10 Bill Sing and Jonathon Peterson, "Northrop's Jones to Retire," *Los Angeles Times*, April 21, 1989; George White, "Maverick Who Helped Build Northrop

Leaves," *Los Angeles Times*, September 20, 1990; Ralph Vartabedian, "Thomas V. Jones," *Los Angeles Times*, January 9, 2014.

11 Jones interview with Westwick. I thank Tony Chong for the correct sales figures for the F-5 and T-38.

12 John Newhouse, *The Sporty Game* (New York: Knopf, 1982), 57; *Northrop Annual Report,* 1974 (ProQuest historical annual reports).

13 Sing and Peterson, "Northrop's Jones to Retire"; White, "Maverick Who Helped Build Northrop Leaves"; Vartabedian, "Thomas V. Jones."

14 *Northrop Annual Report,* 1960 and 1974 (ProQuest historical annual reports); Harold D. Watkins ["weathering"], "Notoriety or Not, Northrop, Jones Going Strong," *Los Angeles Times*, November 30, 1975; "Jones Reinstated as Northrop Chief," *Los Angeles Times*, February 19, 1976.

15 "Technology: A Place in Space."

16 On emergence of the term: *Oxford English Dictionary*, s.v. "aerospace."

17 "SM-62: Analysis of Weapon System Effectiveness," Northrop Corporation, n.d. (c. 1957) (Northrop Grumman historical files [hereafter NGC], box 183, folder 7, Huntington Library); "Snark-infested waters" is in Kenneth P. Werrell, "The Evolution of the Cruise Missile," Air University Press, September 1985 (NGC, box 183, folder 13), and Werrell, "Northrop Snark: The Case Study of Failure," American Aviation Historical Society *Journal* (Fall 1988), 191–204; Jones quoted in Julian Hartt, "This Deterrent Missile Can Force Foe out of Business," *LA Examiner*, October 20, 1959.

18 Moe Star obituary, *Los Angeles Times*, June 3, 2010; Cynthia Sanz, "Brooklyn's Polytech, a Storybook Success," *New York Times*, January 5, 1986. The obituary lists Star's college as City College of New York, but Ken Mitzner says Star went to Brooklyn Poly, which seems a more likely story given its strength in radar electronics. Kenneth Mitzner interview, January 25, 2016.

19 Mitzner interview; John Cashen interview, April 25, 2014 (hereafter Cashen 2); Irv Waaland interview, October 7, 2015.

20 Jones interview with Westwick; David C. Aronstein and Albert C. Piccirillo, *Have Blue and the F-117A: Evolution of the "Stealth Fighter"* (Reston, VA: American Institute of Aeronautis & Astronautics, 1997), 24.

21 J. W. Crispin Jr., R. F. Goodrich, and K. M. Siegel, "A Theoretical Method for the Calculation of the Radar Cross Sections of Aircraft and Missiles," July 1959 (available at http://www.dtic.mil/dtic/tr/fulltext/u2/227695.pdf), 117, 133.

22 John Cashen interview, December 15, 2010 (hereafter Cashen 1); Paul Kaminski interview, September 20, 2017. See also William F. Bahret interview with Squire Brown, May 27, 2009, Wright State University Archives. On British contributions: Bill Sweetman, "Technically Speaking: Stealth before Stealth," *Air and Space Magazine*, April 2016.

23 Fred K. Oshiro and Charles W. Su, "A Source Distribution Technique for the Solution of General Electromagnetic Scattering Problems: Phase I Report,"

Northrop Corporation report NOR-65–271, October 13, 1965 (available at www.dtic.mil/get-tr-doc/pdf?AD=AD0624586), 1.

24 Oshiro and Wu, "A Source Distribution Technique."

25 Denys Overholser telephone interview, March 9, 2018.

26 Northrop Aircraft Division, "Engineering Capabilities," August 31, 1971 (NGC, box 184, folder 25).

27 Cashen 1.

28 Source for this and preceding paragraphs: Cashen 1.

29 Cashen 2; Ben R. Rich and Leo Janos, *Skunk Works: A Personal Memoir of My Years at Lockheed* (New York: Little, Brown, 1994), 306.

30 Waaland interview with Volker Janssen, November 10, 2010.

31 Cashen 1 and 2; Waaland interview with Westwick; Kinnu; Hal Maninger interview, September 28, 2017.

32 Waaland interview with Westwick.

33 Cashen 1; Waaland interview with Westwick.

34 Sybil Francis, "Warhead Politics: Livermore and the Competitive System of Nuclear Weapon Design" (PhD dissertation, MIT, 1996); Anne Fitzpatrick, "Igniting the Elements: The Los Alamos Thermonuclear Project, 1942–1952," Los Alamos National Laboratory, LA-13577-T, July 1999.

35 Paul Ceruzzi, *Beyond the Limits: Flight Enters the Computer Age* (Cambridge, MA: MIT Press, 1989), 20–30.

36 Cashen 2; Ken Dyson and Robert Loschke interview, January 9, 2012.

37 Waaland interview with Westwick.

CHAPTER SIX: SHOWDOWN AT RATSCAT

1 Ryan H. Edgington, *Range Wars: The Environmental Contest for White Sands Missile Range* (Lincoln: University of Nebraska Press, 2014).

2 H. C. Marlow et al., "The RAT SCAT Cross-Section Facility," *Proceedings of the IEEE* 53:8 (1965), 946–54.

3 David C. Aronstein and Albert C. Piccirillo, *Have Blue and the F-117A: Evolution of the "Stealth Fighter"* (Reston, VA: American Institute of Aeronautics & Astronautics, 1997), 31–32; Edward Lovick Jr., *Radar Man: A Personal History of Stealth* (New York: iUniverse, 2010), 191–92; Denys Overholser interview, March 9, 2018.

4 Lovick, *Radar Man*, 193; Carl S. Carter, "White Gypsum Footprints," in *Pioneers of Stealth*, ed. John Griffin (Morrisville, NC: Lulu.com, 2017), 354–55.

5 Lovick, *Radar Man*, 193, 196.

6 John Cashen interview, December 15, 2010 (hereafter Cashen 1).

7 M. P. O'Brien in 1962, quoted in Sherman N. Mullin, "Military Aircraft Engineering Manager: The First Two Years, 1968–1970," unpublished paper.

8   Cashen 1.

9   Bill Sweetman, "Invisible Men," *Air & Space*, April/May 1997, 24.

10 John Cashen interview, April 25, 2014 (hereafter Cashen 2).

11 Cashen 2 (including Rivas quote); Kenneth Mitzner interview, January 25, 2016.

12 E.g., Kai Bird and Martin J. Sherwin, *American Prometheus: The Triumph and Tragedy of J. Robert Oppenheimer* (New York: Vintage, 2005), 256; Richard Rhodes, *The Making of the Atomic Bomb* (New York: Simon & Schuster, 1986); *The Day after Trinity*, documentary, dir. Jon Else (1981). Cashen made the analogy explicit, by consciously modeling Northrop engineering meetings on Oppenheimer's colloquia at Los Alamos (Cashen 1).

13 Irving Waaland interview with Westwick, October 7, 2015.

14 Overholser in Ben R. Rich and Leo Janos, *Skunk Works: A Personal Memoir of My Years at Lockheed* (New York: Little, Brown, 1994), 36.

15 Alan Brown interview, November 15, 2010; Aronstein and Piccirillo, *Have Blue and the F-117A*, 32.

16 Ken Dyson and Robert Loschke interview, January 9, 2012; Brown interview.

17 Overholser interview; Cashen email to Westwick, March 12, 2018.

18 Lovick attributes the ball-bearing idea to Ed Martin (*Radar Man*, 189–90). Overholser attributes it to Merrill Skolnik, a radar expert at Lincoln Lab who brought up the ball bearing as a way to *ridicule* Lockheed's claims (Overholser interview).

19 Lovick, *Radar Man*, 190. Lovick gives the radar frequency as 15 GHz, although that may be too high.

20 Brown interview; Cashen 1; Waaland interview with Westwick. On Damaskos's earlier role on the SR-71: Lovick, *Radar Man*.

21 Alan Brown email to author, September 22, 2018.

22 Cashen 1; Irv Waaland interview with Volker Janssen, November 15, 2010; Brown interview; Ben Rich, handwritten notes on Have Blue, n.d. (Ben Rich papers, box 2, folder 10, Huntington Library).

23 Overholser interview.

24 Waaland interview with Janssen; Cashen 1.

25 Rebecca Grant, *B-2: The Spirit of Innovation*, Northrop Grumman Aeronautical Systems, report NGAS 13–0405 (2013, available at www.northropgrumman .com/Capabilities/B2SpiritBomber/Documents/pageDocuments/B-2-Spirit-of-Innovation.pdf), 11.

CHAPTER SEVEN: HAVE BLUE AND THE F-117A

1   David A. Mindell, *Digital Apollo: Human and Machine in Spaceflight* (Cambridge, MA: MIT Press, 2008); Paul Ceruzzi, *Beyond the Limits: Flight Enters the Computer Age* (Cambridge, MA: MIT Press, 1989), 191–95. On

test pilots as cowboys: Westwick, "An Album of Early Southern California Aviation," in *Blue Sky Metropolis: The Aerospace Century in Southern California*, ed. Peter J. Westwick (Berkeley: University of California Press, 2012), 24.

2   Robert Loschke and Ken Dyson interview, January 9, 2012.

3   Robert Ferguson, *NASA's First A: Aeronautics from 1958 to 2008* (Washington, DC: NASA, 2013), 107–13.

4   Loschke-Dyson interview; Robert Loschke emails to Westwick, January 30 and February 1, 2019.

5   Sherman N. Mullin, "Robert E. Gross and the Rise of Lockheed: The Creative Tension between Engineering and Finance," in Westwick, *Blue Sky Metropolis*, 57–78.

6   Mindell, *Digital Apollo*, 33.

7   Sherman Mullin email to author, October 4, 2013.

8   Mindell, *Digital Apollo*, 51–54; Glenn E. Bugos, *Atmosphere of Freedom: Sixty Years at the NASA Ames Research Center*, NASA SP-4314 (Washington, DC, 2000), 69–72.

9   Loschke-Dyson interview. The simulators were not in Burbank with the rest of the Skunk Works but about 25 miles north, in Rye Canyon. They ran the simulator sessions at night, since they involved pilots and engineers not usually seen around Rye Canyon, and Lockheed didn't want the regular staff to start asking awkward questions.

10   Tom Morgenfeld interview, July 26, 2011

11   Loschke-Dyson interview; David C. Aronstein and Albert C. Piccirillo, *Have Blue and the F-117A: Evolution of the "Stealth Fighter"* (Reston, VA: American Institute of Aeronatics and Astronautics, 1997), 42–43.

12   Loschke-Dyson interview.

13   Michael J. Neufeld, *Von Braun: Dreamer of Space, Engineer of War* (New York: Knopf, 2007), 38, 302.

14   Lou Lenzi quoted in Charles Fishman, "The Insourcing Boom," *Atlantic*, December 2012; Ben Heineman Jr., "Why We Can All Stop Worrying about Offshoring and Outsourcing," *Atlantic*, March 26, 2013.

15   Larry Kibble interview, May 15, 2014.

16   Kibble interview; Ben Rich, handwritten notes on Have Blue, n.d. (Ben Rich papers, box 2, folder 10, Huntington Library)

17   Rich, handwritten notes on Have Blue. For the F-117 the Skunk Works switched to a sprayed-on coating: Les Jonkey interview, March 5, 2009.

18   Rich, handwritten notes on Have Blue; Kelly Johnson quote from Paul Ciotti, "Tempest in a Toy Box," *Los Angeles Times*, October 19, 1986. On titanium ore for the SR-71 from the USSR: Clarence L. Johnson, *Kelly: More than My Share of It All* (Washington, DC: Smithsonian Books, 1985), 186.

19 Kibble interview.

20 Robert Murphy interview with Volker Janssen, August 25, 2009, and Volker Janssen field notes on Murphy interview, August 26, 2009.

21 "Boeing Workers Return; Talks at Lockheed Stalled," *Washington Post*, November 19, 1977; Leon Bornstein, "Industrial Relations in 1977: Highlights of Key Developments," *Monthly Labor Review* 101 (February 1978), 24–31, 30. Lockheed and the striking workers settled on a new contract in late December 1977.

22 Murphy interview; Loschke-Dyson interview.

23 Phil Patton, *Dreamland: Travels inside the Secret World of Roswell and Area 51* (New York: Random House, 1998); Peter W. Merlin, *Images of Aviation: Area 51* (Charleston, SC: Arcadia Publishing Library, 2011); see also Annie Jacobsen, *Area 51: An Uncensored History of America's Top Secret Military Base* (New York: Little, Brown, 2011), 100.

24 Patton, *Dreamland*; Merlin, *Area 51*.

25 Ralph Vartabedian, "Now It Can Be Said—He Has the Right Stuff," *Los Angeles Times*, September 29, 1989; Patton, *Dreamland*, 132–33.

26 Morgenfeld interview.

27 Mindell, *Digital Apollo*, 29.

28 Patton, *Dreamland*, 135–37.

29 "Baja Groom Lake": Merlin, *Images of Aviation*, 105.

30 Morgenfeld interview; Merlin, *Images of Aviation*, 52, 55, 116. On RC model planes: Jacobsen, *Area 51*, 243.

31 Morgenfeld interview.

32 Rich and Janos, *Skunk Works: A Personal Memoir of My Years at Lockheed* (New York: Little, Brown, 1994), 53.

33 Murphy interview.

34 Loschke-Dyson interview.

35 Loschke-Dyson interview; Rich, handwritten notes on Have Blue.

36 Loschke-Dyson interview.

37 Bill Park in Rich and Janos, *Skunk Works*, 57–61; Loschke-Dyson interview.

38 Loschke-Dyson; Loschke email to Westwick, March 11, 2019. The pressure probes and ports were not heated for anti-icing, so neither Have Blue aircraft could be flown in clouds.

39 Loschke-Dyson; "Ken Dyson," in John Griffin, ed., *Pioneers of Stealth* (Morrisville, NC: Lulu.com, 2017), 138–42.

40 Rich, handwritten notes on Have Blue.

41 Paul Kaminski interview, September 20, 2017.

42 Lew Allen interview, December 10, 2001.

43 William J. Perry, *My Journey at the Nuclear Brink* (Stanford, CA: Stanford University Press, 2015), 28–38; Perry phone interview, October 17, 2018;

Richard H. Van Atta and Michael J. Lippitz, *Transformation and Transition: DARPA's Role in Fostering an Emerging Revolution in Military Affairs*, vol. 1, *Overall Assessment*, Institute for Defense Analyses paper P-3698, April 2003 (available at www.fas.org/irp/agency/dod/idarma.pdf), S-2; Robert R. Tomes, "A Historical Review of U.S. Defense Strategy from Vietnam to Operation Iraqi Freedom," *Defense and Security Analysis* 28:4 (2012), 303–15.

44 Kaminski interview.

45 Sweetman, "Invisible Men," 26.

46 Alan Brown, "Color of the F-117," and "Sherman N. Mullin," in Griffin, *Pioneers of Stealth*, 355, 251.

47 "F-117A Cost Performance and Contracts History," n.d. (Ben Rich papers, box 2, folder 10).

48 "F-117A Cost Performance."

49 Rich, handwritten notes on Have Blue.

50 John Newhouse, *The Sporty Game* (New York, 1982), 35, 170–71, 181.

51 "F-117A Cost Performance"; Rich and Janos, *Skunk Works*, 71, 74.

52 Murphy interview; "F-117A Cost Performance"; Rich and Janos, *Skunk Works*, 74; David J. Lynch, "How the Skunk Works Fielded Stealth," *Air Force Magazine*, November 1992, 22–28. On a couple of hundred workers for Have Blue: Loschke-Dyson interview.

53 "F-117A Cost Performance."

54 Merlin, *Area 51*, 113.

55 Alan Brown in Rich and Janos, *Skunk Works*, 84–85.

56 Rich and Janos, *Skunk Works*, 89–90; Mullin in Griffin, *Pioneers of Stealth*, 250.

57 Morgenfeld interview; Vincent T. Baker in Griffin, *Pioneers of Stealth*, 77. The design engineers had planned the plane to be able to fly and land even if one tail fin was missing: Alan Brown, "Lockheed F-117A Design Story" (powerpoint presentation courtesy of Alan Brown).

58 Morgenfeld interview.

59 Sherman N. Mullin, "Aerospace Engineer, the Easy Way" (copy courtesy of Mullin); Mullin in Griffin, *Pioneers of Stealth*, 250–51.

60 Alan Brown emails to Westwick, January 28, 29, 2019; Sherman Mullin interview, January 24, 2019; Aronstein and Piccirillo, *Have Blue and the F-117A*, 95–97. The wires in the grid did not cross at right angles; to avoid radar return from the wires themselves, the grids were aligned with the wing trailing edges.

61 "F-117A Cost Performance."

62 Annie Jacobsen, *The Pentagon's Brain: An Uncensored History of DARPA, America's Top Secret Military Research Agency* (New York: Little, Brown, 2015), 242.

63 Paul Ciotti, "Tempest in a Toy Box," *Los Angeles Times*, October 19, 1986; Patton, *Dreamland*, 150–51, 161; Patricia Trenner, "A Short (Very Short) History of the F-19," *Air & Space Magazine*, January 2008.

64 Melissa Healy, "Pentagon Ends Long Silence on Stealth Fighter," *Los Angeles Times*, November 11, 1988.

65 George C. Wilson, "'Stealth' Plane Used in Panama," *Washington Post*, December 24, 1989; Michael R. Gordon, "Stealth's Panama Mission Reported Marred by Error," *New York Times*, April 4, 1990; Aronstein and Piccirillo, *Have Blue and the F-117A*, 154.

CHAPTER EIGHT: SECRETS AND STRATEGIES

1 Mihir Pandya, "The Vanishing Act: Stealth Airplanes and Cold War Southern California," in *Blue Sky Metropolis: The Aerospace Century in Southern California*, ed. Peter J. Westwick (Berkeley: University of California Press, 2012), 105–26; on the evolution of Stealth's classification, see David C. Aronstein and Albert C. Piccirillo, *Have Blue and the F-117A: Evolution of the "Stealth Fighter"* (Reston, VA: American Institute of Aeronautics and Astronautics, 1997), 33–34.

2 Gus Weiss, "The Farewell Dossier: Duping the Soviets," *Studies in Intelligence* 39:5 (1996, available online at https://www.cia.gov/library/center-for-the-study-of-intelligence/csi-publications/csi-studies/studies/96unclass/farewell .htm). See also Thomas C. Reed, *At the Abyss: An Insider's History of the Cold War* (New York: Ballantine Books, 2004), 266–70.

3 Bulat Galeyev, "Light and Shadows of a Great Life: Leon Theremin, Pioneer of Electronic Art," *Leonardo Music Journal* 6 (1996): 45–48. On daily hassles, see Hugh Gusterson, *Nuclear Rites: A Weapons Laboratory at the End of the Cold War* (Berkeley: University of California Press, 1996), 69–79.

4 Peter Galison, "Removing Knowledge," *Critical Inquiry* 31 (Fall 2004), 229–43. In addition to estimating the number of classified documents, Galison reports that four million people in the US had security clearances at the time of his writing. With a total US population of 292 million, assuming an adult population of 75 percent gives a ratio of about one clearance per 55 adults. See also Brian Fung, "5.1 Million Americans Have Security Clearances," *Washington Post*, March 24, 2014.

5 Pandya, "The Vanishing Act."

6 William Perry phone interview, October 17, 2018; Paul Kaminski interview, September 20, 2017. Sen. Sam Nunn in particular was a crucial advocate for Stealth.

7 Stanley Goldberg, "General Groves and the Atomic West: The Making and the Meaning of Hanford," in *The Atomic West*, ed. Bruce Hevly and John M. Findlay (Seattle: University of Washington Press, 1998), , 61, 65–70.

8 Edward A. Shils, *The Torment of Secrecy* (Glencoe, IL: The Free Press, 1956); Sissela Bok, *Secrets: On the Ethics of Concealment and Revelation* (New

York: Pantheon, 1982); Herbert M. Foerstel, *Secret Science: Federal Control of American Science and Technology* (Westport, CT: Praeger, 1993); Daniel Patrick Moynihan, *Secrecy: The American Experience* (New Haven, CT: Yale University Press, 1998); Judith Reppy, ed., *Secrecy and Knowledge Production*, Cornell University, Peace Studies Program, Occasional Paper 23 (October 1999).

9   John Cashen interview, December 15, 2010.

10 Ed Zardorozni comments at CSULB workshop "The Cold War Home Front," July 30, 2014, Aerospace Legacy Foundation, Downey, CA.

11 "Industry Observer," *Aviation Week & Space Technology*, June 23, 1975, 9.

12 Jim Cunningham, "Cracks in the Black Dike: Secrecy, the Media, and the F-117A," *Airpower Journal*, Fall 1991.

13 CIA Directorate of Intelligence, "US Stealth Programs and Technology: Soviet Exploitation of the Western Press," August 1, 1988 (available at https://www .cia.gov/library/readingroom/docs/DOC_0000500640.pdf), quotes on 2.

14 Transcript of press conference, August 22, 1980, in J. Jones, *Stealth Technology: The Art of Black Magic* (Blue Ridge Summit, PA: AERO, 1989), 3–12; Perry interview; Verne Orr, "Developing Strategic Weaponry and the Political Process: The B1-B Bomber: From Drawing Board to Flight" (PhD diss., Claremont Graduate University, 2005), 100–112.

15 *Leaks of Classified National Defense Information—Stealth Aircraft*, Report of the Investigations Subcommittee of the Committee on Armed Services, House of Representatives, 96th Congress, 2nd session (Washington, DC, 1980).

16 The House Armed Services Committee had a number of strong backers of the B-1, which helps explains its opposition to the Stealth bomber.

17 H. Bruce Franklin, *War Stars: The Superweapon and the American Imagination* (New York: Oxford University Press, 1988); David E. Nye, *American Technological Sublime* (Cambridge, MA: MIT Press, 1994).

18 Perry interview.

19 Jones, *Stealth Technology*, 3–12.

20 V. D. Sokolovskii, *Soviet Military Strategy*, trans. Herbert S. Dinerstein, Leon Gouré, and Thomas W. Wolfe, RAND report R-416-PR (Santa Monica, CA, 1963).

21 E.g., Col. Gen. M. A. Gareyev, "The Creative Nature of Soviet Military Science in the Great Patriotic War," *Voyenno-Istoricheskiy Zhurnal* 7 (July 7, 1985), translation in JPRS UMA-85-060; William Odom, "Soviet Force Posture," *Problems of Communism* 34:4 (1985), 1–14; Dale R. Herspring, "Nikolay Ogarkov and the Scientific-Technical Revolution in Soviet Military Affairs," *Comparative Strategy* 6:1 (1987), 29–59; Andrew Krepinevich, "The Military-Technical Revolution: A Preliminary Assessment," Office of Net Assessment (July 1992, available at www.csbaonline.org); Eliot A. Cohen, "A Revolution in Warfare," *Foreign Affairs* 75:2 (1996), 37–54; Dima Adamsky, *The Culture of Military Innovation: The Impact of Cultural Factors on the Revolution in*

Military Affairs in Russia, the US, and Israel (Stanford, CA: Stanford University Press, 2010), 27–31; Andrew Krepinevich and Barry Watts, *The Last Warrior: Andrew Marshall and the Shaping of Modern American Defense Strategy* (New York: Basic Books, 2015), 194.

22 Williamson Murray and MacGregor Knox, "Thinking about Revolutions in Warfare," in *The Dynamics of Military Revolution, 1300–2015*, ed. Murray and Knox (Cambridge, 2001), 2; Mikkel Nadby Rasmussen, *The Risk Society at War: Terror, Technology, and Strategy in the Twenty-First Century* (Cambridge: Cambridge University Press, 2006), 45–46; Adamsky, *The Culture of Military Innovation*, 39–44.

23 Julian Cooper, "The Scientific and Technical Revolution in Soviet Theory," in *Technology and Communist Culture: The Socio-Cultural Impact of Technology under Socialism*, ed. Frederic J. Fleron (New York: Praeger, 1977), 146–79; Erik P. Hoffmann, "Soviet Views of 'The Scientific-Technological Revolution,'" *World Politics* 30:4 (July 1978), 615–44.

24 Steven J. Zaloga, *The Kremlin's Nuclear Sword: The Rise and Fall of Russia's Strategic Nuclear Forces, 1945–2000* (Washington, DC: Smithsonian Books, 2002), vii.

25 Ogarkov quoted in Leslie Gelb, "Foreign Affairs: Who Won the Cold War?" *New York Times* op-ed, August 20, 1992.

26 Clifford G. Gaddy, *The Price of the Past: Russia's Struggle with the Legacy of a Militarized Economy* (Washington, DC: Brookings Institution Press, 1996), 33–46; Odom, "Soviet Force Posture," 11.

27 Gaddy, *The Price of the Past*, 53–54. Ogarkov had also antagonized the defense minister, Ustinov, by opposing the invasion of Afghanistan.

28 Quoted in Murray and Knox, "Thinking about Revolutions in Warfare," 3.

29 Ron Robin, *The Cold World They Made: The Strategic Legacy of Roberta and Albert Wohlstetter* (Cambridge, MA: Harvard University Press, 2016), quote on 4.

30 Albert Wohlstetter, "Outline for a DoD-Wide Two Year Program on the New Defense Policy and New Technologies," July 11, 1982 (Albert J. and Roberta Wohlstetter papers, box 117, folder 20, Hoover Institution archives; hereafter Wohlstetter, [box]/[folder]).

31 Wohlstetter, notes on improved technology, June–July 1982 (Wohlstetter, 117/16). On Afghanistan ("empty threats"): Wohlstetter, "Notes on Wartime Challenges to Soviet Control," October 22, 1982 (Wohlstetter, 117/22). On the Freeze movement: Wohlstetter notes for talk at New Alternatives workshop, November 22–23, 1982 (Wohlstetter, 86/8).

32 Wohlstetter, notes on improved technology; Wohlstetter, notes for talk at New Alternatives workshop; "Suicidally indiscriminate" quote from Wohlstetter, "The Basic Premises of LRRD II," March 1986 (Wohlstetter, 89/12).

33 Richard Brody, notes on improved technology, June 9, 1982 (Wohlstetter, 117/16).

34 DNA New Alternatives Workshop, "New Strategies, New Technologies and the Changing Threat," November 22–23, 1982 (Wohlstetter, 86/5); DNA New Alternatives Workshop agenda, October 25–26, 1983 (Wohlstetter, 87/14); DNA New Alternatives Workshop agenda, April 24–26, 1984 (Wohlstetter, 88/5); J. J. Martin, memo on DNA New Alternatives Workshop, June 17, 1985 (Wohlstetter, 88/22); Wohlstetter, "The Basic Premises of LRRD II."

35 J. J. Martin to Albert Wohlstetter, May 8, 1986 (Wohlstetter, 89/12).

36 President Ronald Reagan, "Address to the Nation on Defense and National Security," March 23, 1983 (available at reaganlibrary.archives.gov/archives/speeches/1983/32383d.htm).

37 Wohlstetter, "Thoughts after the President's Speech on Defense," March 23, 1983 (Wohlstetter, 180/7).

38 George Keyworth to Fred Iklé, May 16, 1985, SDI collection, box 1, folder 1985, Ronald Reagan Presidential Library, Simi Valley, CA.

39 Wohlstetter, "The Problem of Technology Transfer," June 1982 (Wohlstetter, 117/17).

40 Wohlstetter, "A Note on the Costs and Horrors of Conventional War," July 16, 1983 (Wohlstetter, 117/26).

41 James Fallows, "America's High-Tech Weaponry," *Atlantic* 247 (May 1981), 21; James Fallows, *National Defense* (New York: Random House, 1981); Mary Kaldor, *The Baroque Arsenal* (New York: Hill & Wang, 1981). See also Max Boot, *War Made New* (New York: Gotham Books, 2006), 329.

42 Jeffrey Record, "The Military Reform Caucus," *Washington Quarterly* 6:2 (June 1983), 125–29.

43 On Iklé participation: "Suggested FCI [Fred Iklé] Introduction to NAW [New Alternatives Workshop]: Balanced Offense and Defense to Strengthen Deterrence," April 20, 1984 (Wohlstetter, 88/6).

44 The Commission on Integrated Long-Term Strategy (Fred C. Iklé and Albert Wohlstetter, cochairmen), *Discriminate Deterrence*, January 1988, 8. See also Krepinevich and Watts, *The Last Warrior*, 175–76, and C. Richard Nelson, *The Life and Work of General Andrew J. Goodpaster* (Lanham, MD: Roman & Littlefield, 2016), 267.

45 Stephen I. Schwartz, *Atomic Audit: The Costs and Consequences of U.S. Nuclear Weapons since 1940* (Washington, DC: Brookings Institution Press, 1998).

46 Wohlstetter, "Notes for Bud and for AW/RW [Albert and Roberta Wohlstetter] on Arms Agreements," August 25, 1984 (Wohlsteter, 118/6).

CHAPTER NINE: THE WHALE

1 Michael J. Sterling, "Soviet Reactions to NATO's Emerging Technologies for Deep Attack," RAND report N-2294-AF (December 1985); Richard P. Hallion, *Storm over Iraq: Air Power and the Gulf War* (Washington, DC:

Smithsonian Books, 1992), 75–82; Robert R. Tomes, "An Historical Review of US Defense Strategy from Vietnam to Operation Iraqi Freedom," *Defense and Security Analysis* 28:4 (2012), 303–15.

2 Richard H. Van Atta, Jack Nunn, and Alethia Cook, "Assault Breaker," in Van Atta et al., *Transformation and Transition: DARPA's Role in Fostering an Emerging Revolution in Military Affairs*, vol. 2, *Detailed Assessments*, Institute for Defense Analyses paper P-3698 (Alexandria, VA: Institute for Defense Analyses, November 2003), IV:1–IV:39.

3 Glenn A. Kent, *Thinking about America's Defense: An Analytical Memoir* (Santa Monica, CA: Rand Corporation, 2008), 184–88; John Cashen interview, April 25, 2014 (hereafter Cashen 2).

4 Cashen 2; Irv Waaland interview, October 7, 2015.

5 Cashen comments to Westwick, October 19, 2018.

6 Cashen 2 and Cashen interview, December 15, 2010 (hereafter Cashen 1); Waaland interview, October 7, 2015.

7 Waaland says it was 10 degrees sweep (Waaland interview); Cashen says it was 15 degrees (Cashen 2).

8 Cashen 1.

9 Cashen 1.

10 Albert C. Piccirillo, "The Clark Y Airfoil: A Historical Retrospective," paper presented to World Aviation Conference, October 10–12, 2000 (SAE/AIAA paper 2000-01-5517).

11 Waaland interview; Cashen 1.

12 Waaland interview; Cashen 1.

13 Kenneth Mitzner interview, January 25, 2016.

14 Waaland interview; Cashen 1.

15 Cashen 1 and 2; Mitzner interview.

16 Waaland interview; Cashen 2.

17 Irv Waaland interview with Volker Janssen, November 10, 2010; Cashen 2.

18 Richard Scherrer to David Aronstein, July 17, 1998 (Scherrer personal files).

19 Scherrer to Aronstein.

20 Waaland interview with Janssen; Waaland interview; Cashen 2. Cashen's and Waaland's accounts differ on a few details. In particular, Cashen recalls that DARPA managers specifically suggested Northrop try a flying wing; Waaland doesn't recall DARPA suggesting a specific design but says it was clear that only a flying wing could meet DARPA's target radar-cross-section number.

21 Hal Maninger interview, September 28, 2017.

22 Steven R. Smith interview with Volker Janssen, February 21, 2011. On Lockheed in Iran: Al Stacey interview, June 4, 2012.

23 Cashen 2.

24 On lofting in the aircraft industry: Forrest MacDonald interview, February 2, 2012; Waaland interview with Janssen.

25 Waaland interview with Janssen; Waaland interview; Mitzner interview; Cashen 2.

26 Waaland interview with Janssen; Waaland interview; Cashen 2.

27 Cashen 2.

28 Smith interview.

29 Robert E. Wulf in *Pioneers of Stealth*, ed. John Griffin (Morrisville, NC: Lulu. com, 2017), 346.

30 Cynda Thomas and Velvet Thomas, *Hell of a Ride* (Bloomington:iUniverse, 2008), 141–43.

31 Cashen 2.

32 Thomas and Thomas, *Hell of a Ride*, 3–5, 94–114.

33 Cashen 2.

34 Thomas and Thomas, *Hell of a Ride*, 147–48.

CHAPTER TEN: FACETS VERSUS CURVES

1 Richard Smoke, *National Security and the Nuclear Dilemma*, 3rd ed. (New York: Random House, 1993), 207–15; Donald MacKenzie, *Inventing Accuracy: A Historical Sociology of Nuclear Missile Guidance* (Cambridge, MA: MIT Press, 1993), 225–29.

2 Donald C. Daniel, *The Future of Strategic ASW*, Naval War College technical report 11–90 (Newport, RI, August 1, 1990), 16. On blue-green laser and Gorshkov: Ed Frieman interview, November 28, 2007; on SAR: Peter J. Westwick, *Into the Black: JPL and the American Space Program* (New Haven, CT: Yale University Press, 2007), 97.

3 Kenneth P. Werrell, *The Evolution of the Cruise Missile*, Air University, Maxwell Air Force Base, September 1985 (available at www.dtic.mil/dtic/tr/ fulltext/u2/a162646.pdf), 136–39, 156–64.

4 Nick Kotz, *Wild Blue Yonder: Money, Politics, and the B-1 Bomber* (New York: Pantheon, 1988), 153, 161–68; Verne Orr, "Developing Strategic Weaponry and the Political Process: The B1-B Bomber: From Drawing Board to Flight" (PhD diss., Claremont Graduate University, 2005), 100–12; transcript of Harold Brown at press conference in J. Jones, *Stealth Technology: The Art of Black Magic* (Blue Ridge Summit, PA: Tab Books, 1989), 3–12. Zbigniew Brzezinski, Carter's national security adviser, later claimed that he visited Area 51 a few weeks before the B-1 decision, saw Have Blue, and came away a convert: Ben R. Rich and Leo Janos, *Skunk Works: A Personal Memoir of My Years at Lockheed* (New York: Little, Brown, 1994), 64–66, 314. On the Stealth role in the B-1 decision: William Perry phone interview, October 17, 2018; Paul Kaminski interview, September 20, 2017.

5 Craig Covault, "Advanced Bomber, Missile in Definition," *Aviation Week & Space Technology*, January 29, 1979, 113–21.

6   Bill Sweetman, *Inside the Stealth Bomber* (Osceola, WI: Zenith Press, 1999), 14–16.

7   Alan Brown interview, November 15, 2010.

8   Richard Scherrer to David Aronstein, July 17, 1998 (Scherrer personal files).

9   Denys Overholser phone interview, March 9, 2018; Brown interview; see also Kaminski interview.

10 John Cashen interview, April 25, 2014 (hereafter Cashen 2); Irv Waaland interview with Volker Janssen, November 10, 2010.

11 Cashen 2; Waaland interview with Janssen, November 10, 2010. Cashen recalls Gen. David Jones telling Tom Jones to play ball; Waaland remembers it as Gen. Thomas Stafford.

12 On the cockpit deriving from Oshiro's insight on Tacit Blue: Rebecca Grant, *B-2: The Spirit of Innovation*, Northrop Grumman Aeronautical Systems, report NGAS 13-0405 (2013, available at www.northropgrumman.com/Capabilities/ B2SpiritBomber/Documents/pageDocuments/B-2-Spirit-of-Innovation.pdf), 19.

13 Cashen 2.

14 Richard Scherrer to Westwick, November 24, 2015; Scherrer to Aronstein.

15 Waaland interview.

16 Scherrer to Westwick; Scherrer to Aronstein; Waaland interview.

17 I. T. Waaland, "Technology in the Lives of an Aircraft Designer," 1991 Wright Brothers Lecture, AIAA Aircraft Design and Operations Meeting, September 23, 1991, Baltimore, MD (copy courtesy of Waaland), 12; see also "Low Observables Bomber Study," 1979, reproduced as appendix 4 in John M. Griffin and James E. Kinnu, *B-2 Systems Engineering Case Study*, Air Force Center for Systems Engineering, Wright-Patterson Air Force Base (2007).

18 Grant, *B-2*, 27–28; Waaland interview with Janssen, November 10, 2010; Waaland interview.

19 Waaland interview with Janssen, November 10, 2010; James Kinnu ("stalking horse") interview with Janssen, February 22, 2011. The range and RCS by frequency are in "Low Observables Bomber Study" in Griffin and Kinnu, *B-2 Systems Engineering Case Study*.

20 Waaland interview ("insurance policy").

21 Rich and Janos, *Skunk Works*, 308–9.

22 Kathleen Day, "McDonnell Settles Suit by Northrop for $50 Million," *Los Angeles Times*, April 9, 1985; Kinnu interview.

23 Waaland interview with Janssen, November 10, 2010; Cashen 2; Kinnu interview. The Jones and Wilson quotes were given in similar, though not identical, versions by Waaland and Cashen.

24 Kinnu interview.

25 Rich and Janos, *Skunk Works*, 304–5. Northrop's entry was later dubbed Senior CJ in honor of Connie Jo Kelly, a dedicated secretary in the Air Force

Low Observable Office. Rick Atkinson, "Stealth: From 18-Inch Model to $70 Billion Muddle," *Washington Post*, October 8, 1989.

26 Kinnu interview; Cashen 2.

27 Kinnu interview.

28 Stephen Johnson, *The Secret of Apollo: Systems Management in American and European Space Programs* (Baltimore: Johns Hopkins University Press, 2002); Westwick, *Into the Black*.

29 "Driver" appears in Waaland interview with Janssen, November 15, 2010 and in Hal Maninger interview, September 28, 2017.

30 Kinnu interview.

31 D. Kenneth Richardson, *Hughes after Howard: The Story of Hughes Aircraft Company* (Santa Barbara, CA, 2012), 365–66. Another version of this story has the owl episode taking place at the Gray Butte radar range east of Palmdale. James Uphold, "The Feathered Saboteurs of Gray Butte," in *Pioneers of Stealth*, ed. John Griffin (Morrisville, NC: Lulu.com, 2017), 352–54.

32 Cashen 2; Kinnu interview.

33 Kotz, *Wild Blue Yonder*, 205–9; Orr, "Developing Strategic Weaponry and the Political Process," 112.

34 Tom Jones interview, February 16, 2010; "Washington Roundup," *Aviation Week & Space Technology*, October 12, 1981, 17; "Northrop Wins Stealth Bomber Contract," *New York Times*, October 17, 1981; Sweetman, *Inside the Stealth Bomber*, 31.

35 Rich and Janos, *Skunk Works*, 304–12.

36 Kaminski interview.

37 Lockheed range in Rich and Janos, *Skunk Works*, 305; Northrop range in "Low Observables Bomber Study," in Griffin and Kinnu.

38 Kinnu interview; Grant, *B-2*, 41; Atkinson, "Stealth."

39 "F-117A Cost Performance and Contracts History," n.d. (Ben Rich papers, box 2, folder 10, Huntington Library); Rich and Janos, *Skunk Works*, 70; David J. Lynch, "How the Skunk Works Fielded Stealth," *Air Force Magazine*, November 1992, 22–28. The first negotiated cost for the F-117 was $350 million; that cost was later renegotiated upward several times. "F-117A Cost Performance"; see also David C. Aronstein and Albert C. Piccirillo, *Have Blue and the F-117A: Evolution of the "Stealth Fighter"* (Reston, VA, 1997), 60, 66.

40 Waaland interview with Janssen, November 10, 2010. Waaland gave the wingspan as 172.5 feet, but Northrop's drawings for both aircraft give it as 172 feet even. I thank Tony Chong for the correction.

41 Welko Gasich interview (quote), October 28, 2010; Waaland interview with Janssen, November 15, 2010. Tony Chong, *Flying Wings and Radical Things* (Forest Lake, MN: Specialty Press, 2016), 262, gives Northrop's quote as "Now I know why God has kept me alive all these years," which is similar to Waaland's recollection.

CHAPTER ELEVEN: BUILDING THE B-2

1 James Kinnu interview with Volker Janssen, February 22, 2011.

2 Kinnu interview.

3 Preceding discussion of Red Teams based on Paul Kaminski interview, September 20, 2017.

4 "Low Observables Bomber Study," 1979, reproduced as appendix 4 in John M. Griffin and James E. Kinnu, *B-2 Systems Engineering Case Study*, Air Force Center for Systems Engineering, Wright-Patterson Air Force Base (2007).

5 Kinnu interview (quotes); Irv Waaland interview with Volker Janssen, November 15, 2010; John Cashen interview, April 25, 2014 (hereafter Cashen 2).

6 Griffin and Kinnu, *B-2 Systems Engineering*, 40; Kinnu interview. On Boeing's campaign: Cashen 2; Bud Baker in *Pioneers of Stealth*, ed. John Griffin (Morrisville, NC: lulu.com, 2017), 76.

7 Kinnu interview; Waaland interview with Janssen, November 15, 2010; Waaland interview, October 7, 2015.

8 Rebecca Grant, *B-2: The Spirit of Innovation*, Northrop Grumman Aeronautical Systems, report NGAS 13-0405 (2013, available at www.northropgrumman .com/Capabilities/B2SpiritBomber/Documents/pageDocuments/B-2-Spirit-of-Innovation.pdf), 59.

9 Cashen 2.

10 Cashen 2.

11 K. M. Mitzner, *Incremental Length Diffraction Coefficients*, Air Force Avionics Laboratory, Wright-Patterson Air Force Base, report AFAL-TR-73-296, April 1974; Ken Mitzner interview, January 25, 2016; Cashen 2.

12 Mitzner interview; Cashen 2.

13 Cashen 2.

14 Mitzner interview.

15 Bill Sweetman, *Inside the Stealth Bomber* (Osceola, WI: Zenith Press, 1999), 53; Mitzner interview; on priorities, and acoustics at low altitudes: Cashen interview, December 15, 2010 (hereafter Cashen 1).

16 Grant, *B-2*, 60; on priorities: Griffin and Kinnu, *B-2 Systems Engineering,* xi (on priorities), 15n5 (on renaming as B-2).

17 Mark Twain, *"Pudd'nhead Wilson" and "Those Extraordinary Twins"* (New York, 1894), 145.

18 Waaland interview with Janssen; Cashen 2.

19 Wayne King, "One Charged with Spying Aided FBI, Affidavit Says," *New York Times*, June 30, 1981; Philip M. Boffey, "What Exactly Are Russians Getting?" *New York Times*, October 5, 1982; Ralph Vartabedian, "Stealth Job Is Living Up to Its Name," *Los Angeles Times*, May 26, 1987. Another Northrop engineer who worked on the B-2 was later arrested and convicted

of charges of selling Stealth secrets to China: Cashen; US Justice Department press release, "Hawaii Man Sentenced to 32 Years in Prison for Providing Defense Information and Services to People's Republic of China," January 25, 2011 (available at www.justice.gov/opa/pr/hawaii-man-sentenced-32-years-prison-providing-defense-information-and-services-people-s).

20 Nick Kotz, *Wild Blue Yonder: Money, Politics, and the B-1 Bomber* (New York: Pantheon, 1988), 231.

21 Kaminski interview.

22 Rick Atkinson, "Unraveling Stealth's 'Black World,'" *Washington Post*, October 9, 1989.

23 Tim Weiner, *Blank Check: The Pentagon's Black Budget* (New York: Grand Central Publishing, 1990), 94.

24 Weiner, *Blank Check*, 94–96; House staffer Anthony Battista quoted in Atkinson, "Unraveling Stealth's Black World."

25 Weiner, *Blank Check*, 94–96.

26 Griffin and Kinnu, *B-2 Systems Engineering*, 39; Kinnu interview.

27 Kinnu interview; Grant, *B-2*, 66–67; Atkinson, "Unraveling."

28 Vartabedian, "Stealth Job Living Up to Its Name."

29 Sweetman, *Inside the Stealth Bomber*, 47–48.

30 Griffin and Kinnu, *B-2 Systems Engineering*, 26; Grant, *B-2*, 45; Ralph Vartabedian, "Northrop Practically Telling and Showing All to Salvage the B-2," *Los Angeles Times*, June 20, 1990; Richard M. Scofield and John M. Griffin, "The B-2 Spirit Bomber," in Griffin, *Pioneers of Stealth*, 60.

31 Cashen 1 and 2; Waaland interview with Janssen, November 10, 2010.

32 Ralph Vartabedian, "Northrop to Build 250-Acre Desert Complex," *Los Angeles Times*, May 9, 1984; statistic on forty thousand workers from Scofield and Griffin, "The B-2 Spirit Bomber," 54–55.

33 Griffin and Kinnu, *B-2 Systems Engineering*, 9–10; Vartabedian, "Northrop Practically Telling and Showing All to Salvage the B-2"; Chris Cochran, *The Aerospace Industry in California*, Office of Economic Research, California Department of Commerce, August 1988.

34 Cochran, *Aerospace Industry*; Philip Scranton, afterword to *Blue Sky Metropolis: The Aerospace Century in Southern California*, ed. Peter J. Westwick (Berkeley: University of California Press, 2012), 279. The actual number of aerospace jobs in LA varies widely depending on how one defines aerospace—especially whether one includes electronics, measuring and control devices, and other related SIC (Standard Industrial Classification) categories. Thus in 1988 the Commerce Department counted Southern California aerospace employment at 257,000; the Aerospace Industries Association said it was 451,000; and the State of California had 754,000. Cochran, *Aerospace Industry*, 203.

35 Ralph Vartabedian, "Two Strong-Willed Adversaries Square Off over the MX," *Los Angeles Times*, July 19, 1987.

36 Les Lackman interview, September 7, 2017.

37 Kinnu interview; original schedule in Griffin and Kinnu, *B-2 Systems Engineering*, 26.

38 Weiner, *Blank Check*, 98–99; Ralph Vartabedian, "Northrop's Stealth Role Is under Review," *Los Angeles Times*, July 8, 1987.

39 Grant, *B-2*, 73, 77.

40 Weiner, *Blank Check*, 76, 94–96.

41 Vartabedian, "Northrop's Stealth Role Is under Review" ; Michael D. Rich, "When Should We Start High-Rate Production of the B-2?," statement included in National Defense Authorization Act for Fiscal Years 1992 and 1993, Amendment no. 1056, August 2, 1991 (available at fas.org/nuke/guide/usa/bomber/910802-2-cr.htm); Michael Rich, remarks at Pioneers of Stealth reunion, National Museum of the US Air Force, September 29, 2017 (I thank Michael Rich for a copy of his remarks).

42 Ralph Vartabedian, "Northrop—A Company in Turmoil," *Los Angeles Times*, December 20, 1987; Vartabedian, "Northrop Delays Initial Flight of Stealth Bomber for 4 Months," *Los Angeles Times*, January 5, 1988; Rick Atkinson, "How Stealth's Consensus Crumbled," *Washington Post*, October 10, 1989.

43 Vartabedian, "Northrop—A Company in Turmoil"; Ralph Vartabedian, "Northrop Official Terms as 'Nonsense' Allegations of MX Missile Flaws," *Los Angeles Times*, June 19, 1987; Vartabedian, "Northrop Charged with Fraud, Conspiracy in Defense Work," *Los Angeles Times*, April 12, 1989. On the competition for staff: Kent Kresa interview, December 7, 2018.

44 Bill Sing and Jonathon Peterson, "Northrop's Jones to Retire," *Los Angeles Times*, April 21, 1989; Atkinson, "How Stealth's Consensus Crumbled"; George White, "Maverick Who Helped Build Northrop Leaves," *Los Angeles Times*, September 20, 1990.

45 Vartabedian, "Stealth Bomber Unveiled amid Pomp, Huzzahs," *Los Angeles Times*, November 23, 1988; Weiner, *Blank Check*, 73–74.

46 Bill Sweetman, "1988: B-2 Stealth Unveiled," *Aviation Week & Space Technology*, December 7, 2013.

47 Don Oberdorfer, *The Turn: From the Cold War to a New Era: The United States and the Soviet Union, 1983–1990* (New York: Poseidon Press, 1991), 23, 299.

48 Waaland interview.

49 Scofield and Griffin, "The B-2 Spirit Bomber," on 62–63; Robert E. Wulf in Griffin, *Pioneers of Stealth*, 347.

50 Ralph Vartabedian, "First Flight Creating 'as Much Hype as Batman Movie,'" *Los Angeles Times*, July 15, 1989; Vartabedian, "Fuel System Glitch Forces Scrapping of B-2 Test Flight," *Los Angeles Times*, July 16, 1989; Vartabedian,

"Stealth Bomber Makes First Flight," *Los Angeles Times*, July 18, 1989; Bruce Van Voorst, "The Stealth Takes Wing," *Time*, July 31, 1989; Grant, *B-2*, 81–82; John Griffin, "Kiss My 'What'?'" in Griffin, *Pioneers of Stealth*, 365.

CHAPTER TWELVE: FROM THE SHADOWS TO
THE SPOTLIGHT

1 Richard P. Hallion, *Storm over Iraq: Air Power and the Gulf War* (Washington, DC: Smithsonian Books, 1992), 128, 166–76; Annie Jacobsen, *The Pentagon's Brain: An Uncensored History of DARPA, America's Top Secret Military Research Agency* (New York: Little, Brown. 2015), 271–72.

2 Hallion, *Storm over Iraq*, 174, 177.

3 Bombing accuracy from Charles W. McArthur, *Operations Analysis in the U.S. Army Eighth Air Force in World War II* (Providence, RI: American Mathematical Society, 1990), 112–15; attrition rate of 5 percent of sorties for 1943 from Mark K. Wells, *Courage and Air Warfare: The Allied Aircrew Experience in the Second World War* (London: Frank Cass & Co., 1995), 101.

4 Hallion, *Storm over Iraq*, 192, 249; Paul Kaminski interview, September 20, 2017.

5 See testimonials in Edward P. Baldwin papers, box 1, folder F-117 (Udvar-Hazy Center, National Air and Space Museum).

6 Annie Leibovitz and Susan Mercandetti, "Vanity Fair's 1991 Hall of Fame," *Vanity Fair* 54:12 (December 1991), 181, 201.

7 Ralph Vartabedian, "Northrop Practically Telling and Showing All to Salvage the B-2," *Los Angeles Times*, June 20, 1990; Tim Weiner, *Blank Check: The Pentagon's Black Budget* (New York: Grand Central Publishing, 1990), 106–7; Chad Garland, "B-2 Stealth Bomber Made Its Maiden Flight 25 Years Ago," *Los Angeles Times*, July 17, 2014.

8 Bruce Van Voorst, "The Stealth Takes Wing," *Time*, July 31, 1989.

9 General Accounting Office, *B-2 Bomber: Cost and Operational Issues*, GAO/NSIAD-97-181, August 1997.

10 John M. Griffin and James E. Kinnu, *B-2 Systems Engineering Case Study*, Air Force Center for Systems Engineering, Wright-Patterson Air Force Base (2007), 12; Richard M. Scofield and John M. Griffin, "The B-2 Spirit Bomber," in *Pioneers of Stealth*, ed. John Griffin (Morrisville, NC: Lulu.com, 2017), 63. On the F-117 shot down in Serbia: Bill Sweetman, "Unconventional Weapon," *Air & Space Magazine*, January 2008.

11 Ben Rich, "Senior Prom," September 9, 1992 (Ben Rich papers, box 3, folder 5, Huntington Library); Cashen 2; Bradley Graham, "Missile Project Became a $3.9 Billion Misfire," *Washington Post*, April 3, 1995.

12 Alan Brown email to Westwick, September 29, 2018.

13 James P. Stevenson, *The $5 Billion Misunderstanding: The Collapse of the Navy's A-12 Stealth Bomber Program* (Annapolis, MD: Naval Institute Press, 2001).

14 Sherman N. Mullin, *Winning the ATF*, Mitchell Paper 9, Mitchell Institute Press (2012). The seven competitors in the first round: Boeing, General Dynamics, Grumman, Lockheed, McDonnell Douglas, Northrop, and North American–Rockwell.

15 Sherman Mullin in Griffin, *Pioneers of Stealth*, 251.

16 Ralph Vartabedian, W. J. Hennigan, and Samantha Masunaga, "A Top Secret Desert Assembly Plant Starts Ramping Up to Build Northrop's B-21 Bomber," *Los Angeles Times*, November 10, 2017.

17 David Fulghum and Bill Sweetman, "Stealth over Afghanistan," *Aviation Week & Space Technology*, December 14, 2009; Amy Butler and Bill Sweetman, "Secret New UAS Shows Stealth, Efficiency Advances," *Aviation Week & Space Technology*, December 6, 2013; Zach Rosenberg, "Unmasked: Area 51's Biggest, Stealthiest Spy Drone Yet," *Foreign Policy*, December 6, 2013.

18 Sean D. Naylor, "Mission Helo Was Secret Stealth Black Hawk," *Army Times*, May 4, 2011; David Axe, "Aviation Geeks Scramble to ID bin Laden Raid's Mystery Copter," *Wired*, May 4, 2011; Ed Darack, "The Drone That Stalked bin Laden," *Air & Space Magazine*, April 2016.

19 Bill Sweetman, "Cloak and Dagger: The Development of Stealth and Counterstealth," *Aviation Week & Space Technology*, September 14–27, 2015; Thomas Grove, "The New Iron Curtain," *Wall Street Journal*, 23 Jan 2019.

20 Robert F. Schoeni, Michael Dardia, Kevin F. McCarthy, and Georges Vernez, *Life After Cutbacks: Tracking California's Aerospace Workers*, RAND report MR-688-OSD (Santa Monica CA, 1996), xii–xiii, 8–9.

21 William J. Perry, *My Journey at the Nuclear Brink* (Stanford, CA: Stanford University Press, 2015), 83–84; John Mintz, "How a Dinner Led to a Feeding Frenzy," *Washington Post*, July 4, 1997; Leslie Wayne, "The Shrinking Military Complex," *New York Times*, February 27, 1998.

22 John Cashen interview, December 15, 2010 (hereafter Cashen 1).

23 John Mintz, "Is Conversion a Wash?" *Washington Post*, June 27, 1993.

24 Hal Maninger interview, September 28, 2017.

25 Ralph Vartabedian, "U.S. Objects to Merger of Lockheed, Northrop," *Los Angeles Times*, March 10, 1998; Tony Chong, *Flying Wings and Radical Things* (Forest Lake, MN,: Specialty Press, 2016), 214.

26 Ralph Vartabedian, "Job Stress Catches Up with 'Dr. Stealth' of Aerospace," *Los Angeles Times*, February 26,1993.

27 US patent 5,250,950 (October 5, 1993).

28 US Patent D314,366 (February 5, 1991); Irv Waaland interview, October 7, 2015; Cashen interview, April 25, 2014.

29 Cashen 1 ("you won't believe it"); Alan Brown interview ("the enemy is using my stuff"), November 15, 2010; Ken Mitzner interview, January 25, 2016.

30 Pyotr Ufimtsev interview, October 12, 2016.

CONCLUSION: THE SECRET OF STEALTH

1 Malcolm Browne, "2 Rival Designers Led the Way to Stealthy Warplanes," *New York Times*, May 14, 1991.

2 Cf., e.g., Joshua Wolf Shenk, *Powers of Two: Finding the Essence of Innovation in Creative Pairs* (New York: Mariner Books, 2014).

3 Robert C. McFarlane and Zofia Smardz, *Special Trust* (New York: Cadell & Davies, 1994); Peter Schweizer, *Victory: The Reagan Administration's Secret Strategy That Hastened the Collapse of the Soviet Union* (New York: Atlantic Monthly Press, 1994); Mira Duric, *The Strategic Defence Initiative: US Policy and the Soviet Union* (Aldershot, UK: Ashgate Publishing, 2003). See also Hendrik Hertzberg, "Laser Show," *New Yorker*, May 15, 2000; Peter J. Westwick, "'Space-Strike Weapons' and the Soviet Response to SDI," *Diplomatic History* 32:5 (November 2008), 955–79.

4 Mikkel Nadby Rasmussen, *The Risk Society at War: Terror, Technology, and Strategy in the Twenty-First Century* (New York: Cambridge University Press, 2006), 46n6.

5 Noel E. Firth and James H. Noren, *Soviet Defense Spending: A History of CIA Estimates, 1950–1990* (College Station: Texas A&M University Press, 1998), 108–9. The 8 percent increase began in 1985.

6 Views of the 1970s as a pivotal decade include Edward Berkowitz, *Something Happened: A Political and Cultural Overview of the Seventies* (New York: Columbia University Press, 2007); Dominic Sandbrook, *Mad as Hell: The Crisis of the 1970s and the Rise of the Populist Right* (New York: Knopf, 2011); Daniel T. Rodgers, *Age of Fracture* (Cambridge, MA: Harvard University Press, 2011).

7 The most persistent proponent of this view was Seymour Melman: see *Pentagon Capitalism: The Political Economy of War* (New York: McGraw-Hill, 1970), *The Permanent War Economy* (New York, 1974), and *The Demilitarized Society: Disarmament and Conversion* (Nottingham, 1988). On the pork-barrel perspective, see Tim Weiner, *Blank Check: The Pentagon's Black Budget* (New York: Grand Central Publishing, 1990).

8 Mihir Pandya, "The Cold War Present: The Logic of Defense Time," in *Anthropology and Global Counterinsurgency*, ed. J. Kelly, B. Jauregui, S. T. Mitchell, and J. Walton (Chicago: University of Chicago Press, 2010), 137–45; see also Peter J. Westwick, "The International History of the Strategic Defense Initiative: American Influence and Economic Competition in the Late Cold War," *Centaurus* 52 (Fall 2010), 338–51.

9   Eisenhower's farewell address is available at https://www.ourdocuments.gov /doc.php?flash=true&doc=90.

10 Fred Block, "Swimming against the Current: The Rise of a Hidden Developmental State in the U.S.," *Politics & Society* 36:2 (2008), 169–206; Mariana Mazzucato, *The Entrepreneurial State: Debunking Public vs. Private Sector Myths* (New York: Public Affairs, 2014); "innovation hybrids" in Linda Weiss, *America Inc.? Innovation and Enterprise in the National Security State* (Ithaca, NY: Cornell Univesity Press, 2014), 7. On MITI: Chalmers Johnson, *MITI and the Japanese Miracle: The Growth of Industrial Policy, 1925–1975* (Stanford, CA: Stanford University Press,1982).

11 For an example of military support leading to the personal computer: John Markoff, *What the Dormouse Said: How the Sixties Counterculture Shaped the Personal Computer* (New York: Penguin Books, 2005). On the internet: Arthur L. Norberg and Judy O'Neill, *Transforming Computer Technology: Information Processing for the Pentagon, 1962–1986* (Baltimore: Johns Hopkins University Press, 1996); Janet Abbate, *Inventing the Internet* (Cambridge, MA: MIT Press, 1999).

12 See the various contributions in John Griffin, ed., *Pioneers of Stealth* (Morrisville, NC: Lulu.com, 2017).

13 Sherman Mullin in Griffin, *Pioneers of Stealth*, 250.

INDEX

For the benefit of digital users, indexed terms that span two pages (e.g., 52–53) may, on occasion, appear on only one of those pages.

Note: Page references followed by an "*f*" indicate figure.